DELICIOUSNESS. EXPERIMENTATION. PERFECTION. TARTINE.

With more than 120 recipes for breakfast pastries, tarts, pies, cakes, cookies, and so much more, this is the only baking book you need.

The cookbook *Tartine* has become a go-to resource for home bakers since it was published. Now this classic baking book has been updated and expanded with 68 new recipes that reflect how home bakers have developed. And Tartine— once a single storefront in the Mission District of San Francisco with a line around the block—has transformed itself with changing tastes and times to become a global empire with a cult-like following.

Known for the brilliance and creativity of its bakers, Tartine is a place where otherworldly treats are produced, both in the bakeries and in this book. For the first time ever, you'll find the most-requested recipe in Tartine history: the Tartine Morning Bun. This updated edition also contains dozens of recipes perfect for beginning bakers, including banana muffins, thumbprint cookies, brownies with a rocky road topping, peanut butter honey cookies, and pound cake.

Here are more old-fashioned desserts reimagined, including a Dutch apple pie sweetened with apple butter, diner-classic chocolate pudding pie, homey cakes, and a marvel of a cheesecake with a gluten-free crust. But there's a twist: modern flavors and ingredients—matcha, einkorn, buckwheat—upend our expectations and result in surprisingly delicious treats. Recipe variations include natural sweeteners, such as coconut sugar and maple syrup, and heritage grains, such as teff and rye—to satisfy curiosity, dietary restrictions, or a not-so-sweet tooth. More than 25 recipes are gluten-free.

There are also projects to satisfy the most serious bakers: a stunner of an updated bûche de noël (featuring beautiful white chocolate mushrooms) and the classiest pig in a blanket you've ever eaten. More than 115 gorgeous photographs by the renowned Gentl + Hyers provide mouthwatering visual inspiration and instruction.

Tartine is a masterwork of baking.

TARTINE

TARTINE

A CLASSIC REVISITED

68 All-New Recipes + 55 Updated Favorites

ELISABETH PRUEITT + CHAD ROBERTSON

FOREWORD BY ALICE WATERS

Photographs by
GENTL + HYERS

With editorial collaboration from
CAROLYN NUGENT, LYNN ECHEVERRIA + MARIA ZIZKA

CHRONICLE BOOKS
SAN FRANCISCO

Library of Congress Cataloging-in-Publication Data:

Names: Prueitt, Elisabeth M., author. | Robertson, Chad., author.
Title: Tartine : A Classic Revisited / authors Elisabeth M. Prueitt and
    Chad Robertson.
Description: San Francisco : Chronicle Books, [2019] | Includes
    index.
Identifiers: LCCN 2019001090 | ISBN 9781452178738 (hc : alk. paper)
Subjects: LCSH: Desserts. | Pastry. | Tartine (Bakery) | LCGFT:
    Cookbooks.
Classification: LCC TX773 .P96 2019 | DDC 641.86--dc23 LC record
    available at https://lccn.loc.gov/2019001090

Manufactured in China.

Editing by Sarah Billingsley.
Design by Vanessa Dina.
Typesetting by Frank Brayton.

10 9 8 7 6 5 4 3 2 1

Chronicle books and gifts are available at special quantity
discounts to corporations, professional associations, literacy
programs, and other organizations. For details and discount
information, please contact our premiums department at
corporatesales@chroniclebooks.com or at 1-800-759-0190.

Chronicle Books LLC
680 Second Street
San Francisco, California 94107
www.chroniclebooks.com

CONTENTS

BASIC BAKERY RECIPES

FOREWORD

The word *authentic* has been overused by food writers, who have turned it into a catchall in praise of just about anything that tastes good. But whenever I see this word, another similar word springs to mind—*author*—and the food I recognize as authentic is real food that is unmistakably its creator's own, as genuine as a handwritten manuscript. Such food is rare, so when I first saw the handmade fruit tarts and bread loaves from the wood-fired brick oven of Elisabeth Prueitt and Chad Robertson, I did an excited double take.

That was nearly twenty-five years ago, when Liz and Chad had started their tiny Bay Village Bakery in Point Reyes Station in Marin County. Twice a week, they hauled their bread to the Berkeley farmers' market in big, eye-catching, vintage wooden boxes, and before long Berkeley shoppers were queuing up for bread before the market had even opened. The bread was that good. It had that remarkable village-bakery quality that comes from stone-ground organic flour, native yeasts, coarse gray sea salt, a wood fire, and loving hands. Call it authenticity.

Soon after I discovered them at the farmers' market, I went to see the bakery. It was in a little Victorian cottage, and the brick oven was in a 15-square-foot [1.4-square-meter] kitchen in the back of the house, where Chad baked as much as he could in the limited space. At the time, I was staying in a friend's house in the fog of Bolinas, not far from Point Reyes Station, so I had the luxury of visiting their bakery often. I remember thinking that Liz and Chad's little tarts and rustic loaves felt like they were of another world, like the France of a hundred years ago—where freshness was measured in hours rather than days or weeks and where honest food was grown and prepared by human hands—a world that, even in France, has largely disappeared now. That summer, I visited Liz at the bakery one afternoon as she was stacking boxes of apricot tarts to take to market; I remember the sun streaming down and the apricots glistening, their edges just slightly caramelized, and the entire scene took my breath away. The magic tableau said everything that needs to be said about food and the joy of living.

I've never been much of a baker or pastry cook, and so whenever family birthdays rolled around in the years that followed, I came to entrust Liz and Chad with baking the cake, one of which floats into my mind's eye as a kind of Platonic ideal of a birthday cake: layers of airy cake separated by thinner layers of strawberry jam; a rose geranium–flavored red wine syrup; perfectly whipped cream; and little sprigs of just-picked *fraises des bois*, the fragile, intensely aromatic European woodland strawberries rarely grown in California gardens, arranged around the glazed top. It is a cake so classically restrained in appearance and so impetuously romantic in flavor that it is the finest birthday present I can imagine receiving.

Many more birthdays have raced by, and today Liz and Chad are the proprietors of the bustling bakery in San Francisco's Mission District that gives this book its name—as well as two expansive, ambitious Tartine Manufactories in San Francisco and Los Angeles. There is even a Tartine Bakery now in Seoul, South Korea! On the surface, these establishments may appear to be the urban antitheses of the tiny, bucolic Victorian cottage in which Liz and Chad began their journey. Yet these bakers have preserved their quiet artisanal authority and integrity without making any compromises: that delicious country bread of theirs has redefined and influenced so many of the breads made in the Bay Area and around the country; their sandwiches and salads are perfectly balanced and highlight the ripest ingredients; and the desserts are full of light and air. They are lavish in their use of seasonal fruits and judicious in their deployment of sugar and decoration, and, best of all, nearly all the ingredients used are grown nearby and produced sustainably, so that everything that comes out of the kitchen is fresh, unfussy, simple, and alive. Tartine Bakery opened in 2002, and in the intervening 17 years, it has become an anchor for the neighborhood, a defining institution for the city of San Francisco, and a beacon of taste and flavor for people the whole country over.

In short, Tartine is about as authentic—and indispensable—as a bakery and café can get. No wonder people are still lining up.

Alice Waters

INTRODUCTION

At the time of this book's release, it has been 13 years since the first *Tartine* book was published, 17 years since we first opened our doors in San Francisco, and almost 25 years since we started our first bakery in the west Marin town of Point Reyes Station. We started our business with just the two of us, baking early mornings and then driving to the East Bay farmers' markets to sell our bread and pastries, hot out of the oven.

We've had many milestones to celebrate along the way, including the birth of our daughter, winning a James Beard award, and expanding to a second San Francisco location. We are happily in a business that people come to when they have something to celebrate. Customers who have met in our line have since married; employees have married each other and have families of their own now. We've been a part of decades' worth of birthdays, bar mitzvahs, Thanksgivings, Passovers, Christmases, and celebrations of life. It's an honor specific to owning a bakery. Even when the Twin Towers came down and businesses temporarily closed around us, we remained open to offer people a communal place to gather, eat, grieve, and feel connection to each other. Whether a happy or sad occasion, or part of the routine of your day, is there anything more comforting than being in your favorite bakery, with your favorite book or person, eating your favorite food?

As the title indicates, this edition contains more than 67 new recipes with some changes here and there to old favorites. Because the first book is a static snapshot of our baking up to 2006, we jumped at the chance to update it. As opposed to a "volume two," this book is an update, since that's how we have looked at the progression and evolution of our recipes from the beginning.

We use a wider variety of grains now, and I've been baking more and more gluten-free goods over the years to reflect how I and others have to eat. We have also minimized the amount of sugar in some recipes to reflect how our approach has changed at the bakery (the Lemon Meringue Cake is one–a favorite, but a bit less sweet now). Amongst the changes, we've also added many things that people will invariably ask me when they discover I own a bakery, the number one request being "Do you make cheesecake?" Here you have, finally, Tartine Cheesecake. I hope it makes its way to whatever celebration you have in mind, or just offers the unique satisfaction and comfort only found in the perfect cheesecake.

In this book, you will also find recipes for many of Tartine's best-loved breakfast pastries. Some are simple constructions, perfect for a quick bite with coffee, and others are more elaborate creations meant to be savored over a long breakfast or brunch. Still others are the way to end a meal on a decadent note, and a few are good for gift giving. The bakery always stocks a variety from each of these categories, with seasonal changes to keep the baker and eater interested, challenged, and anticipating what is coming next throughout the year.

These recipes are more than simply ingredients lists and general directions for assembling and baking. It is important to know how and why a recipe works, too, so recipes include both an introductory note, usually on how the recipe came to be or how it looks and tastes when it is on the table, and sections called Kitchen Notes, bits of practical advice or insider's know-how. This latter text is typically something about the recipe that I or others have learned in the kitchen as we worked.

It has been said that the skill of a cook can be measured in how he or she makes an omelet, a seemingly simple exercise. Putting together an omelet assesses the cook's understanding of eggs and how they react not only to heat, but also to whisking, seasoning, the addition of ingredients, timing, and various pieces of equipment. The same is true in pastry making. When cooks try out for a position in the Tartine kitchen, the first thing they do is make a batch of pastry cream and a génoise, two relatively easy tasks but with enough variables to make them challenging tests of the baker's skill and focus. All of the senses are involved in these two recipes, and adjustments must be made quickly and precisely throughout the process. This is true for every recipe we make in the Tartine kitchen and every recipe you will make at home.

Many of the recipes are our versions of such classics as brownies or shortbread that are found in countless other bakery counters. But what sets our brownies apart from what you will find in most other display cases is our bakers' understanding of the correct technique for making these ubiquitous favorites. You can have the best brownie recipe in the world, but if a brownie is slightly overbaked, it will not have the proper texture. In other words, while it will still be a decent brownie, it won't be a Tartine brownie. This is true of all the recipes. In general, we are not doing things radically differently than what many other bakeries and restaurants do, but we strive to be conscious of every detail as we work. And we are extremely resolute on two aspects of everything we make: we use only the best-quality ingredients, and we adhere to exacting standards of production. Attention to both is what makes the difference between something good and something exceptional emerging from the oven.

The formal, gilded pastries seen in many pastry shops look and feel rigid—labored over by too many hands for too much time. In contrast, the Tartine philosophy is that our pastries should look natural, rather than contrived, that everything we make should be an honest expression of the marriage of first-rate ingredients and experienced hands and minds. We see the nuances of flavor as another essential component of good pastry making, one that elsewhere is often ignored or buried under layers of sugar. We regularly experiment with flavors to gain a better understanding of the way they work together. For example, at the bakery we might add a squeeze of lemon juice to strawberries or a pinch of black pepper to the batter for a ginger tea cake to heighten the "true" flavor of the berries or the batter. Or, there are times when I will add a dash of orange flower water to a Bavarian batter if I know that I am going to be serving it with a citrus compote after a Middle Eastern main course.

The flavor combinations and rules of preparation for most traditional recipes are grindingly pedantic. I remember being a young, tentative baker who slavishly followed each and every pinch and cupful, whether or not it seemed right. Even though I may have thought the recipe needed something more, I was afraid to stray from the formula on the page. Now I know that almost anything folded into croissant dough, from smoked ham, cheese, or chocolate to fresh fruit, results in a batch of delicious pastries. And I know that the same is true for scones, quiches, and countless other items.

I have also learned never to discriminate against any part of a fruit. A friend who runs a fresh juice stand at one of the local farmers' markets was having a hard time getting her watermelon juice to taste right. Using only the ripe, sweet pink flesh of the melon didn't do the trick; the result was a slushy, sugary drink without good melon flavor. She kept experimenting until she discovered that simply adding some puréed watermelon seeds to the drink produced a true watermelon flavor— the taste of the seeds completed the picture. If we make a peach dessert at the bakery, for example, we often leave the skins on the fruits. The same is true for apples for a tart, if they are nice and fresh and the skins haven't toughened from storage. Apple skins have a lot of flavor, and by leaving a little bit of skin on, you can end up with a more interesting texture and flavor than if you used soft-cooked peeled apples alone.

Because fruits play a big role in our kitchen, we are always thinking about ways to enhance their texture in what we make. We rarely strain berry purées, for example, for two reasons: an unstrained purée creates contrast on the palate and for the eye, and it clues the eater in to what the purée is made from, rather than it simply being a generic "red berry" sauce. Or, roasting strawberries whole for topping a bread pudding or as a garnish for ice cream is an unusual and a delicious alternative to using them fresh. The juices that come from roasting run clear, making a beautiful sauce; the fruit turns soft and luscious but stays intact; and the contrast of texture and temperature is wonderfully satisfying.

Newborn ideas come from things freshly looked at and learned, and of course, from memories of desserts past. Some of the recipes in this book are classic, like fruit cobbler or shortbread, and should always be that way. They were perfected long ago and don't need to be changed. Some others, like Steamed Gingerbread Pudding or Lemon Cream Tart, are the product of new ways to make old favorites. As a baker, I am always intrigued by the use of different techniques to make something

familiar, and as an eater, I am equally intrigued by the different texture and flavor that result from such changes.

In these pages, I have tried to pass along the enthusiasm we all have at Tartine for what we do and the knowledge we have gained baking over the years. I hope that what you find here will inspire you, whether a novice or a seasoned baker, not only to bake more but to learn more, too.

A Note on the Measurements

I have included two measuring systems for recipe ingredients: standard American volume measures in cups and metric milliliters and grams. American cooks traditionally use volume measures for both wet and dry ingredients, and you will achieve perfect results with the recipes if you use these measures consistently. Note that the metric measurements have been rounded off, usually to the nearest gram. For accuracy, we recommend weighing ingredients.

Liz Prueitt

CHAPTER ONE

BREAKFAST

BANANA MUFFINS WITH VARIATIONS

YIELDS 18 TO 20 MUFFINS

CRUMBLE

Rolled oats	1²/₃ cups	160 g
Almond flour	1²/₃ cups	120 g
Sugar	³/₄ cup	90 g
Ground cinnamon	1¹/₂ tsp	
Salt	1 tsp	
Unsalted butter, melted and cooled	³/₄ cup	210 g
Walnuts, coarsely chopped	1¹/₂ cups	160 g

CAKE

Unsalted butter, at room temperature	6 Tbsp	85 g
Sugar	³/₄ cup	150 g
Large eggs	2	
Very ripe bananas, mashed	2	200 g
Crème fraîche	¹/₃ cup + 1 Tbsp	95 g
Vanilla extract	1 tsp	
Oat flour	1 cup	105 g
Almond flour	6 Tbsp	40 g
Brown rice flour	¹/₃ cup	45 g
Baking soda	³/₄ tsp	
Salt	¹/₂ tsp	
Ground cinnamon	¹/₂ tsp	
Walnuts, coarsely chopped	1 cup	120 g

This muffin passes the test I give all of my gluten-free recipes: Can you tell it's gluten free? It is for this reason you will rarely find a gluten-free baguette or light, holey pizza crust. Doughs that rely very heavily on gluten formation and structure are the most challenging and disappointing. However, in pastry-making, the replacements are much easier, and a soft crumb is practically guaranteed when made with ingredients that add moisture. This is a very moist, chunky muffin; the crumble adds a salty, spicy crunch.

. . . . . .

Preheat the oven to 350°F [180°C]. Line the wells of two 12-cup muffin tins with paper liners.

To make the crumble, in the bowl of a stand mixer fitted with the paddle attachment, combine the oats, almond flour, sugar, cinnamon, and salt. Reduce the speed to low and pour in the butter. Gently stir in the walnuts until coated. Spread the mixture on a baking sheet in a thin layer and freeze for 1 hour. Break into chunks.

Alternatively, put the dry ingredients in a medium bowl and, using a pastry cutter or your fingers, cut the butter into the dry ingredients until the clumps are pea-size.

To make the cake, in the bowl of a stand mixer fitted with the paddle attachment, cream the softened butter and the sugar on medium-high speed until fluffy, about 2 minutes. Add the eggs, one at a time, mixing well after each addition. Add the mashed bananas and beat until the mixture is smooth. Scrape down the sides of the bowl with a rubber spatula. Stir in the crème fraîche and vanilla.

In a separate bowl, sift together the oat flour, almond flour, brown rice flour, baking soda, salt, and cinnamon. Add to the banana mixture with the walnuts, beating on low until just combined.

Using an ice-cream scoop or large spoon, portion the batter into the wells, filling each three-quarters full. Top with the crumble. Bake for 25 to 30 minutes, until a tester inserted into the center of the largest muffin comes out clean.

Cool on a wire rack for 5 minutes. Remove the muffins from the tins to cool completely. Store, well wrapped, at room temperature for up to 4 days.

Summer Berries Variation: Switch out ½ cup plus 2 Tbsp [140 g] applesauce for the bananas and add about 1 pint [560 g] fresh blueberries or raspberries.

Autumn Apple Variation: Switch out ½ cup plus 2 Tbsp [140 g] applesauce for the bananas and add 1 cup [115 g] peeled and grated apple or pear.

ENGLISH MUFFINS

YIELDS TWELVE 2½ IN [6 CM] MUFFINS

POOLISH

Bread flour	1 cup	130 g
Cold water	1 cup	240 ml
Instant yeast	¼ tsp	

DOUGH

Bread flour	3¾ cups	510 g
Warm water	1½ cups	360 ml
Yeast	¾ tsp	
Salt	1½ tsp	
Olive oil	1 Tbsp + 1 tsp	
Cornmeal for sprinkling		
Unsalted butter for the pan		

This is an adaptation of the English Muffin recipe in *Tartine Bread*. Our head baker, Jen, created this wonderful recipe, which has a light, moist, and tender interior that slices easily and an open-textured crumb to hold butter and jam. The key to making muffins with the lightest texture is to handle the dough as little as possible and not skimp on the rise time.

. . . . . .

The night before you want to make the muffins (about 8 hours ahead of baking), mix the poolish. Mix the flour, cold water, and yeast in a bowl by hand until well combined. Cover with a clean, damp towel and let rise in a cool spot overnight. In the morning it should have doubled in size and be very bubbly. If you're not going to use it right away, keep it in the refrigerator, covered, for up to 6 hours.

Place the flour, warm water, and poolish in the bowl of a stand mixer fitted with the dough hook. Mix on low speed until the ingredients are just combined, about 3 minutes. Rest for 30 minutes, allowing the flour to gently become hydrated (in baker's terms, this is called the "autolyse"). If your kitchen is cool, remove the bowl from the mixer and keep it someplace warm for the duration of the rest period. A turned-off oven with a pan of hot water placed in the bottom is a great resting spot.

Return the mixing bowl to the machine if you've removed it and add the yeast to the dough. Mix (still using the dough hook) for 3 minutes on medium speed. Add the salt and mix for 3 more minutes on medium speed. Drizzle the olive oil into the dough as the mixer is running. Mix for 3 more minutes, until the olive oil is all absorbed and the dough is smooth and supple. It will be slightly sticky but should form a cohesive ball.

Place the bowl in a warm spot (again, a turned-off oven with a bowl of hot water works very well). Allow to rise for 1 hour. The dough should maintain a constant temperature of 77 to 80°F [25 to 27°C].

Gently fold the dough over itself a few times, keeping the shape generally a ball. Allow to rise for another 30 minutes, until it has grown significantly in size and is showing signs of fermentation, such as air bubbles and a yeasty smell.

Sprinkle a baking sheet liberally with cornmeal.

continued

Turn the dough out onto a lightly floured work surface. Pat it out until the dough is roughly ½ in [12 mm] thick. Use a widemouthed water glass or a large round cutter to cut the dough into circles. Flour the cutter as needed to prevent sticking. Place the muffins on the prepared baking sheet. Rest for 20 minutes.

Heat a cast-iron skillet over medium-high heat. Melt just enough butter to cover the bottom of the pan and place a few muffins at a time in the skillet. Cook until the bottoms are golden brown, then flip and cook until both sides are golden brown. Continue until all the muffins are cooked.

These are best the day they are made. Serve warm, or store in an airtight container at room temperature for up to 5 days, reheating or toasting before serving.

BUTTERMILK SCONES

YIELDS 12 SCONES

Zante currants	3/4 cup	100 g
All-purpose flour	5 1/4 cups	680 g
Baking powder	1 Tbsp	
Baking soda	3/4 tsp	
Granulated sugar	1/2 cup	100 g
Salt	1 1/4 tsp	
Unsalted butter, very cold	1 cup + 2 Tbsp	255 g
Buttermilk	1 1/2 cups plus more as needed	360 ml
Lemon zest	1 tsp	

TOPPING

Unsalted butter, melted	3 Tbsp	45 g
Large crystal sugar or granulated sugar for sprinkling		

Scones are made like biscuits, their delicate and flaky texture the result of carefully cutting in the butter and using a light hand to mix in the rest of the ingredients just until it all comes together; the key is not overworking the dough, which activates the gluten, just as you mix pie dough. In the winter we make these with the traditional Zante currants or chopped candied ginger, although we vary the recipe in spring and summer with blueberries, raspberries, strawberries, or peaches. The same dough makes a very good cobbler topping dropped on top of lightly sweetened fruit, or cut into rounds for berry shortcakes.

KITCHEN NOTES: If you decide to use fresh berries, start with about 1 cup [140 g] of fruit. Hull and coarsely chop strawberries, but leave raspberries or blueberries whole. Freeze the whole berries or berry pieces in a single layer on a small baking sheet, then add them to the dough after you add the buttermilk. Take care not to mash the berries into the dough, or you will color it with their juice.

· · · · · ·

Preheat the oven to 400°F [200°C]. Butter a baking sheet.

Place the currants in a small bowl and pour in enough warm water to cover. Set aside for about 10 minutes, until the currants are plumped. Drain well.

While the currants are plumping, sift the flour, baking powder, and baking soda into a large mixing bowl if making by hand, or into the bowl of a stand mixer fitted with the paddle attachment. Add the granulated sugar and salt and stir to mix. Cut the butter into ½ in [12 mm] cubes and scatter the cubes over the dry ingredients. If you are mixing by hand, use a pastry blender or two butter knives to cut the butter into the dry ingredients. If you are using the mixer, pulse on and off so that you don't break down the butter too much. You want to end up with a coarse mixture with pea-size lumps of butter visible.

Add the buttermilk all at once, along with the lemon zest and currants, and mix gently with a wooden spoon by hand or on low speed if using the mixer. Continue to mix just until the dough holds together. If the mixture seems dry, add a little more buttermilk. You still want to see some of the butter pieces at this point, which will add to the flakiness of the scones once they are baked.

Dust your work surface with flour, and turn the dough out onto it. Using your hands, pat the dough into a rectangle about 18 in [46 cm] long, 5 in [12 cm] wide, and 1½ in [4 cm] thick. Brush the top with the melted butter and then sprinkle with the large crystal sugar. Using a chef's knife, cut the dough into twelve triangles. Transfer the triangles to the prepared baking sheet.

Bake the scones until the tops are lightly browned, 25 to 35 minutes. Serve warm.

Scones are best the day they are baked, but can be stored in an airtight container for up to 2 days. Reheat or toast before serving.

SAVORY SCONES

Pastry flour, sifted	2½ cups	275 g
Bread flour, sifted	2 cups + 2 Tbsp	275 g
Baking powder	1 Tbsp + ¼ tsp	
Baking soda	1 tsp	
Salt	1 tsp	
Black pepper, freshly ground	¼ tsp	
Unsalted butter, cold	11 Tbsp	155 g
Bacon fat, chilled	3 Tbsp + 1 tsp	50 g
Buttermilk, chilled	1⅔ cups	400 ml
Bacon, cooked and chopped (reserving the fat, see above)	about 6 slices	160 g
Grated Gruyère cheese	1½ cups	160 g
Fromage blanc	¾ cup + 2 Tbsp	175 g
Chives, finely chopped	5 Tbsp	75 g

TOPPING

Large egg, beaten	1	
Flaky sea salt, such as Maldon		

Scone dough works really well as a vehicle for savory ingredients, especially highly flavored, lower moisture ones such as Gruyère and other firm cheeses, chopped chives, sautéed mushrooms, bacon, and ham. Spanish *pimentón* or fresh herbs make really good additions as well. As with sweet scones, use a very light hand when mixing, and you'll be rewarded with a light, flaky scone.

......

Preheat the oven to 375°F [190°C]. Line a baking sheet with parchment paper or a nonstick liner. If using parchment paper, have a second sheet available.

To make the dough, sift the flours, baking powder, baking soda, salt, and pepper into the bowl of a stand mixer fitted with the paddle attachment. Cut the butter into ½ in [12 mm] cubes and scatter the cubes over the dry ingredients. On low speed, pulse the butter and chilled bacon fat into the dry ingredients, keeping a close eye on the mixture, so that you don't break down the butter too much. You want to end up with a coarse mixture with pea-size lumps of butter visible. Add the buttermilk all at once and stir on low speed for 5 seconds. Stop the mixer and, using your hands or a spatula, pull all the dry ingredients that have not yet been incorporated up to the top. Stir again on low speed for another 5 seconds. Repeat this process once more, or until all the dry ingredients are incorporated and the mixture looks hydrated, but not fully combined. Using a spatula, scrape the dough into a large mixing bowl. Add the bacon, Gruyère, fromage blanc, and chives, and knead by hand to incorporate all of the mix-ins.

Transfer the dough to the prepared baking sheet and shape the dough by hand into a rectangle about 2½ in [6 cm] high. Freeze the dough, on the baking sheet, for about 20 minutes to thoroughly chill it. Dust your work surface with flour, and turn the dough out onto it. Cut the dough into twelve equal portions. Line the baking sheet with a fresh sheet of parchment paper, and transfer the scones to it. Brush the scones with the beaten egg, and sprinkle with the flaky sea salt.

Bake the scones until the tops are golden brown, 20 to 25 minutes. Remove from the oven and let cool for 10 minutes before serving.

Scones are best the day they are baked, but can be stored in an airtight container for up to 2 days. Reheat or toast before serving.

EINKORN DOUGHNUTS

YIELDS 15 DOUGHNUTS

Canola oil for frying

Einkorn flour	4¼ cups	500 g
All-purpose flour	1½ cups + 2 Tbsp	210 g
Baking soda	2 tsp	
Baking powder	1 tsp	
Ground cinnamon	½ tsp	
Granulated sugar	1 cup	200 g
Salt	1¼ tsp	
Lemon zest	2 tsp	
Unsalted butter, melted and cooled slightly	½ cup	115 g
Large eggs	2	
Buttermilk	2 cups	480 ml

SUGAR GLAZE

Confectioners' sugar, sifted	3¼ cups	400 g
Water	6 Tbsp	90 ml

One of our bakers, Kelsey, developed these cake-style doughnuts to serve for dessert at Manufactory, where they are freshly fried and paired with ice cream. Einkorn is lower in protein and therefore softer than all-purpose flour, and gives dough a light texture and delicious flavor. It is well worth seeking out to try as a replacement for a portion of flour in other cake or cookie recipes. If you prefer a classic cinnamon-sugar coating to the glaze, dredge the doughnuts in a mixture of 3 Tbsp granulated sugar and 1 Tbsp cinnamon after frying.

KITCHEN NOTES: You need a small doughnut cutter or small round cookie cutter for this recipe.

If you don't have a deep-fat thermometer, you can test the temperature of the oil by dropping a small piece of scrap dough into the pot. When at temperature, the oil will appear shimmery and the dough should momentarily sink to the bottom of the pot before rising to the surface a few seconds later, with the oil bubbling vigorously around the dough.

. . . . . .

Line a 13 by 18 in [33 by 46 cm] baking sheet with parchment paper and another with a wire cooling rack. You can also use a paper towel–lined sheet tray instead of a wire rack to absorb the excess oil.

Fill a 4 qt [3.8 L] pot with enough canola oil to reach 2½ to 3 in [6 to 7.5 cm] up the sides of the pot. Heat the canola oil to 380°F [190°C].

To make the doughnut dough, combine the flours, baking soda, baking powder, and cinnamon in a medium bowl. Whisk to combine and set aside. Combine the granulated sugar, salt, and lemon zest in the bowl of a stand mixer fitted with the paddle attachment. While mixing on medium speed, slowly pour in the melted butter and then slowly add the eggs and continue to mix until emulsified. With a rubber spatula, scrape down the bowl to ensure all ingredients are incorporated, and then add the buttermilk. Add the dry ingredients and mix just until the dough comes together.

continued

Dust your work surface with flour, and turn the dough out onto it. Dust the top with flour and roll it out to ½ in [12 mm] thick. Lightly dust the work surface with additional flour as needed to prevent sticking. Using a 2½ in [6 cm] doughnut cutter, punch out the doughnuts and holes, utilizing as much of the dough as you can. Place the doughnuts on the parchment-lined baking sheet. The scrap doughnut holes may be gently pushed together and re-rolled (chill the scraps as needed if the dough seems too warm).

Before frying, check that the oil has reached 380°F [190°C]. Using a slotted spoon, lower the doughnuts into the oil, frying two or three doughnuts at a time to prevent overcrowding. Flip each doughnut two or three times, until both sides are dark golden brown and the doughnut has almost doubled in thickness, 4 to 5 minutes. Remove from the oil and place on the cooling rack. To check for doneness, once the doughnut has cooled slightly, tear off a piece—the crumb should be soft and delicate but not doughy. Let the doughnuts cool completely before glazing. (If rolling the fried doughnuts in sugar rather than glazing them, do so while they are still warm, otherwise the sugar won't stick.)

To make the glaze, place the confectioners' sugar in a small bowl and gradually whisk in the water, working out any lumps. Once the doughnuts have cooled completely, dunk them into the glaze, flipping the doughnut two or three times with a fork so it is glazed all over. Let the glazed doughnuts dry on a cooling rack until the glaze has hardened to the touch. Serve immediately.

SOUR CREAM COFFEE CAKE

YIELDS ONE 9 IN [23 CM] CAKE

STREUSEL

Brown rice flour	¼ cup	35 g
Sweet rice flour	1½ Tbsp	
Potato starch	2 Tbsp + 1 tsp	
Sugar	¼ cup	50 g
Ground cinnamon	1 tsp	
Baking powder	¼ tsp	
Unsalted butter, at room temperature	4 Tbsp	60 g
Walnuts, pecans, or almonds, chopped	⅔ cup	80 g

CAKE

Almond flour	2½ cups	240 g
Sweet rice flour	2 Tbsp	
Tapioca flour	2 Tbsp	
Baking powder	¾ tsp	
Salt	½ tsp	
Large eggs	2	
Sugar	7 Tbsp	90 g
Sour cream	¾ cup	180 g

This is a reliable, back-pocket recipe, old-school in its cinnamon-y streusel taste and appearance. It's a classic cake-style breakfast pastry that also happens to be gluten free, with a delicious scent and toothsome-ness from the hefty amount of almond flour and sour cream. Add spoonfuls of jam over the batter before topping with the streusel, and it will bake up into little pockets that make a tasty and attractive cross-section in the cake when sliced. Cornstarch can always be substituted for tapioca flour.

......

To make the streusel, mix all the ingredients together by hand in a bowl or with a mixer on medium-low speed just until it all becomes a slightly clumpy mass. To acheive uniform streusel, sand it between your palms, rubbing tablespoon-size amounts of streusel using a back-and-forth rubbing motion, rolling and breaking the clumps into smaller pea-size pieces. Set aside.

To make the cake, preheat the oven to 350°F [180°C]. Butter the sides and bottom of a 9 in [23 cm] round cake pan. In a large bowl, whisk together the almond flour, sweet rice flour, tapioca flour, baking powder, and salt. Set aside.

Using a handheld mixer or a stand mixer fitted with the whisk attachment, beat the eggs and sugar on high speed until the mixture is very thick, light in color, and leaves a ribbon trailing when the whisk is lifted, about 3 minutes. Mix in the sour cream.

Pour the wet ingredients into the dry, and mix together with a rubber spatula just until smooth and blended.

Transfer the batter to the prepared pan. Scatter the streusel, distributing it evenly across the top. Using your fingertips, very gently push the streusel into the batter here and there.

Bake until golden brown around the edges and a cake tester comes out clean, about 25 minutes. Cool for 15 minutes before removing the cake from the pan. The cake will keep, tightly wrapped, for up to 3 days at room temperature or 1 week in the refrigerator.

CROISSANTS AND VARIATIONS

YIELDS 12 TO 16 CROISSANTS (3 LB 11 OZ [1.6 KG] DOUGH)

POOLISH

Reduced-fat milk	¾ cup	180 ml
Active dry yeast (not instant)	½ tsp	
Bread flour	1⅓ cups	175 g

DOUGH

Active dry yeast (not instant)	2 tsp	
Reduced-fat milk	1¾ cups	420 ml
Sugar	⅓ cup	70 g
Salt	1 Tbsp + 1 tsp	
Bread flour	6¼ cups	810 g
Unsalted butter, melted	1 Tbsp	

BUTTER BLOCK

Unsalted butter, at cool room temperature	2⅔ cups	600 g

EGG WASH

Large egg yolks	3
Heavy cream	2 Tbsp
Salt	pinch

Since the late 1990s, there has been a proliferation of small, local bakeries in most cities, and croissants have become one of the benchmarks of showing a baker's knowledge and deft hand. Although there are a number of origin stories, with details hard to pin down, what is known is that croissants weren't originally leavened. Raising croissants with yeast didn't come about until the turn of the twentieth century; before this they were crescent shaped and laminated, made with a puff pastry-style dough. Like craft beer, cheese making, or bread making at home, dedicated bakers will find this dough very satisfying to make, with unlimited ways of rolling and flavoring and an improvement in lamination each time making the dough.

The real test of perfection is in the basic unadorned croissant, however. Most of the croissants you see today aren't actually crescent shaped as the name implies they should be. At some point a straight-shaped croissant without the ends pointed in toward each other became known as an all-butter pastry, with the curved version indicating it was made with vegetable shortening. The cross section of a perfectly made croissant should have a center like honeycomb, with a discernible swirl pattern and a buttery, wheat-y, lightly yeasted scent. The outside should be shatteringly crisp, contrasted with a center that is pillowy soft. Should you have leftover croissants, they make a remarkable bread pudding; you also can use them to make almond croissants. Crossant dough can be made, shaped, and frozen for use in one project or various projects using this dough. Mixing matcha tea powder into the croissant dough produces a beautiful interior shade of green, and lightly scents the pastry.

......

To make the poolish, in a small saucepan, warm the milk only enough to take the chill off (80 to 90°F [25 to 30°C]). Pour the milk into a mixing bowl, sprinkle the yeast over the milk, and stir to dissolve the yeast. Add the flour, mixing with a whisk until a batter

continued

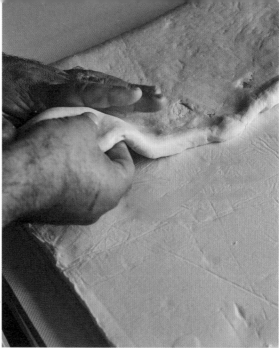
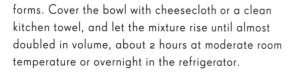

forms. Cover the bowl with cheesecloth or a clean kitchen towel, and let the mixture rise until almost doubled in volume, about 2 hours at moderate room temperature or overnight in the refrigerator.

To make the dough, transfer the poolish to the bowl of a stand mixer fitted with the dough hook. While mixing on low speed, add the yeast and mix until incorporated. Pour in half of the milk, and all of the sugar and salt. Add the flour and mix on low speed for 15 to 20 seconds, until the mixture is 80 percent incorporated. Stop the mixer, and using a rubber spatula, scrape down the sides and bottom of the bowl. With the mixer on low, pour in the rest of the milk and mix for 30 seconds, then add the melted butter. Continue to mix on low speed until a loose dough forms, about 2 minutes. Rest the dough, covered, for 30 minutes.

Mix the dough on low speed for 7 to 8 minutes, until smooth and elastic.

Dust your work surface with flour and turn the dough out onto it. Press the dough into a rectangle 2 in [5 cm] thick. Wrap the rectangle in plastic wrap, or slip it into a plastic bag and seal. Place the dough in the refrigerator to chill for 6 to 8 hours.

For the butter block, about 1 hour before you are ready to start laminating the dough, remove the

2½ cups [595 g] butter from the refrigerator. Ten minutes before laminating the dough, put the butter between two pieces of waxed paper or parchment paper, or slip it into a large plastic bag and seal. With a rolling pin, pound the butter into a rectangle 8 by 12 in [20 by 30 cm]. This is the butter block.

Dust your work surface with flour. Remove the chilled dough from the refrigerator and turn it out onto the floured surface. Roll out the dough into a rectangle measuring 12 by 18 in [30 by 46 cm]. Unwrap the butter block and place it in the center of the dough rectangle so the butter covers the dough, top to bottom, leaving 5 in [12 cm] of the dough exposed on each side of the butter. Fold the left third of the dough over the butter to the middle of the butter block; repeat with the right-hand third. Both sides of the dough should meet in the middle and completely cover the butter block. Using your fingers, push down along the middle seam to make a seal, then seal the top and bottom seams.

Give the block a quarter turn so that the top and bottom seams are to the right and left. Roll out the dough into a rectangle 28 by 12 in [71 by 30 cm]. Fold over the right third of the dough to the center, then fold the left third over the center, as if folding a business letter. The resulting rectangle should be 8 by 12 in [20 by 30 cm]. Wrap the dough in plastic

wrap or slip into a plastic bag and seal, and refrigerate for 1½ to 2 hours to relax the gluten in the dough before you make the last fold or "turn."

Clean the work surface, dust again with flour, and remove the dough from the refrigerator. Unwrap, and place the top and bottom seams to the sides on the floured surface. This time the dough will need to be a little longer, to make a "double turn." Roll out the dough into a rectangle 28 by 12 in [71 by 30 cm]. Fold the right side in to meet the middle of the dough; fold the left side in to meet in the center next to the right. Then fold the left side on top of the right (like closing a book). The dough should measure 7 by 12 in [18 by 30 cm]. Wrap in plastic wrap or slip into a plastic bag and seal. Immediately place in the freezer to chill for at least 1 hour. If you intend to make the croissants the next morning, transfer the dough from the freezer to the fridge to thaw for 8 hours before shaping. Or you can leave the dough in the freezer for up to 1 week; just remember to transfer to the refrigerator to thaw overnight before using.

When you are ready to roll out the dough, dust the work surface with flour. Roll out the dough into a rectangle 10 by 30 in [25 by 76 cm] and 3/8 in [1 cm] thick. Using a pizza wheel or chef's knife, cut the dough into long triangles measuring 10 in

[25 cm] on each side and 3 to 4 in [7.5 to 10 cm] along the base.

Line a baking sheet with parchment paper or a non-stick liner. To shape each croissant, position a triangle with the base facing you. Positioning your palms on the two outer points of the base, carefully roll the base toward the point. To finish, grab the point with one hand, stretching it slightly, and continue to roll, tucking the point underneath the rolled dough so that the croissant will stand tall when you place it on the baking sheet. If you have properly shaped the croissant, it will have six or seven ridges. At this point, you can freeze the shaped pastries. Take them out the morning of or the day before baking, 12 to 18 hours in the refrigerator. They will hold in the refrigerator for up to 48 hours without rising.

As you form the croissants, place them, point-side down and well spaced, on the prepared baking sheet. Set the sheet in a draft-free area with relatively high humidity and let the pastries rise for 2 to 3 hours. The ideal temperature is 75°F [24°C]. A bit cooler or warmer is all right, as long as the temperature is not warm enough to melt the layers of butter in the dough, which would yield greasy pastries. Cooler is preferable, and will increase the rising time and with it the flavor development. A turned-off oven with a pan of hot water placed in the bottom

continued

is a good place to proof yeasted pastries. To make sure that no skin forms on the pastries during this final proofing, refresh the pan of water halfway through the rising.

During this final rising, the croissants should at least double in size and look noticeably puffy. If, when you press a croissant lightly with a fingertip, the indentation fills in slowly, the croissants are almost ready to bake. At this point, they should still be slightly "firm" and holding their shape and be neither spongy nor starting to slouch. If you put the croissants in the oven to rise, remove them now and set the oven to 425°F [220°C] to preheat for 20 to 30 minutes.

Ten minutes before you are ready to bake the croissants, make the egg wash. In a small bowl, whisk together the egg yolks, cream, and salt until you have a pale yellow mixture. Using a pastry brush, lightly and carefully brush the yolk mixture on the ridges of the croissants, being careful not to allow the egg wash to drip onto the sheet.

Place the croissants into the oven, immediately turn down the temperature to 400°F [200°C], and leave the door shut for the first 10 minutes. Then, working quickly, open the oven door and rotate the sheet 180 degrees, and close the door. This rotation will help the pastries bake evenly. Bake for 6 to 10 minutes longer. The croissants are done when they are a deep golden brown on the top and bottom, crisp on the outside, and feel light when they are picked up, indicating that the interior is baked through.

Remove the croissants from the oven and place them on a wire rack to cool. They are best if eaten while slightly warm. If they have cooled completely, you can rewarm them in a 375°F [190°C] oven for 6 to 8 minutes to recrisp them before serving. You can also store leftover croissants in an airtight container at room temperature for 1 day, and then afterward in the refrigerator for up to 3 days.

continued

PAIN AU JAMBON VARIATION

Smoked ham	1 thin slice per croissant
Gruyère cheese, cut into batons	1 oz [30 g] per croissant

We call for Gruyère, but you can use any sharp, firm cheese here.

· · · · · ·

Following the process on page 37, after you cut the dough into triangles, lay one slice of ham over two-thirds of each triangle. Leave the pointed tip (the remaining one-third) uncovered. Place several batons (about 1 oz [30 g]) of Gruyère on top of the ham. Roll up the pastry carefully, encasing the ham and cheese (see photo, facing page). Proceed as directed for plain croissants.

CROISSANTS AUX AMANDES VARIATION

BRANDY SYRUP

Granulated sugar	½ cup	100 g
Water	⅓ cup	80 ml
Brandy	2 Tbsp	
Frangipane Cream (page 304)	1 recipe	
Sliced almonds	¾ cup + 2 Tbsp	75 g
Confectioners' sugar		

We sell so many of these that we make ours from fresh croissants, but traditionally making croissants aux amandes is a wonderful use of day-old croissants.

· · · · · ·

Bake the plain croissants as directed on page 37. When cool, split each croissant in half (like a bagel).

Line a baking sheet with parchment paper. Preheat the oven to 350°F [180°C].

Prepare the brandy syrup by combining the granulated sugar and water in a small saucepan over medium heat, stirring until the sugar dissolves. Add the brandy and remove from the heat.

Moisten both cut sides of each croissant with the brandy syrup. Spread the bottom half of each croissant with Frangipane Cream, replace the top half, and spread more cream on top. Top each croissant with sliced almonds. Arrange the croissants on the prepared baking sheet and bake until hot throughout, crispy, and golden, 20 to 35 minutes.

Serve warm from the oven, dusted with confectioners' sugar.

MATCHA DOUGH VARIATION

Matcha powder	3 Tbsp	20 g
Water	3 Tbsp	45 ml

Whisk together the matcha powder and water to make a paste. Following the recipe that begins on page 37, just after you warm the milk for the poolish, whisk the matcha paste into the milk until smooth. Proceed with the recipe to add the milk to the dough as directed.

PAIN AU CHOCOLAT VARIATION

Bittersweet chocolate batons or pastilles	1 oz [30 g] per croissant

For double-chocolate, use 2 oz [60 g] of chocolate per croissant.

• • • • • •

Roll out the dough as directed in the recipe that begins on page 37, but cut it into 6 by 4 in [15 by 10 cm] rectangles rather than triangles. Place 1 to 2 oz [30 to 60 g] bittersweet chocolate batons in the center of each rectangle. Starting from a long side, roll up each rectangle carefully, encasing the batons in the center, and proceed as directed for plain croissants.

MATCHA-GLAZED VARIATION

MATCHA GLAZE

Confectioners' sugar	4 cups	510 g
Matcha powder	1 Tbsp	
Water	6 Tbsp	90 ml

We've been experimenting with matcha tea powder, which is made from ground, premium green tea leaves from Japan, in ice cream, cookies, and pastries—anything we can think of to take advantage of its beautiful bright hue and subtle, but mild green tea flavor. This glaze would be delicious and beautiful on simple butter cookies, éclairs, or a not-too-sweet cake. It is a basic "water icing" of confectioners' sugar mixed with water and matcha powder to flow over pastry. We dip our croissants in it, but you can also drizzle it. You can thicken it with more sugar or thin it with water, depending on its use, and it sets to a pretty, shiny finish. This glaze yields 2 cups [475 ml], enough to coat 12 croissants.

KITCHEN NOTES: We've tried mixing lemon juice into the icing, but it reacts with the tea and muddies the beautiful, bright, natural color of matcha. The croissants are coated two times in a thinner glaze as opposed to once in a thicker glaze; the dough is so flaky that the outer layers tend to break off into the glaze if it is too thick.

. . . . . .

Bake the plain croissants as directed on page 37.

Combine the sugar, matcha powder, and water in a medium bowl. Whisk until smooth, 20 to 30 seconds.

To glaze the croissants, tilt the bowl to one side so the glaze pools. Holding the croissant by one end and starting on one side, dip the croissant into the glaze and roll to the other side. Allow the excess to drip off the croissant for a few seconds before transferring to a wire rack to set. This should result in a croissant that is glazed on one half, a great contrast to the flaky layers on the other half. For a smoother, thicker finish, dip the croissants a second time after the croissants have rested for at least 10 minutes.

Once the glaze has dried, the croissants can be stored in an airtight container for 1 day.

TARTINE MORNING BUNS

Croissant dough (page 37)	1 recipe	
Unsalted butter, melted	½ cup	115 g
Sugar, plus more for the pan	1⅓ cups	285 g
Orange zest	¼ cup	55 g
Ground cinnamon	1 Tbsp	

COATING

Sugar	1 cup	200 g

Morning buns are one of the most popular breakfast pastries we make, and yet they were not included in our first bakery book. Here they are—finally!—our orange-cinnamon, crispy-on-the-outside, soft-on-the-inside morning buns.

Whereas croissants are a show of a baker's technique in perfect lamination, painstaking rolling, proofing, and baking, there's some leeway in the preparation of morning buns. You can even use re-rolled scraps left over from croissant-making and they will bake up into the most delicious, caramelized buns with an incredible scent. Make sure the sugar is well caramelized to a beautiful deep brown for the best flavor.

KITCHEN NOTES: You'll need two medium oranges to yield ¼ cup [55 g] of zest.

. . . . . .

Make the croissant dough as directed on page 37, through the resting, chilling, and freezing steps.

Generously butter the 12 cups of a standard muffin pan, making sure to also butter the top of the pan, using about 3 Tbsp [45 g] total. Measure ¼ tsp of sugar into each muffin cup and set the pan aside.

In a small bowl, mix together the sugar, orange zest, and cinnamon until thoroughly combined. Set aside.

On a floured work surface, working quickly, roll out the prepared dough to a 10 by 32 in [25 by 81 cm] rectangle ¼ in [6 mm] thick. Using a pastry brush, spread the melted butter evenly over the top of the entire pastry. Generously sprinkle the sugar and orange zest mixture over the top of the entire pastry, patting the sugar down with the palm of your hand to make it adhere, ensuring it stays in place.

Starting at the left top corner of the pastry, roll down the first ½ in [12 mm] of dough all along the top of the pastry, moving to the right. Starting back at the top left corner, roll down the second 1 in [2.5 cm] of dough along the top of the pastry. Repeat all the way to the bottom of the pastry; you will end up with a log with a sugar spiral inside. Use a small amount of flour underneath the roll to prevent sticking to the work surface.

Pull the left side of the roll lightly to the left, and the right side lightly to the right; the dough should feel relaxed and not tight. You don't want the dough to spring back when cut. The log should measure about 36 in [91 cm] long and about 2 in [5 cm] in diameter. Using a sharp chef's knife, cut the roll crosswise every 3 in [7.5 cm], moving to the right; you should end up with twelve individual rolls. Transfer each roll to the prepared muffin pan, tucking in the bottom flap and placing the cut side of the roll into the muffin cup on top of the sugar.

continued

Set the pan in a draft-free area and let the pastries rise for 2 to 3 hours. The temperature should not exceed 75°F [24°C]. A cool temperature will increase the rising time and with it the flavor development (for more information, see Croissant recipe method, page 37). Morning buns are ready to bake when they've risen and the layers begin to open up.

Preheat the oven to 400°F [200°C]. Line a baking sheet with parchment paper. Set the pan on the prepared baking sheet (the parchment paper will catch any sugar or butter drips) and place in the oven. Halfway through the baking time (20 minutes or so), rotate the baking sheet 180 degrees, and, using a metal spatula, lightly push down the tops of each bun so the center stays in.

Morning buns are done baking when they are a dark golden brown, about 45 minutes. Working carefully so as not to burn yourself, remove the baking sheet with the muffin pan from the oven, and turn out the baked buns onto the parchment-lined baking sheet. Let rest until cool to the touch, then toss them in a bowl of sugar to coat. These are best eaten slightly warm, but they can be stored in an airtight container for up to 2 days. To serve, reheat in a 375°F [190°C] oven for 6 to 8 minutes.

CROISSANT BAKLAVA KNOTS AND WREATH

YIELDS 16 KNOTS OR ONE 10 IN [25 CM] WREATH

Croissant dough (page 37)	1 recipe	

BAKLAVA FILLING

Pistachios	2 cups + 2 Tbsp	285 g
Walnuts	1½ cups	170 g
Granulated sugar	¾ cup	140 g
Ground cinnamon	2 tsp	
Salt	1 tsp	
Orange zest	2 Tbsp	
Lemon zest	1 tsp	
Lemon juice	2 Tbsp	
Unsalted butter, melted	1 cup	225 g
Orange blossom water	2 Tbsp	

ORANGE-HONEY GLAZE (FOR THE KNOTS)

Honey	½ cup	170 g
Orange blossom water	¼ cup	60 ml
Lemon juice	2 Tbsp	

ORANGE BLOSSOM ICING (FOR THE WREATH)

Confectioners' sugar	1 cup	115 g
Water	2 Tbsp	
Orange blossom water	½ tsp	

The flavors of honey, orange flower water, and cinnamon, plus a mixture of pistachios and walnuts, remind me of the Middle Eastern bakeries on Atlantic Avenue in Brooklyn, where my parents took me as a child. The counters were filled with large tins of flaky, sweet pastries soaking in honey syrup.

This is another take on versatile croissant dough. Fill individual knots in one version; fill and twist it as you would a Danish wreath in the other. Brushing with an orange-honey syrup after baking (as you would baklava) gives these a beautiful shine and scent. The flakiness of the dough pairs well with the light sweetness and spice of the filling.

......

Make the croissant dough as directed on page 37, through the resting, chilling, and freezing steps.

To make the baklava filling, in the bowl of a food processor, combine the pistachios, walnuts, granulated sugar, cinnamon, salt, zests, and lemon juice. Pulse the mixture for 30 seconds to grind the nuts and combine the ingredients. Process again for 45 seconds, pouring in the melted butter and orange blossom water. When finished, the texture should be a soft paste with medium pieces of nuts. Refrigerate until ready to use, for up to 2 days.

To assemble the knots, line two 12-cup muffin pans with tall parchment paper liners. Or generously butter the 12 cups of a standard muffin pan, making sure to also butter the top of the pan.

To shape the knots, lightly flour a work surface. Place the dough on the work surface and roll out the dough into a rectangle measuring 12 in [30 cm] long, 24 in [60 cm] wide, and ½ in [12 mm] thick. Using a ruler, measure 6 in [15 cm] from the top on both sides, mark the dough with a knife, and cut the dough in half horizontally. Measure and cut each rectangle into eight equal pieces, with each piece 3 in [7.5 cm] wide by 6 in [15 cm] long. Make two 5 in [12 cm] cuts in each rectangle, leaving 1 in [2.5 cm] uncut at the top;

continued

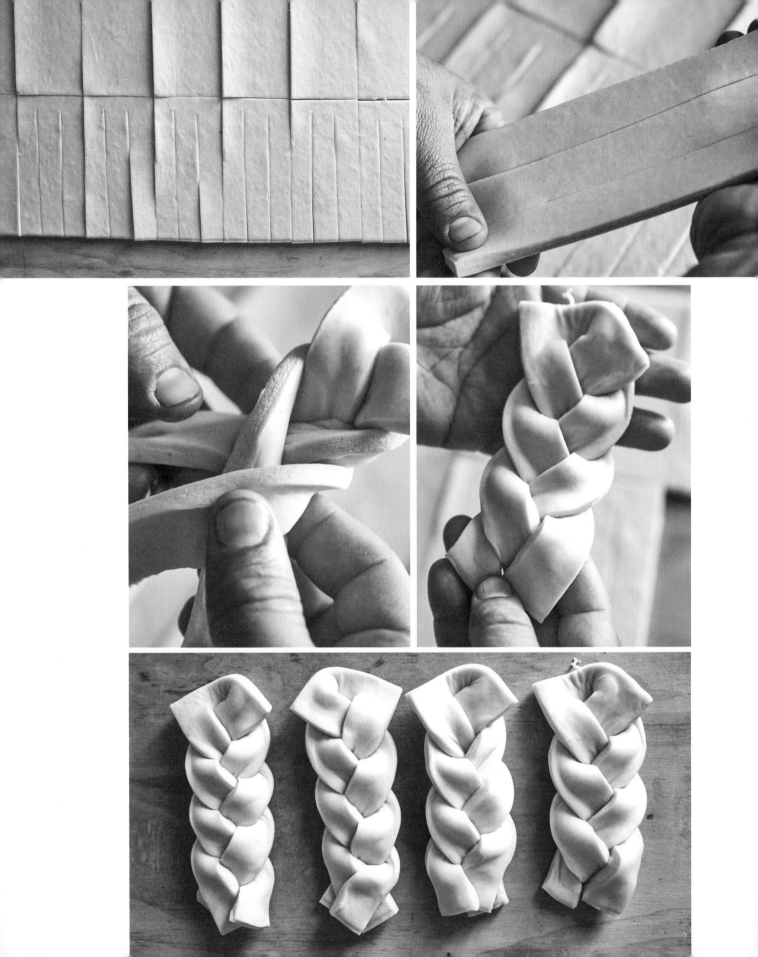

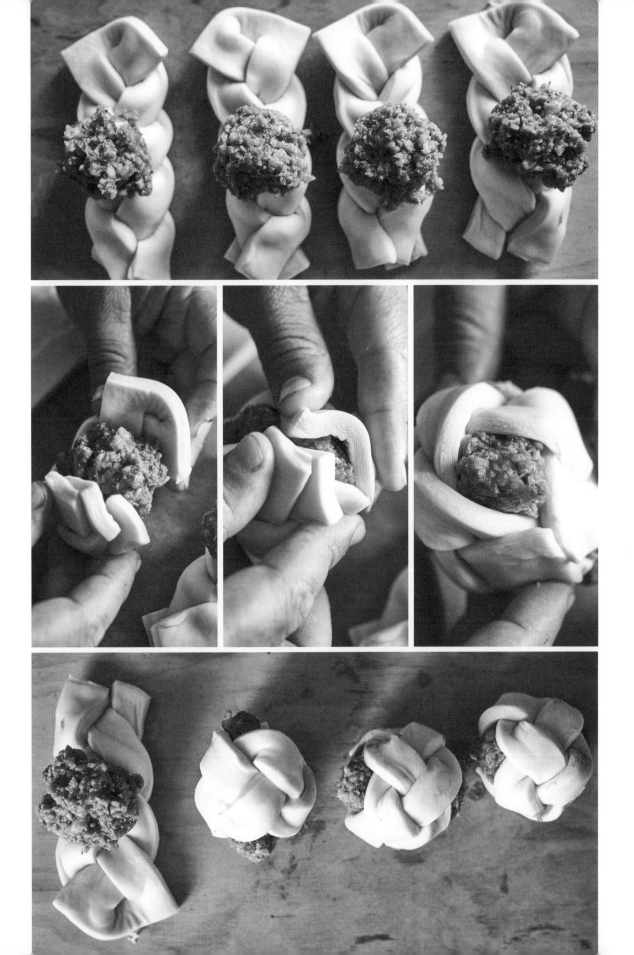

each cut strip should measure 1 in [2.5 cm] wide. Braid the three strips on each rectangle. Stretch the dough slightly and lay flat on the table. Place ¼ cup [about 50 g] of baklava filling on the top of each braid. Roll the braids from the bottom up, ending on top of the uncut piece. Place each rolled knot into the prepared muffin pans.

Set the pan in a draft-free area and let the pastries rise for 2 to 3 hours. The temperature should not exceed 75°F [24°C]. A cool temperature will increase the rising time and with it the flavor development (for more information, see Croissant recipe method, page 37). Twenty minutes before the knots finish proofing, preheat the oven to 375°F [190°C]. Bake the knots until golden brown, 25 to 30 minutes. Transfer the knots to a wire rack and let cool completely.

To make the glaze for the knots, in a small saucepan, heat the honey, orange blossom water, and lemon juice until warm. Brush the tops of each knot with the glaze.

The knots are best eaten the same day, but will keep in an airtight container for 2 days.

To assemble the wreaths, line a baking sheet with parchment and lightly flour a work surface. Make sure your dough is well chilled. Place the dough on the prepared work surface. Roll out the dough to a rectangle measuring 24 in [60 cm] long, 8 in [20 cm] wide, and ¼ in [6 mm] thick. Using an offset spatula or knife, spread the baklava filling onto the surface of the dough.

To start the roll, fold the top ½ in [12 mm] of the dough over the filling and continue to roll toward you, as you would a jelly roll. Use a small amount of flour underneath the roll to prevent sticking to the work surface. If the dough is becoming too soft, it's best to chill the dough further in the refrigerator before shaping.

Using a very sharp knife, split the rolled log down the center lengthwise into two pieces. Starting at the center (see photos, pages 56–57), fold one piece over the other, like an X. Continue to twist the two pieces together on either side of the X. Shape the twisted roll into a wreath, firmly pressing the two ends together. Place on the prepared baking sheet.

Set the pan in a draft-free area and let the pastries rise for 2 to 3 hours. The temperature should not exceed 75°F [24°C]. A cool temperature will increase the rising time and with it the flavor development (for more information, see Croissant recipe method, page 37).

Preheat the oven to 375°F [190°C]. Bake the wreath until golden brown, 40 to 45 minutes. Cool completely.

To make the icing, combine the confectioners' sugar, water, and orange blossom water in a small bowl; whisk until smooth. With a spoon, drizzle the icing over the wreath; let the icing set for about 30 minutes.

The wreath is best if eaten the same day, but can keep, wrapped tightly in plastic wrap (after the icing dries) at room temperature, for 3 days.

CROISSANT-WRAPPED SPIRAL DOGS

YIELDS 12 CROISSANT-WRAPPED HOT DOGS

Croissant dough (page 37)	⅓ recipe	
Twelve 3 oz [85 g] hot dogs or sausages		

MUSTARD AIOLI

Large egg yolk	1	
Dijon mustard	3 Tbsp	45 g
Whole-grain mustard	1 Tbsp	
Cayenne pepper	1 tsp	
Garlic powder	1 tsp	
Salt	½ tsp	
White wine	2 Tbsp	
Lemon juice	2 tsp	
Olive oil	½ cup	120 ml

Our head of *viennoiserie*, Fausto, has an expert hand with laminated doughs, and came up with an ingenious new way of cutting croissant dough. Instead of rolling it, he cuts thin strips off of the block of dough so that when it's laid down like a ribbon on the workbench, you see the cross section of hundreds of layers of butter and dough. Wrapped around hot dogs and baked, the layers expand as they normally do in croissants—part steam trapped in between layers, part yeast—but when cut this way they "rise" sideways, creating filo-like flakiness, encasing the filling with bands of crispy flakes of dough. It is striking, shatteringly crunchy, and creates a whole new type of *viennoiserie* just by turning dough on its side. Try this with hot links, sausage, kielbasa, or breakfast sausage. Mustard is delicious with these, or try Fausto's mustard aioli, which you'll want to slather on everything you can think of, it's so good.

This recipe calls for only one-third of a batch of croissant dough. Freeze the remainder, as directed in the Croissant recipe (page 39) to use in any of the other croissant recipes.

......

Make the croissant dough as directed on page 37, through the resting, chilling, and freezing steps.

Line two baking sheets with parchment paper.

To prepare the croissant strips, lightly flour a work surface. Roll the dough out to a rectangle measuring 18 in [46 cm] wide, 8 in [20 cm] long, and ⅜ in [1 cm] thick. Using a rolling cutter or a sharp knife, cut the dough horizontally into twelve ⅜ in [1 cm] strips. Lightly stretch each strip to measure 30 in [76 cm] long.

continued

To wrap the hot dogs, turn a dough strip cut-side up, so you can see the layers of dough. Press the edge of the dough firmly against one end of the hot dog to secure it in place. Moving quickly, start wrapping the dough around the hot dog with no gaps between the dough, moving from one end to the other. If the dough is a little too long, cut off the end of the dough and discard. If you need a little extra dough to reach the end, unwrap the hot dog slightly and stretch the dough a little more. Press the dough firmly against the hot dog at the end to secure it. Place on the prepared baking sheet. Repeat with the remaining dough, spacing the wrapped hot dogs 2 in [5 cm] apart (six per baking sheet).

Set the pan in a draft-free area and let the pastries rise at warm room temperature for 1 hour.

Preheat the oven to 375°F [190°C]. Bake until golden brown, 30 to 35 minutes.

They are best eaten the same day, but can be refrigerated and reheated in a 350°F [180°C] oven for 10 minutes before serving with the mustard aioli.

To make the aioli, combine the egg yolk, both mustards, cayenne pepper, garlic powder, salt, white wine, and lemon juice in a blender or food processor fitted with the steel blade. With the blender on high speed, drizzle in the olive oil and mix until thickened and smooth, about 1 minute. The aioli will keep for 5 days in an airtight container in the refrigerator.

BRIOCHE

POOLISH

Instant yeast	¼ tsp	
Water, warmed to 75°F [24°C]	¾ cup	180 ml
Bread flour	1 cup + 2 Tbsp	150 g

DOUGH

Instant yeast	1 Tbsp	
Whole milk, chilled	⅓ cup + 2 Tbsp	110 ml
Large eggs, chilled	4	
Large egg yolks, chilled	5	
Bread flour	2⅓ cups + 1 Tbsp	315 g
All-purpose flour	1⅓ cups + 1 Tbsp	185 g
Sugar	¼ cup	50 g
Salt	¾ Tbsp	
Unsalted butter, at room temperature	1½ cups + 1 Tbsp	350 g

EGG WASH

Large egg yolks	4	
Heavy cream	¼ cup	60 ml
Salt	pinch	

This lightly textured yet rich French bread likely originated in Normandy, which has long been known for its high-quality butter, and is the first cousin to other enriched doughs, such as challah, panettone, Swedish *vetebröd*, and Finnish *pulla*. Different types of brioche dough are made depending on how the dough will be used, with formulas varying primarily in the percentage of butter and length of fermentation.

Baker Alen Ramos developed this recipe, which qualifies to be called *brioche mousseline*, meaning it is made with at least 50 percent butter (some recipes have as much as 80 percent) and is used for making coffee cakes, individual pastries, buns (such as Conchas, page 79), or plain loaves. Of all the enriched bread doughs, brioche has the softest, most meltingly tender crumb. French toast made from this bread fries up with a center like pudding, and, when sliced and toasted, it's a classic accompaniment for paté, caviar, or foie gras. Leftover brioche makes exceptional bread pudding.

KITCHEN NOTES: Because brioche has a high ratio of butter, the dough must be well chilled when you form it into loaves. If the dough becomes too warm, the butter will begin to melt out of the dough, becoming soft and sticky; place it back in the refrigerator to firm up if this happens. To keep the dough from sticking to your fingers, lightly oil them before shaping.

· · · · · ·

To make the poolish, sprinkle the yeast over the water in a small bowl and stir with a spoon. Measure the flour into the bowl of a stand mixer. Add the water and yeast mixture to the flour and mix with a rubber spatula or a wooden spoon to combine. Cover with plastic wrap and allow to ferment at room temperature for 2 hours until doubled in size, with active bubbles forming on the surface.

continued

While the poolish is fermenting, measure out the rest of the ingredients. Cut the butter into ½ in [12 mm] chunks.

To mix the dough, place the mixing bowl containing the poolish on the stand mixer and attach the dough hook. Sprinkle the yeast over the cold milk in a small bowl and mix with a spoon to combine. Pour the cold milk-yeast mixture, eggs, and yolks into the bowl with the poolish, all at once. Mix on the lowest speed for about 1 minute to break up the ingredients. Turn the mixer off, and add the flours, sugar, and salt to the liquid ingredients, all at once. Place the bowl back onto the mixer and mix on low speed until the dough begins to form and the dry ingredients are no longer visible on the side of the mixing bowl, about 2 minutes. Increase the mixer speed to medium-low and mix for 6 minutes. Begin adding the butter, one piece at a time, with no waiting between pieces. Once all of the butter has been added, continue to mix for 4 minutes to incorporate the fat into the dough. Stop the mixer and scrape the sides of the bowl, pushing any excess butter back down into the dough to incorporate it into the mixture. Increase the mixer speed to medium for 8 minutes to finish incorporating the butter and to continue strengthening the dough. When the last of the butter has disappeared, increase the mixer speed to medium-high for 1 minute. The dough will be smooth and shiny.

Transfer the dough to a large bowl and cover with a tea towel or plastic wrap. Allow to proof at room temperature for 1 hour.

When the dough has doubled in size, turn it out onto a lightly floured surface. Fold it in half, then in quarters. Lightly oil a large baking sheet. Gently pat the dough into a 1½ in [4 cm] thick round on the prepared sheet. Dust the top lightly with flour and wrap with plastic wrap. Put the sheet in the freezer for at least 1 hour to quickly lower the temperature of the brioche dough and slow fermentation. Then transfer to the refrigerator overnight, if baking the next morning. If you want to bake the same day, put the pan in the freezer for 2 hours and then transfer to the refrigerator for 3 to 5 hours before shaping the dough. Alternatively, you can freeze the dough for a few days before baking: transfer it to a wide, shallow airtight container, slip it into the freezer for several days, and then thaw it overnight in the refrigerator before using.

Brush three 9 by 5 in [23 by 12 cm] loaf pans with melted butter. Remove the chilled dough from the refrigerator and place on a lightly floured work surface in a cool kitchen. Divide the dough into three equal portions. Press each portion into a rectangle the length of a loaf pan and slightly wider than the pan. Starting from a narrow end, roll up the rectangle tightly, pinch the ends and seam to seal, and place seam-side down in a prepared pan. The pan should be no more than about one-third full. The dough increases substantially in volume during rising, and if you fill the pan any fuller, the brioche will bake up too large for the pan. When the pans are filled, place them in a draft-free area with relatively high humidity and an ideal temperature of 75 to 80°F [24 to 27°C]. Let rise for 2 to 3 hours. During this final rising, the brioche dough should at least double in size and look noticeably puffy but still be resilient to the touch.

Preheat the oven to 425°F [220°C] for at least 20 minutes. Then about 10 minutes before you are ready to begin baking, make the egg wash. In a small bowl, whisk together the egg yolks, cream, and salt until you have a pale yellow mixture. Using a pastry brush, brush the yolk mixture on the tops of the loaves. Let the wash dry slightly, about 10 minutes, before baking.

Place the loaves in the oven and bake for 15 minutes. Reduce the oven temperature to 350°F [180°C] and bake until the loaves are a uniformly dark golden brown on the bottom, sides, and top, about 45 minutes longer. Remove the pans from the oven, immediately rap the bottoms on a countertop to release the loaves, and then turn the loaves out onto wire racks to cool. The loaves can be eaten warm from the oven or allowed to cool and eaten that day at room temperature or toasted. If you keep them longer than a day, wrap them in plastic wrap or parchment paper and store them for up to 3 days in the refrigerator, then toast or warm to serve.

BACON AND EGG BRIOCHE BUNS

YIELDS 20 BUNS

Brioche dough (page 61)	1 recipe
Bacon slices	20
Large eggs	20

EGG WASH

Large egg yolks	2
Heavy cream	2 Tbsp
Salt	pinch

Fresh herbs, grated firm cheese,
olive oil, chili flakes, sea salt,
or pimentón for garnish

I love a baking puzzle, and this bun presented one that was very satisfying to figure out. How could we bake a savory pastry using brioche dough with 1. an egg with a soft center, 2. the bacon cooked perfectly crisp, and 3. a dough that rose to cup these ingredients perfectly within? Here is an all-in-one egg sandwich that isn't all that hard once you realize how the ingredients are arranged, with precooked bacon creating a little insulated nest for the egg to be broken into and baked. Top with herbs, chili flakes, grated cheese, or *pimentón*, a smoked Spanish paprika.

KITCHEN NOTES: Breaking the eggs directly into a measuring cup will save you the trouble of fishing out any egg shells from your buns if need be, or trying to replace an egg with a broken yolk.

Make the brioche dough as directed on page 61, through the resting and chilling steps.

Preheat the oven to 350°F [180°C]. Line a rimmed baking sheet with foil.

Place the sliced bacon in a single layer on the prepared baking sheet. Bake until the bacon is halfway cooked, with some of the fat rendered out, but still light in color, and bendable without breaking, about 15 minutes. Allow to cool on the sheet.

Brush the cups of an extra-large muffin pan with melted butter, or line with extra-large liners.

Transfer the dough to a floured work surface. Using a knife or a bench scraper, cut the dough into twenty 3 oz [80 g] pieces and shape each one into a ball by rolling them by hand in a circular motion against the floured surface. Place one brioche ball into each muffin cup and, with floured hands, gently press into a disk shape, pressing right to the edges of each cup. Place a tea towel or plastic wrap over the pan and proof at room temperature until doubled in size, about 2 hours.

Preheat the oven to 350°F [180°C]. For the egg wash, whisk together the yolks, cream, and salt. When the brioche is ready, gently brush each bun with egg wash, using care not to press or poke the proofed dough with the brush, as this will cause it to deflate. With wet hands, use your fingers to form a cavity by pressing directly into the center and pushing outward, again using care to not deflate the dough. The cavity should be deep and large enough to hold an egg without overflowing. Press each bacon slice into a ring inside the cavity, overlapping the edges to

continued

match the size of the cavity in each bun. Crack one egg at a time into a small measuring cup or ramekin and gently transfer each egg to the center of the bacon ring. Sprinkle with cheese, if using.

Place the pan in the oven on the center rack and bake until the egg white is completely opaque but still quite jiggly, the yolk is bright yellow, the bacon has crisped, and the brioche is golden brown, 15 to 18 minutes. Remove from the oven and allow the buns to cool in the pan for 10 minutes before transferring them to a cooling rack. Garnish each bun with chopped fresh herbs, olive oil, chili flakes, sea salt, or *pimentón*—whatever is your preference. These are best eaten fresh and warm from the oven or within the next 2 to 3 hours.

BRIOCHE JAM BUNS

YIELDS 24 JAM BUNS

Brioche dough (page 61)	1 recipe	
EGG WASH		
Large egg yolks	2	
Heavy cream	2 Tbsp	
Salt	pinch	
Jam or preserves	3¼ cups	910 g
Pastry Cream (page 300)	3¼ cups	720 g
Sugar for sprinkling		

Like thumbprint cookies, these soft, plump buns are a vehicle for your favorite jam. There is a little pastry cream spooned on top, giving the buns extra flavor and moisture, with the brioche dough rising up and enveloping the filling as it bakes. You can make a salty/sweet variation by spooning jam into prosciutto. The edges of the prosciutto get lacy and crisp around the sweet center.

. . . . . .

Make the brioche dough as directed on page 61, through the resting and chilling steps.

Preheat the oven to 350°F [180°C]. Brush the cups of two muffin top pans with melted butter, or arrange 24 round, wide, shallow, paper baking molds on a baking sheet. Lightly flour a work surface.

Turn the chilled brioche dough out onto the floured surface and cut into twenty-four 2¼ oz [65 g] pieces. Shape the dough pieces into balls and place in the cups or molds. Use floured fingers to gently and

slightly flatten each piece into a disk shape to the edge of the mold. Cover the muffin pan or tray with a kitchen towel or plastic wrap and allow to rest at room temperature until doubled in size, for about 2 hours.

To make the egg wash, whisk together the yolks, cream, and salt. Use a pastry brush to gently brush the dough with the egg wash. With wet fingers, gently create a small well in the center of the brioche round, slowly pushing out from the center, so as to not deflate the dough. Use a small spoon to fill each round first with 2 Tbsp of jam topped by 2 Tbsp of pastry cream. Sprinkle liberally with sugar.

Bake until golden and fragrant, 12 to 15 minutes. Cool on a wire rack for at least 5 minutes before unmolding. These are best served at room temperature on the day they are made.

Brioche Suisse Variation: After brushing with the egg wash, make a well and fill each bun with 2 Tbsp of pastry cream and top with 1 Tbsp of chopped dark chocolate or chocolate chips. Bake as directed.

Prosciutto Variation: Use 1 slice of prosciutto per bun. After brushing with egg wash, make a well with your fingers in the dough as described above and line it with the prosciutto, allowing some to rest over the sides. Spoon in 1 Tbsp of jam per bun, and omit the sugar. Bake as directed.

BOSTOCK

SYRUP

Water	¼ cup	60 ml
Granulated sugar	¼ cup	50 g
Orange liqueur	2 Tbsp	
Orange juice	¼ cup	60 ml
Orange zest	1 Tbsp	

Brioche slices (page 61), each ½ in [12 mm] thick	6	
Apricot jam, at room temperature	¾ cup	210 g
Frangipane Cream (page 304), at room temperature	¾ cup	175 ml
Sliced almonds	¾ cup	65 g
Confectioners' sugar for dusting		

Although it is traditionally eaten for breakfast or brunch, Bostock would make an exceptional dessert, prepared ahead of time and popped into the oven a half hour before serving. It is made from thick brioche slices that are moistened with a syrup of orange juice and orange liqueur; topped with apricot jam (and/or fresh fruit, as pictured), almond cream, and sliced nuts; and baked until toasted and crunchy. It would be equally good made with other enriched or plain breads, such as challah, panettone, or basic good sliced white bread.

KITCHEN NOTES: Make sure that your jam and frangipane cream are at room temperature so that they are easy to spread. This recipe makes very good use of day-old bread. If you can find sliced natural almonds (with the skin on), they are more visually interesting than blanched almonds, but either works.

Preheat the oven to 375°F [190°C].

To make the syrup, in a small saucepan over medium heat, combine the water, granulated sugar, orange liqueur, orange juice, and orange zest, stirring just until the sugar dissolves. Remove from the heat and let cool to room temperature.

While the syrup is cooling, line a baking sheet with parchment paper or a nonstick liner. Arrange the bread slices on the prepared pan, and brush evenly with the syrup. Using an offset spatula or knife, spread 2 Tbsp of the jam over each slice, and then spread 2 Tbsp of the cream over the jam. Finally, scatter 2 Tbsp of the almonds evenly over each slice.

Bake the brioche slices until the almonds are golden brown and the edges of the bread slices are toasted, 20 to 25 minutes. Remove from the oven and, using a fine-mesh sieve, dust with confectioners' sugar. Serve immediately.

BRIOCHE BREAD PUDDING

YIELDS ONE 9 BY 5 IN [23 BY 12 CM] PUDDING; 6 TO 8 SERVINGS

Brioche slices (page 61), each 1 in [2.5 cm] thick	6	

CUSTARD

Large eggs	8	
Sugar	¾ cup + 3 Tbsp	185 g
Whole milk	4 cups	1 L
Vanilla extract	1½ tsp	
Salt	½ tsp	

We make countless, huge, deep pans of this bread pudding every day. It is one recipe that doesn't suffer from being made in a really large batch—in fact, it only gets better. If you have some left over, you can chill it, slice it, and fry as you would French toast. We serve it topped with seasonal fresh fruit such as cherries, peaches, or thinly sliced apples or pears, and lightly sauté it in butter with a little caramel. When we use blueberries, we heat them briefly with a little maple syrup and a bit of butter and immediately spoon them over each serving. For alternative toppings, try warmed caramel, chocolate sauce, or fresh, lightly sweetened berry purée. I like to see little pockets of custard between the bread slices, and a nice crusty top; the more distinction between soft and eggy interior with crusty top, the better. You can also use leftover croissants, chocolate croissants (or tuck chunks of chocolate into the croissants), or any rich egg bread, such as challah, panettone, or Swedish *vetebröd*.

KITCHEN NOTES: Make sure you don't crowd the bread; they are like sponges in the custard and need room to soak up the liquid or you'll have a dry pudding. You can use just about any size or shape of mold, just realize that if you go with a deep mold, you will have a lower crust-to-pudding ratio. If you have leftover custard, pour it into ramekins and bake in a hot double boiler in a 350°F [180°C] oven, or refrigerate, covered, for up to 2 days and use for French toast.

Preheat the oven to 350°F [180°C]. Butter a 9 by 5 in [23 by 12 cm] glass loaf dish.

Arrange the brioche slices on a baking sheet. Place in the oven until lightly toasted, 4 to 10 minutes, depending on the freshness of the bread. Remove from the oven and set aside to cool.

To make the custard, crack the eggs into a mixing bowl and whisk until blended. Add the sugar and whisk until smooth. Add the milk, vanilla, and salt and whisk until fully incorporated. Pour the custard through a fine-mesh sieve held over a pitcher or a measuring cup with a spout (to make pouring it into the dish easier).

Place the toasted bread slices in the prepared loaf dish, cutting the slices to fit as needed. If the bread extends over the top of the loaf pan, trim the slices to fit. Pour the custard evenly over the bread, filling the dish to the top. You may not be able to add all of the custard at this point. Let sit for about 10 minutes, so that the bread can absorb the custard.

continued

(Or, you can make the pudding up to this point, cover, and refrigerate overnight and then bake the next day. Cover and refrigerate any extra custard for adding just before baking if the mixture does not reach the rim of the dish.)

Just before baking, top off the dish with more of the custard if the previous addition has been completely absorbed. (See Kitchen Notes for a suggestion on how to use any leftover custard.) Cover the dish with aluminum foil, place in the oven, and bake the pudding for about 1 hour. (If you have refrigerated the pudding overnight before baking it, it will take 20 to 30 minutes longer to bake.) To test for doneness, uncover the dish, slip a knife into the center, and push the bread aside. If the custard is still very liquid, re-cover the dish and return the pudding to the oven to bake for about 10 more minutes. If only a little liquid remains, the pudding is ready to come out of the oven. The custard will continue to cook after it is removed from the oven and it will set up as it cools.

Let the pudding cool for about 10 minutes before serving. You can serve the bread pudding by slicing it and removing each slice with an offset spatula, or by scooping it out with a serving spoon. Store leftovers, covered, in the refrigerator for up to 4 days. Serve cold, at room temperature, or reheated.

SAVORY BREAD PUDDING

Country bread, or any type of good crusty bread, preferably day old	12 oz	340 g
Olive oil	2 Tbsp	
Yellow onion or leek, chopped	3/4 cup	100 g

CUSTARD

Large eggs	5	
Salt	3/4 tsp	
Whole milk	4 cups	1 L
Heavy cream	4 cups	1 L
Black pepper, freshly ground	1/2 tsp	
Nutmeg, freshly grated	1/4 tsp	
Sliced smoked ham, cut into strips	4 oz	115 g
Fresh thyme, chopped	2 Tbsp	
Swiss chard or other braising green, chopped (optional)	1 cup	85 g
Grated Gruyère, Cheddar, or other good melting cheese	3/4 cup	85 g

TOPPING

Grated cheese, as above	1/2 cup	55 g
Black pepper, freshly ground		

We go through a lot of sliced bread at the bakery and Manufactory for sandwiches, and always end up with lots of ends and unusable holey pieces. We toast them and combine with any number of savory ingredients such as fresh mushrooms, smoked ham or bacon, chard, asparagus, onion or leek, and, of course, cheese.

KITCHEN NOTES: You can bake the bread pudding in a heavy 10 in [25 cm] skillet, preferably cast iron. If you decide to use the skillet, you can sauté the onion or leek in it and then use it for baking the pudding without washing it first. The bits left behind in the bottom of the pan add more flavor to the pudding. You can also substitute 4 oz [115 g] sliced bacon, cut into strips, for the ham, and sauté it in the skillet before the onion or leek, making the olive oil for cooking the onion or leek unnecessary.

· · · · · ·

Preheat the oven to 350°F [180°C]. Oil a 9 by 13 in [23 by 33 cm] baking dish with olive oil.

Cut the bread into 1½ in [4 cm] cubes. If the bread is fresh, spread the pieces on a baking sheet, and toast for a few minutes to dry them out. Set aside.

In a skillet, heat the olive oil over medium-high heat. Add the onion or leek and sweat, stirring, for 3 to 5 minutes. Remove from the heat and set aside.

continued

To make the custard, whisk together the eggs and salt. Add the milk and cream, whisk to combine, and then whisk in the pepper and nutmeg.

In a large mixing bowl, combine the bread, custard, ham, thyme, chard (if using), sautéed onion or leek, and cheese and mix well. Carefully pour the mixture into the prepared baking dish. The custard should come right up to the top but not cover the highest pieces of bread.

Top the pudding evenly with cheese and then grind a light dusting of pepper over the surface. Place in the oven and bake until the custard is no longer runny in the center, 1 to 1½ hours. Check, after 1 hour. If the top starts to get too dark before the pudding is done, cover the dish with aluminum foil. Serve hot or at room temperature. Store any left-overs in the refrigerator, covered, for up to 4 days.

CONCHAS

YIELDS 12 CONCHAS

Brioche dough (page 61)	1.3 lb	600 g

CONCHA TOPPING

Unsalted butter, at room temperature	½ cup	115 g
Sugar	½ cup + 4 tsp	115 g
All-purpose flour	1 cup + 1 Tbsp	140 g
Salt	⅛ tsp	
Baking powder	⅛ tsp	

EGG WASH

Large egg, lightly beaten	1	
Milk	1 Tbsp	

These rich, light buns, made with our brioche dough, were popularized in Mexico City and are found all over the Mission District in San Francisco and most Latin American neighborhoods in the United States. Conchas were on the breakfast table every Sunday morning in the childhood home of Scarlett, one of our bakers who grew up in the Mission. She likes to split them and fill them with pastry cream (page 300) or chocolate pudding (page 310).

Traditionally, enriched dough, called pan dulce, is formed into a small bun with a thin cookie-like coating draped over the top before baking. The pastries are scored to mimic the striations of a seashell, and bake up crisp on the outside, soft bun underneath. They're usually flavored with cinnamon, vanilla, or chocolate, or made with brightly colored sugars.

KITCHEN NOTES: Conchas should be eaten very fresh, as the small size makes them stale quickly.

. . . . . .

Make the brioche dough as directed on page 61, through the resting and chilling steps.

Cut the brioche dough into twelve equal pieces (approximately 1.75 oz [50 g] per concha). Line two baking sheets with parchment paper.

On a lightly floured work surface, sprinkle the dough with flour and, using the side of your palm, roll each dough portion in a clockwise motion until it forms a smooth ball. Place the dough balls about 3 in [7.5 cm] apart on the prepared baking sheets. Cover lightly with plastic wrap. Set the pan in a draft-free area and let the pastries rise for about 1 hour.

Check after 45 minutes. You want the dough balls to have proofed halfway before you cover them with the topping. They should have grown in size but still have a spring to them when gently touched with your finger.

Meanwhile, make the topping. In the bowl of a stand mixer fitted with the paddle attachment, combine the butter, sugar, flour, salt, and baking powder. Mix on medium-low speed until all the ingredients are well incorporated and a smooth dough forms. Wrap in plastic wrap until ready to use.

Cut the topping into twelve equal pieces. Between two pieces of parchment paper, roll out each portion into a 3 in [7.5 cm] circle. With a sharp knife, cut the topping into shapes that mimic the ridges of a seashell.

continued

To make the egg wash, combine the lightly beaten egg and milk in a small bowl. Brush the brioche dough balls with the egg wash.

Transfer the cut strips of topping one by one, or use a bench scraper to transfer all the strips for each bun at once, and gently adhere to the brioche. Let the conchas rest in a warm place for 1 to 1½ hours to finish rising. To check the rise, gently touch the dough with your finger (you can wet your finger if the dough is sticky). They are ready when the indent in the dough from your finger springs back very slowly.

Preheat the oven to 350°F [180°C]. Bake until light golden brown, 15 to 18 minutes.

OPTIONAL: To preserve the color of the concha topping, lightly tent with foil after 10 minutes of baking and return to the oven to finish baking. Allow to cool, uncovered, for 5 minutes.

Conchas are best eaten the day they are baked, but can be kept in an airtight container at room temperature for up to 2 days.

FLAVOR AND FILLING VARIATIONS

To flavor or color the topping, use 2 Tbsp less flour than the recipe calls for and add 2 Tbsp of cocoa powder, matcha powder, or ground freeze-dried strawberries or mango (grind using a spice grinder). You can also add 1 tsp cinnamon to the topping recipe. To color the topping, add drops of food coloring until the desired hue is reached.

To fill the conchas, slice the pastry in half horizontally and sandwich with chocolate pudding (page 310) or pastry cream (page 300). Eat within hours of filling.

QUICHE

YIELDS ONE 10 IN [25 CM] QUICHE; 6 TO 8 SERVINGS

Fully baked and cooled 10 in [25 cm] Flaky Tart Dough shell baked in a deep tart pan or a pie pan (page 286)	1	
Large eggs	5	
All-purpose flour	¼ cup	30 g
Crème fraîche	1 cup	240 g
Whole milk	1 cup	240 ml
Salt	1 tsp	
Black pepper, freshly ground	½ tsp	
Fresh thyme, finely chopped	1 Tbsp	
Grated sharp cheese, such as Gruyère or Cheddar	1 cup	115 g

Quiche is the queen of breakfast and brunch, and it is ideal when you don't want to short-order cook eggs and want to have something made ahead of time. There are two small but important differences between this quiche filling and most others. The first is that part of the liquid is crème fraîche, which makes the filling a little richer but with a slight tartness for balance. The other is that we add a small amount of flour. These details come from Boulangerie Artisinale des Maures, a bakery in the Var region of France, where we both apprenticed in 1994. We learned this recipe there and many others, each of which had some particular extra ingredient or technique to it.

KITCHEN NOTES: We often add 1 cup [85 g] of uncooked, coarsely chopped leafy greens, such as chard or spinach, to the egg mixture. It's a small enough amount that any liquid exuded during cooking doesn't affect the set of the filling; you have to precook and wring out greens when they are added in larger quantity. If you have difficulty filling the shell entirely and then transferring it to the oven without spills, fill it three-quarters full, transfer to the oven, and bake until the top is ever so slightly set. Pour in the rest to fill and continue baking.

. . . . . .

Have the pie shell ready for filling. Preheat the oven to 375°F [190°C].

Place 1 egg and the flour in the bowl of a stand mixer fitted with the paddle attachment or in a large mixing bowl and mix at high speed or by hand with a whisk until smooth. Mix or whisk in the remaining 4 eggs until blended. In a medium bowl, whisk the crème fraîche until it is perfectly smooth and then whisk in the milk. Pour the egg mixture through a fine-mesh sieve held over the milk mixture. Whisk in the salt, pepper, and thyme. Mix in the cheese. (You can prepare the custard up to 4 days in advance before baking; cover and refrigerate. The flour will settle to the bottom of the container, so whisk well before using.)

Pour the egg mixture into the pie shell. Place in the oven and bake for 10 minutes. Reduce the oven temperature to 325°F [160°C] and bake until the filling is just set, about 30 minutes longer. The center of the quiche should feel slightly firm, rather than liquidy, when touched. Let cool on a wire rack for at least 20 minutes to allow the custard to set up, so that it will slice neatly. It can be served warm or at room temperature. To serve a fully cooled quiche warm, cover it with aluminum foil and reheat it in a 325°F [160°C] oven for about 15 minutes.

Store, tightly wrapped, in the refrigerator for up to 4 days. Serve cold, at room temperature, or reheated as suggested.

GOUGÈRES

YIELDS ABOUT THIRTY 1½ IN [4 CM] HORS D'OEUVRES, OR EIGHT TO TEN 4 IN [10 CM] PASTRIES

CHOUX PASTE

Nonfat milk	1¼ cups	300 ml
Unsalted butter	10 Tbsp	140 g
Salt	1 tsp	
All-purpose flour	1 cup	140 g
Large eggs	5	
Grated Gruyère cheese, plus more for sprinkling	¾ cup	85 g
Black pepper, freshly ground	1 tsp	
Fresh thyme, minced	1 Tbsp	

EGG WASH

Large egg	1
Salt	pinch

Gougères are made from one of the mainstays of French classical baking, pâte à choux, or choux paste. It is what éclair shells, crullers, and cream puffs are made from, the dough rising from the large amount of egg mixed in, and the steam that forms as it bakes, raising the elastic dough. They are crisp on the outside, and soft and eggy inside, creating the perfect form to fill like a sandwich with sliced meat or charcuterie, or greens. These have a hefty amount of black pepper to balance the richness of the cheese in the dough; we use Gruyère, but Cheddar, Swiss, or any of the lower-moisture cheeses work well. The dough is very forgiving, so you can add or subtract flavors easily and make the recipe yours. Try duxelles (minced sautéed mushrooms and shallot), caramelized onions, chopped herbs, *pimentón*, or curry. They are best eaten the day they are baked, but you can refresh them in a hot oven for a few minutes if older than a day.

KITCHEN NOTES: Don't be tempted to use whole milk instead of nonfat. Because of the amount of butter and cheese, the batter is rich, and the whole milk will cause the Large-Size Gougères to fall. If you do not have nonfat milk, use half water and half whole milk, or just water. To make them ahead, spoon the batter onto the baking sheet, freeze, and store covered in the freezer. The small 1 in [2.5 cm] gougères can be baked straight from the freezer (increase the baking time by 5 to 10 minutes), whereas larger ones need to be defrosted prior to baking.

Preheat the oven to 350°F [180°C]. Butter a baking sheet or line with parchment paper.

To make the choux paste, combine the milk, butter, and salt in a heavy saucepan, and place over medium heat until the butter melts and the mixture comes to a full boil. Add the flour all at once, stirring vigorously with a wooden spoon. Keep stirring until the mixture has formed a smooth mass, it pulls away from the sides of the pan, and some of the moisture has evaporated. This will take about 3 minutes.

Transfer the paste to the bowl of a stand mixer fitted with the paddle attachment or to a heatproof mixing bowl. If using a mixer, add the eggs one at a time and mix on medium speed, incorporating each egg before adding the next. When all the eggs

continued

have been added, the mixture will be very thick, smooth, and shiny. Remove the bowl from the mixer stand, add the cheese, pepper, and thyme, and mix in with a rubber spatula. If making by hand, add the eggs one at a time to the bowl and mix with a wooden spoon, incorporating each egg before adding the next one, then proceed as directed for the mixer method.

Transfer the contents of the bowl to a pastry bag fitted with a ½ in [12 mm] (no. 6 or 7) plain tip, adding only as much to the bag as is comfortable to work with. Pipe 1 in [2.5 cm] mounds onto the prepared baking sheet, spacing them about 1½ in [4 cm] apart. Or, use a spoon to drop the dough in 1 in [2.5 cm] mounds.

To make the egg wash, in a small bowl, whisk together the egg and salt, and then gently brush the top of each pastry with the egg wash. Lightly sprinkle the top of each pastry with a little cheese.

Place the pastries in the oven immediately and bake until they have puffed, are nicely browned, and feel light for their size, about 25 minutes. These are delicious served hot or warm, or are also good at room temperature. Or, let cool completely, store in an airtight container in the refrigerator for up to a few days, and recrisp in a 350°F [180°C] oven for 5 minutes.

Large-Size Gougères Variation: To make 4 in [10 cm] gougères, use a large spoon to form 3 in [7.5 cm] rounds about 1 in [2.5 cm] high on the prepared baking sheet, spacing them about 2 in [5 cm] apart. Brush with the egg wash and top with the cheese. Bake until they have puffed, are light for their size, and are golden brown, 35 to 45 minutes. Remove from the oven and poke a small hole in the side of each pastry to allow steam to escape. Releasing the steam keeps them from collapsing (this step is unnecessary for the small ones). If splitting and filling, let cool to room temperature; otherwise, they may be served hot, warm, or at room temperature.

GRANOLA BARK

Coconut sugar	1/3 cup + 1 Tbsp	75 g
Maple syrup or honey	1/4 to 1/2 cup	80 to 170 g
Water	1/4 cup	60 ml
Salt	1/2 tsp	
Rolled oats	3 1/3 cups	300 g
Almonds or hazelnuts, chopped	1 1/4 cups	175 g
Unsweetened shredded coconut	2/3 cup	60 g
Almond or hazelnut flour	1/2 cup + 2 Tbsp	60 g
Flax or chia seeds	1/2 cup	80 g
Sesame seeds	1/4 cup	35 g
Ground cinnamon	1 1/2 tsp	
Olive oil	1/3 cup	80 ml
Large egg white, beaten	1	
Vanilla extract	1 tsp	

This is the ultimate crispy-crunchy granola bar, packed with delicious nuts and seeds, perfect for a child's lunch or crumbled over yogurt. For the compacting step, I stand on the top baking sheet to really get a good compression. Use the upper range of maple syrup if you like a sweeter granola.

• • • • • •

Preheat the oven to 325°F [160°C]. Line a 13 by 18 in [33 by 46 cm] rimmed baking sheet with parchment paper.

In a small saucepan over medium heat, bring the coconut sugar, maple syrup, water, and salt to a boil. Stir until the sugar is dissolved, remove from the heat, and cool.

Combine the oats, almonds, coconut, almond flour, flax seeds, sesame seeds, and cinnamon in a large bowl. Stir the olive oil, egg white, and vanilla into the cooled syrup-sugar mixture and pour over the oat-nut mixture. Mix until well coated and spread evenly on the prepared baking sheet.

Using a heavy pot or another baking sheet of the same size, press the mixture firmly to compact it. Bake until dark golden brown, about 45 minutes total, rotating the sheet after 15 minutes. Open the oven door two or three times during baking to release steam.

Cool on a baking rack until crisp. If the surface is tacky to the touch after 15 minutes, return the pan to the warm oven and allow the bark to crisp for another 10 minutes. Once cool, break the bark into pieces. Store in an airtight container at room temperature for up to 2 weeks.

CHAPTER TWO

TARTS, PIES, FRUIT

LEMON CREAM TART

YIELDS ONE 9 IN [23 CM] TART OR TWELVE 4 IN [10 CM] TARTLETS; 8 TO 12 SERVINGS

Fully baked and cooled 9 in [23 cm] Sweet Tart Dough shell or twelve 4 in [10 cm] tartlet shells (page 290)	1	
Lemon Cream (page 306)	2⅓ cups	560 ml
Heavy cream, very cold	1 cup	240 ml
Sugar	2 tsp	
Fresh flowers or Candied Fennel (page 314) for decorating		

Most lemon tarts are a baked lemon custard or curd in a sweet or flaky tart shell. This one calls for our basic Lemon Cream recipe, which you make with a generous amount of butter on the stove top. This technique creates an even softer, more luscious and delicate filling than a typical curd (no surprise then that innovative French pastry chef Pierre Hermé developed it). I use his technique for this cream, although our recipe has more lemon bite and a little less butter than his. The method is genius and yet obvious and common sense: after making the curd, you "mount" butter into the very warm mixture as you would for a buerre blanc sauce, whisking continuously as it melts, which keeps the butter in emulsion and creates the softer, lighter look of this lemon cream. The resulting filling is a little less tart than curd, and is softer, creamier, and more unctuous and will set just enough to slice but without being at all stiff. We use the same lemon cream in a number of ways, including mixing it with whipped cream to make a light-textured filling for a fresh fruit tart and using it as a filling for Lemon Meringue Cake (page 155).

I've also frozen it in popsicle molds, creating a sort of lemon pudding pop. If you fold it with an equal volume of whipped cream, it makes a luscious cake filling as well, a bit lighter and more mousse-like than the straight lemon cream.

KITCHEN NOTES: If you are using chilled, already-made lemon cream, you need to soften it so that you can pour it into the tart shell and create a smooth finish on top. Spoon it into a stainless-steel bowl and set up a double boiler (see page 306). Stir it constantly over simmering water. This will keep the butter in emulsion, which is what makes this filling so smooth and creamy. If the butter "breaks," or comes out of emulsion, it won't have as light a texture, although it will still be delicious.

......

Have the tart shell ready for filling. Pour the lemon cream directly into the cooled tart shell. Shake the tart pan gently to smooth out the top of the filling. Chill the tart until firm, about 2 hours, before serving. It will keep for up to 3 days in the refrigerator.

To serve the tart, whip the heavy cream until thickened. Add the sugar and whip until the cream holds soft peaks. Top the chilled tart with the whipped cream and decorate with fresh flowers or candied fennel.

BANANA CREAM PIE
WITH CARAMEL AND CHOCOLATE

YIELDS ONE 10 IN [25 CM] PIE; 8 TO 12 SERVINGS

Fully baked and cooled 10 in [25 cm] Flaky Tart Dough shell (page 286)	1	
Bittersweet chocolate, coarsely chopped	3 oz	85 g
Heavy cream, very cold	1 cup	240 ml
Sugar	2 Tbsp	
Caramel Sauce (page 309)	5 Tbsp	75 ml
Pastry Cream (page 300), cold	2½ cups	600 ml
Ripe bananas, sliced into ¼ in [6 mm] thick rounds	2	
Bittersweet chocolate bar for making curls	3 oz	85 g

This is a very American pie using very French components: a flaky crust and a silky pastry cream filling. It is so popular at the bakery that it's even offered at Thanksgiving alongside the more traditional holiday pies. I like a cream pie with a filling that is not so stiffened with cornstarch that the cut edges stand straight when the pie is sliced. This one oozes a bit, but the tradeoff is a lovely, light, creamy contrast to the crisp shell and chunks of bananas. We line our pie shell with melted chocolate to protect it from becoming soggy, and providing a little foil to the richness of the other ingredients.

KITCHEN NOTES: If you prefer your pastry cream a little thicker, use the larger amount of cornstarch indicated in the Pastry Cream recipe. When making the chocolate curls, it is easiest to work with a large bar, which should be at room temperature, optimal for making curls successfully. Rubbing your palm

over the chocolate is all that is needed to bring it to the right temperature.

. . . . . .

Have the pie shell ready for filling.

Pour water to a depth of about 2 in [5 cm] into a saucepan, place over medium heat, and bring to a simmer. Put the chopped chocolate into a large stainless-steel bowl that will rest securely on the rim of the pan and place it over, but not touching, the water. Heat, stirring occasionally with a rubber spatula, just until the chocolate melts and is smooth. Remove from the heat.

Using an offset spatula, pastry brush, or the back of a spoon, spread the melted chocolate evenly over the bottom of the pie shell. If using a pastry brush, make sure it is completely dry. Any moisture will make the chocolate seize, or become grainy and hard. Refrigerate for 10 minutes to set the chocolate.

While the chocolate is setting, pour the heavy cream into a mixing bowl and whip with a whisk or in a stand mixer fitted with the whisk attachment until thickened. Add the sugar and continue to whip until it holds medium-firm peaks.

Remove the pie shell from the refrigerator and drizzle the caramel evenly over the chocolate. Add the pastry cream to the shell. (It's not necessary to whisk the pastry cream to smooth it for this tart.) Arrange the banana slices evenly over the pastry cream, and then lightly press them into the cream.

Using an offset or rubber spatula, spread the whipped cream on top.

continued

To make the chocolate curls, place the chocolate bar, with the smooth side facing you, on the counter-top. If the chocolate is cool, warm it slightly by lightly rubbing it with your palm. Position the bar on the edge of the counter to stabilize it, and use your body to block the bar from falling off the counter (I wear an apron while doing this). Now, using long strokes, scrape the warm surface with a chef's knife to form curls. Scatter the curls over the top of the pie.

Chill the pie until the pastry cream is set, at least 3 hours. Serve the pie cool. It will keep in the refrigerator for up to 4 days.

Banana Coconut Cream Pie Variation: Fold 1¼ cups [100 g] unsweetened small-flake dried coconut into the pastry cream before filling the pie shell. Chill the tart for several hours before serving to allow time for the coconut to absorb moisture from the pastry cream, which will thicken the cream and hydrate and soften the coconut.

CHOCOLATE PUDDING PIE

Fully baked and cooled 9 in [23 cm] Gluten-Free Crumb Crust (page 298)	1	
Chocolate Pudding (page 310)	3½ cups	800 g

TOPPING

Heavy cream, very cold	1½ cups	360 ml
Vanilla extract	2 tsp	
Confectioners' sugar	1 Tbsp	
Chopped bittersweet chocolate or chocolate shavings	¼ cup	60 g

In adding more pies to this new book, a classic Chocolate Pudding Pie was a clear top choice, considering the Chocolate Pudding that first appeared in the original Tartine Bakery cookbook. When cold, the pudding has a thick texture, much like pot de crème, and is firm enough to hold a spoon upright, making it a good choice for a sliceable pie and reminiscent of real-deal East Coast diners, where you can find every kind of pudding pie.

Have the pie shell ready for filling. Follow the directions to prepare the Chocolate Pudding and immediately pour it into the prepared pie shell. Refrigerate until the surface is cold and set, about 1½ hours.

To prepare the soft cream topping, chill the bowl and whisk attachment of a stand mixer (or a medium bowl, if making by hand) in the freezer for 5 minutes. Pour the cold cream and vanilla into the chilled bowl, and add the confectioners' sugar. Whisk on medium speed, or briskly by hand, until the whipped cream holds medium to firm peaks. Using an offset or rubber spatula, spread the whipped cream on top of the chocolate pudding, just to the edges of the crust. Scatter the chocolate shavings evenly over the top of the pie.

Chill the pie until the cream is set, about 1 hour. Serve the pie cool. It will keep in the refrigerator for up to 4 days.

CHOCOLATE CHESS PIE

YIELDS ONE 9 IN [23 CM] PIE; 8 TO 12 SERVINGS

Partially baked and cooled 9 in [23 cm] Einkorn Flaky Tart Dough shell (page 287)	1	
Unsalted butter	¼ cup	60 g
Dark chocolate, coarsely chopped	2½ oz	70 g
Large eggs	2	
Evaporated milk	⅔ cup	160 ml
Vanilla extract	1 Tbsp	
Sugar	1¾ cups	350 g
Cocoa powder	½ cup	50 g
Salt	½ tsp	

Chess pies, originally from England, were introduced to New England in the late 1800s, but are mostly associated with the Southern states. They are low, single-crust pies that are sweeter than pudding or fruit pies, and are set from a mixture of eggs, butter, and sugar. They're firm enough to travel—a pie you can take on a picnic. Carolyn created this chocolate version, which is velvety smooth and wants some unsweetened whipped cream to go with it.

KITCHEN NOTES: This pie filling would work well with any partially baked pie dough in the book. We thought the flavors matched the best with the einkorn flour.

Preheat the oven to 350°F [180°C]. Have the pie shell ready for filling.

Pour water to a depth of about 2 in [5 cm] into a small saucepan, place over medium-low heat, and bring to a gentle simmer. Put the butter and chocolate in a small heatproof bowl that will rest securely on the rim of the pan and place it over, but not touching, the water. Melt the butter and chocolate, stirring with a rubber spatula, until smooth, and remove from the heat. Add the eggs, evaporated milk, and vanilla to the chocolate-egg mixture and whisk to combine.

In a medium bowl, whisk together the sugar, cocoa powder, and salt. Add the chocolate-egg mixture to the sugar mixture and whisk until smooth.

Pour the batter into the prepared crust and bake until a paring knife inserted into the center of the pie comes out clean, about 1 hour. Transfer to a wire rack to cool. Refrigerate for 4 to 6 hours before serving. This pie will keep, well wrapped, in the refrigerator for 1 week.

MILLIONAIRE'S CHOCOLATE CARAMEL TART

YIELDS ONE 9 IN [23 CM] TART OR SIX TO EIGHT 4 IN [10 CM] TARTLETS; 8 TO 12 SERVINGS

Fully baked and cooled 9 in [23 cm] Chocolate Buckwheat Tart Dough shell or six to eight 4 in [10 cm] tartlet shells (page 292)	1	

CARAMEL

Heavy cream	2/3 cup	160 ml
Water	2 Tbsp	
Corn syrup	1/4 cup	85 ml
Sugar	3/4 cup	150 g
Unsalted butter, cold	1/4 cup	60 g
Flaky sea salt, such as Maldon	1 tsp	

DARK CHOCOLATE GANACHE

Bittersweet chocolate chunks	1 1/4 cups	180 g
Heavy cream	scant 1 cup	225 ml
Corn syrup	2 Tbsp	
Unsalted butter, at room temperature	2 Tbsp	

One of our bakers, Carolyn, developed this rich, delicious tart for the dessert bar we presented at the 2018 Oscars after-party we catered. They were sized as little two-bite rounds and topped with gold leaf to reflect the occasion. If making a larger tart, serve it in slivers. The layers of caramel and chocolate are delicious and beautiful sprinkled with large-flake sea salt. The salty caramel, chocolate, and crunch from the shell make this an addictive and very elegant dessert.

KITCHEN NOTES: Make sure to caramelize your sugar to a nice, deep color. It's the darker caramel that saves the tart from being overly sweet or rich, as counterintuitive as that sounds. A very light caramel hasn't cooked out enough of the sweetness of the sugar.

. . . .

Have the tart shell ready for filling on a baking sheet.

To make the caramel, pour the cream into a small, heavy saucepan. Place over medium heat and bring to just under a boil. Reduce the heat to the lowest possible setting and keep warm.

In a medium, heavy saucepan, combine the water, corn syrup, and sugar. Bring to a boil over medium heat, gently swirling the pot to dissolve the sugar. Then cook, without stirring, until the mixture is a dark amber color, 7 to 8 minutes. Once it turns amber, watch it carefully as it burns quickly. Remove from the heat, add half of the butter, and swirl into the caramel, then slowly and carefully add the warmed cream. The mixture will boil vigorously at first. Let the mixture settle, then whisk until smooth. Add the rest of the butter, whisk again to combine, and place the pot over medium-low heat. Let the caramel gently boil for 30 seconds to thicken. Remove from the heat. Pour the caramel into the prepared tart shell and allow to cool and set, about 2 hours. Sprinkle the sea salt evenly over the surface of the caramel.

continued

To make the ganache, pour water to a depth of about 2 in [5 cm] into a medium saucepan, place over medium-low heat, and bring to a gentle simmer. Put the chocolate in a medium heatproof bowl that will rest securely on the rim of the pan and place it over, but not touching, the water. Melt the chocolate, stirring with a rubber spatula, until smooth, and remove from the heat. Pour the cream and corn syrup into a small saucepan. Place over medium heat and bring to a simmer. Pour the cream over the chocolate, and stir gently with a rubber spatula (to incorporate as little air as possible) until smooth. Stir in the butter.

Pour the ganache over the caramel layer, and turn, tilt, and gently tap the tart pan if necessary to create an even layer. Allow the chocolate to set at room temperature, about 2 hours.

Slice with a knife that has been warmed with hot water and wiped dry between each slice. Serve at room temperature. The tart will keep, wrapped, at room temperature for up to 3 days.

CHOCOLATE HAZELNUT TART

YIELDS ONE 9 IN [23 CM] TART OR SIX TO EIGHT 4 IN [10 CM] TARTLETS; 8 TO 12 SERVINGS

Fully baked and cooled 9 in [23 cm] Sweet Tart Dough shell or six to eight 4 in [10 cm] tartlet shells (page 290)	1	
Bittersweet chocolate, coarsely chopped	6 oz	170 g
Unsalted butter	½ cup	115 g
Brandy (optional)	¼ cup	60 ml
Sugar	⅔ cup	135 g
Large eggs	3	
Orange zest	½ tsp	
Salt	⅛ tsp	

TOPPING

Hazelnuts, lightly toasted and skins rubbed off	1 cup	140 g

Although the filling for this tart calls for a substantial amount of chocolate, it is light textured due to the eggs that are whipped to a ribbon with the sugar before they are folded in. Chocolate will usually overwhelm all other flavors, but the tiny amount of orange zest and the brandy complement the toasty hazelnuts. Although this is the version we almost always make, I love to fiddle with alternatives. Try making it with coffee and walnuts, using an equal amount of each, or arranging Armagnac-soaked prunes in the crust before filling instead of using brandy and hazelnut.

Have the tart shell ready for filling. Preheat the oven to 325°F [160°C].

Put the chocolate in a heatproof mixing bowl. In a saucepan, combine the butter, brandy (if using), and ⅓ cup [70 g] of the sugar. Place over medium-low heat and stir until the butter melts and the sugar dissolves. Pour the butter mixture over the chocolate and stir with a rubber spatula until the chocolate melts.

In a large mixing bowl, combine the remaining sugar, the eggs, zest, and salt. Using a stand mixer fitted with the whisk attachment on medium speed or a whisk, beat the mixture until it is a very pale yellow, light, and flows off the whisk in a thick ribbon when the whisk is lifted out of the bowl. This will take about 3 minutes.

Pour one-third of the egg mixture into the melted chocolate, whisk to lighten the mixture, and then fold in the remaining egg mixture with a rubber spatula. Pour the filling into the tart shell and smooth the surface with an offset spatula. This filling can be made in advance and stored in the refrigerator. When needed, scoop it into the tart shell, smoothing the top, and proceed with the recipe.

Arrange the hazelnuts evenly on top of the tart. Bake the tart until the surface of the filling loses some of its shine, 7 to 9 minutes. Remove from the oven and let cool completely on a wire rack. Serve at room temperature. The tart will keep, well wrapped, in the refrigerator for up to 5 days.

FRANGIPANE TART

YIELDS ONE 9 IN [23 CM] TART OR SIX TO EIGHT 4 IN [10 CM] TARTLETS; 8 TO 12 SERVINGS

Unbaked 9 in [23 cm] Flaky Tart Dough shell or six to eight 4 in [10 cm] tartlet shells (page 286)	1	
Frangipane Cream (page 304) or Frangipane Cream Variation (page 305)	3 cups + 3 Tbsp	750 ml
Fruit, such as sliced apricots, plums, or peaches or whole raspberries or blackberries	2 cups	300 g
Apricot jam	3 Tbsp	55 g
Sliced almonds (optional)	3/4 cup	65 g

This humble-looking tart reminds me of some of the less-sweet tarts you often see in Italy, meant to be eaten with a cappuccino. The downside is that many of those tarts are so dry they require a beverage to have with them. The filling of this tart has pastry cream as its base, which keeps it moist, with sliced almonds added for texture. If you don't happen to have pastry cream on hand, there is a version of the filling without it—or you could always make a batch of éclairs or a trifle if you want to use up leftover, freshly made pastry cream.

The fruits that work best with this almond filling are the juicier ones that have a bit of acidity to balance the nuts and richness in the cream: stone fruit such as peaches, cherries, or apricots, or berries such as raspberries. Poached pear halves arranged in the filling, or sliced and fanned over the tart, are classic. Poached quince would be a beautiful fall or winter fruit to use as well.

KITCHEN NOTES: We remove the bottom from a tart pan and bake with the ring only, right on a baking sheet.

The direct contact with the pan conducts the heat more efficiently, ensuring a crisp tart bottom.

......

Have the tart shell ready. Line a baking sheet with parchment paper or a nonstick liner. Place the tart shell on the prepared pan. Preheat the oven to 375°F [190°C].

Fill the tart shell with the frangipane cream, smoothing the top with a rubber spatula. Arrange the fruit and almonds, if using, on top. Bake the tart until the crust is golden brown and the filling is set, about 1 hour and 20 minutes. The filling should feel firm and slightly springy to the touch and the fruit should be tender. Transfer the tart to a wire rack and let cool until warm. To unmold, use a wide metal spatula to lift the tart onto a surface slightly smaller in diameter than the tart ring. The ring will fall away.

While the tart is baking, in a small saucepan, warm the jam over low heat just until it is liquid, then strain through a medium-mesh sieve to make a glaze. Brush the glaze over the fruit when the tart comes out of the oven. The tart tastes best served warm or at room temperature. It will keep in the refrigerator for up to 3 days.

FRUIT PIES

As soon as each kind of fruit comes into season, the first thing I want to make is a fruit pie that showcases the simplest, cleanest fruit flavor. If I make more than one, it's experimentation time, but the first is always the simplest, cleanest fruit flavor.

Be mindful that fruit varies tremendously in water and sugar content depending on the season and where in the country it's grown. Maine blueberries are tiny and more flavorful than our plump California ones. The first strawberries of the year are usually not the most flavorful or the sweetest, and the first-pick apples in the fall are the best. Our suggestions for sugar and thickener are general parameters to use. If your peaches are extraordinarily juicy, you may want to use a little more thickener and less sugar, but then again, you may like a super-juicy pie. There are blackberry patches that I've picked from out on the coast that get very little water and have fruit that is notably smaller and drier—but much more flavorful—than the farmed ones at the supermarket; these would be ideal berries to mix in with a juicier fruit like plums or nectarines or in a multi-berry pie.

Fruit is an ingredient that is impossible to quantify in a book, as it entirely relies upon your judgment, and it is my favorite thing to work with in terms of flavor and rewarding pastry-making. There is nothing that makes one feel as prideful as a well-made fruit pie.

DUTCH APPLE PIE

YIELDS ONE 9 IN [23 CM] PIE; 8 TO 12 SERVINGS

Unbaked 9 in [23 cm] Flaky Tart Dough shell (page 286)	1	

CRUMBLE TOPPING

All-purpose flour	¾ cup	100 g
Walnuts, finely chopped	⅓ cup	40 g
Sugar	6 Tbsp	75 g
Rolled oats	¼ cup	20 g
Salt	⅛ tsp	
Ground cinnamon	⅛ tsp	
Unsalted butter, cold	7 Tbsp	100 g

FILLING

Apples, cored, half peeled, and cut into ¼ in [6 mm] slices	2 lb	910 g
All-purpose flour	2 Tbsp	
Sugar	2 Tbsp	
Salt	½ tsp	
Lemon juice	2 Tbsp	
Lemon zest	from ½ lemon	
Unsalted butter, cold	2 Tbsp	
Apple Butter (page 150)	⅔ cup	160 g

We've revised our apple pie over the years, from the original two-crust, to a crunchy all-almond top crust version, and now, Dutch Apple. With its nutty, spicy crumble topping, this pie delivers an irresistable layer of flavor and texture not found in pies with a traditional top crust. The apples are partially cooked before the pie is baked, so they form a generous mound in the pie shell that stays impressively high rather than sinking after cooling. Lynn, who devised this recipe, also adds apple butter, which intensifies the natural flavor of whichever apple variety you use.

KITCHEN NOTES: If you don't have apple butter, substitute applesauce and add ½ tsp vanilla extract, ¼ tsp cinnamon, and a generous pinch each of cloves, nutmeg, and allspice.

. . . . . .

Preheat the oven to 350°F [180°C]. Prick the bottom of the pie shell evenly with a fork and place the shell in the refrigerator until ready to fill.

To prepare the crumble topping, combine the flour, walnuts, sugar, oats, salt, and cinnamon in a small bowl and stir with a wooden spoon to combine. Cut the butter into ⅛ in [3 mm] cubes and scatter the cubes over the dry ingredients. Using your fingers, combine the butter with the dry ingredients until all of the butter is dispersed, the dry ingredients are hydrated, and small clumps form. Place in the refrigerator until ready to use. The crumble can be made in advance and stored, covered, in the refrigerator for up to 5 days.

To prepare the filling, place the apples in a large bowl. Separately, in a small bowl, combine the flour, sugar, salt, lemon juice, and lemon zest and mix well with a spoon to combine. Add the flour mixture to the apples and toss together until the apples are well coated. Cut the butter into ¼ in [6 mm] cubes. Add the butter cubes and apple butter and mix well with a wooden spoon or a rubber spatula until the apple butter is distributed evenly into the apple mixture.

continued

Remove the prepared pie shell from the refrigerator and gently fill it with the apple mixture. Arrange some of the apples against the sides of the pie shell to fill in any gaps, and create a large, packed, mound of apples in the center of the pie, compressing and arranging them evenly. Distribute the crumble topping evenly over the apple mixture, and press gently to adhere. Refrigerate the pie for 15 minutes.

Place the pie on a baking sheet and bake until the crust and top of the pie are golden brown, and the filling is bubbling gently, 1 hour to 1 hour and 20 minutes. If the top is browning too quickly, cover with a piece of aluminum foil. Let the pie cool on a wire rack for at least 2 hours before slicing. Serve slightly warm, at room temperature, or cold, with whipped cream or ice cream. The pie will keep in the refrigerator for up to 4 days.

STRAWBERRY-RHUBARB PIE

YIELDS ONE 10 IN [25 CM] TRADITIONAL ROUND PIE
OR ONE 9 BY 13 IN [23 BY 33 CM] SLAB PIE; 8 TO 10 SERVINGS

ROUND PIE

Chilled Einkorn Flaky Dough for Slab Pies rounds, each 12 in [30 cm] in diameter and ⅛ in [3 mm] thick (page 289)	2	
Cornstarch	5 Tbsp	35 g
Salt	⅛ tsp	
Vanilla bean	½ bean	
Granulated sugar	¾ cup	150 g
Strawberries, hulled and quartered	1½ lb	715 g
Rhubarb, cut into ¼ in [6 mm] slices	15 oz	425 g
Orange zest	2 tsp	
Large egg	1	
Coarse sugar for sprinkling (optional)		

SLAB PIE

Chilled Einkorn Flaky Dough for Slab Pies rectangles, each 11 by 15 in [28 by 38 cm] and ⅛ in [3 mm] thick (page 289)	2	
Cornstarch	⅓ cup + 1 Tbsp	45 g
Salt	¼ tsp	
Granulated sugar	1 cup	200 g
Strawberries, hulled and quartered	2 lb	910 g
Rhubarb, cut into ¼ in [6 mm] slices	1 lb 2.5 oz	525 g
Vanilla bean	1 bean	
Orange zest	1 Tbsp	
Large egg	1	
Coarse sugar for sprinkling (optional)		

This is a standard that warrants remaking every spring, when strawberries and rhubarb are plentiful and in their first blush. Even when I think of new things to do with rhubarb in cakes, ice cream, and jams, its tannic tartness in contrast to the sweetness of strawberries can't be matched. Our baker, Carolyn, has developed the perfect level of sweetness and amount of thickener to work in either a classic round or a slab pie.

continued

KITCHEN NOTES: The round pies are deep-dish pies, and the baking is on the long side, from 75 minutes to 2 hours. Check for color and juices starting to bubble. It takes the thickeners a long time to work, so for the full effect, allow to cool for 4 to 6 hours.

· · · · · ·

Position the racks in the middle and lower thirds of the oven. Preheat the oven to 400°F [200°C]. Butter a 10 in [25 cm] round pie dish or a 9 by 13 in [23 by 33 cm] rimmed baking sheet.

Gently fold one chilled flaky dough round or rectangle in half, then in half again, and place in the pie dish or baking sheet with its point at the center. Unfold the dough so it covers the bottom of the dish or baking sheet, carefully adjusting the dough into place, and pressing it lightly with your fingers, so as not to stretch or pull it. There should be about 1 in [2.5 cm] of dough hanging over the edge. Place in the refrigerator until ready to use.

In a small bowl, add the cornstarch and salt and mix well. With a small knife, split and scrape the seeds from the pod of the vanilla bean, reserving the pod for another use. Rub the seeds into the sugar. In a large bowl, toss the strawberries and rhubarb together with the orange zest and sugar until combined and well distributed. Add the cornstarch mixture to the fruit, mixing gently.

Remove the unbaked pie shell from the refrigerator and transfer the fruit to the shell. Arrange the fruit in an even layer and smooth the surface by lightly pressing the fruit down with your fingers or a rubber spatula. (The more even the layer of fruit, the less likelihood an air gap will form between the fruit and crust in the finished pie.) Using a pastry brush or your finger, dampen the overhanging dough with water to act as "glue" for the top crust. For a round pie, roll the second piece of dough around a rolling pin, and unroll it over the top of the pie, gently repositioning it if necessary. For a slab pie, drape the second rectangle of dough over the first, trimming the edges to line up with the edges of the bottom sheet of dough.

Press the top and bottom crusts together to seal the fruit inside. Using kitchen shears or a sharp paring knife, trim off the excess dough using the edge of the pie dish as a guide. Crimp the edges or press with the tines of a fork to create a decorative pattern. Place the pie in the freezer for 15 minutes to chill.

While the pie is chilling, prepare the egg wash by whisking the egg in a small bowl until the yolk and white are completely blended. Place the pie onto a baking sheet lined with parchment paper or aluminum foil. Brush the surface of the pie with the egg wash and sprinkle lightly with coarse sugar, if desired. Using a sharp paring knife, cut a few decorative slits in the top crust for air vents to ensure a crisp crust.

Place the pie on the lowest oven rack and reduce the oven temperature to 350°F [180°C]. After 30 minutes, move the dish to the middle rack, and rotate it 180 degrees for even browning. Check the pie after another 45 minutes—when done it should be deep gold on top with the filling bubbling (visible through the vents, and a sign that the cornstarch has thickened the juices). If needed, continue checking every 15 minutes. If the edges of the pie crust are becoming too dark before the pie is fully baked, cover them with aluminum foil.

When the pie is done, remove it from the oven and place on a wire rack to cool at room temperature for at least 4 to 6 hours for the filling to set. Once the pie is cool, it can be wrapped in plastic wrap and refrigerated before slicing, which will ensure a cleaner cut (otherwise you'll have to contend with more juice when the pie is sliced). Once baked, the pie can be stored in the refrigerator, wrapped in plastic wrap, for up to 4 days.

All-Berry Pie Variation: For the fruit filling, you can substitute a mix of strawberries, all types of raspberries, tayberries (a cross between a blackberry and a raspberry), blackberries, and blueberries. Use care when folding the sugar-starch mixture into the fruit—bush berries are much more fragile and will easily break down with too much agitation. Proceed as directed for assembling, baking, and cooling the pie.

BLUEBERRY PIE

YIELDS ONE 10 IN [25 CM] TRADITIONAL ROUND PIE
OR ONE 9 BY 13 BY 1 IN [23 BY 33 BY 2.5 CM] RECTANGULAR SLAB PIE; 8 TO 10 SERVINGS

ROUND PIE

Chilled Einkorn Flaky Dough for Slab Pies rounds, each 12 in [30 cm] in diameter and 1/8 in [3 mm] thick (page 289)	2	
Granulated sugar	3/4 cup	150 g
Cornstarch	1/4 cup	30 g
Salt	1/8 tsp	
Blueberries	2 1/4 lb	1.1 kg
Lemon juice	1 1/2 tsp	
Lemon zest	1 tsp	
Large egg	1	
Coarse sugar for sprinkling (optional)		

SLAB PIE

Chilled Einkorn Flaky Dough for Slab Pies rectangles, each 11 by 15 in [28 by 38 cm] and 1/8 in [3 mm] thick (page 289)	2	
Granulated sugar	1 1/3 cups	255 g
Cornstarch	1/3 cup + 1 Tbsp	45 g
Salt	1/8 tsp	
Blueberries	3 lb	1.4 kg
Lemon juice	2 1/2 tsp	
Lemon zest	1 1/2 tsp	
Large egg	1	
Coarse sugar for sprinkling (optional)		

Blueberry—the king of pies—represents pie-making in its most elemental form: fresh berries, sugar, a little thickener, and perfect crust. Our baker Carolyn's method of mashing a portion of the berries first is ingenious. It solves the issue of blueberries sinking into themselves when baked (a common problem) and it evenly distributes the thickener and sugar; these normally fall to the bottom of the baking dish.

......

Position the oven racks in the lowest and middle spaces. Preheat the oven to 400°F [200°C]. Butter a 10 in [25 cm] round pie dish or a 9 by 13 in [23 by 33 cm] rimmed baking sheet.

Gently fold one chilled flaky dough round or rectangle in half, then in half again, and place in the pie dish or baking sheet with its point at the center. Unfold the dough so it covers the bottom of the dish or pan, carefully adjusting the dough into place, and pressing it lightly with your fingers, so as not to stretch or pull it. There will be about 1 in [2.5 cm] of dough hanging over the edge. Place in the refrigerator until ready to use.

In a small bowl, combine the granulated sugar, cornstarch, and salt and mix well with a spoon to combine. Place one-third of the blueberries in a large bowl and, using your hands, crush them until they are mostly burst and pulpy, but not liquefied. Add the remaining blueberries, lemon juice, and lemon zest and fold gently to combine. Add the cornstarch mixture to the fruit, folding gently with a rubber spatula to coat the blueberry filling.

continued

Remove the unbaked pie shell from the refrigerator and transfer the fruit to the shell. Arrange the fruit in an even layer and smooth the surface by lightly pressing the fruit down. (The more even the layer of fruit, the less likelihood an air gap will form between the fruit and crust in the finished pie.) Dampen the overhanging dough with water to act as "glue" for the top crust. For a round pie, roll the second round of dough around a rolling pin, and unroll it over the surface of the pie, gently repositioning it if necessary. For a slab pie, drape the second rectangle of dough over the first, trimming the edges to line up with the edges of the bottom sheet of dough.

Press the top and bottom crusts together to seal the fruit inside. Using kitchen shears or a sharp paring knife, trim off the excess dough, using the edge of the dish as a guide. Evenly roll the dough edges away from the pie and tuck into the edge of the pie dish. Crimp the edges or press with the tines of a fork to create a decorative pattern. Then, place the pie in the freezer for 15 minutes to chill.

While the pie is chilling, prepare the egg wash by whisking the egg in a small bowl until the yolk and white are completely blended. Place the pie onto a baking sheet lined with parchment paper or aluminum foil. If making the slab pie, use a next-size-up cookie sheet to catch drips. Brush the surface of the pie with the egg wash and sprinkle lightly with coarse sugar, if desired. Using a sharp paring knife, cut a few decorative slits in the top crust to create air vents to ensure a crisp crust.

Place the pie on the lowest oven rack and reduce the oven temperature to 350°F [180°C]. After 30 minutes, move the pie to the middle rack, and rotate it 180 degrees for even browning. Check the pie after another 45 minutes—when done it should be deep gold on top with the filling bubbling (visible through the vents, and a sign that the cornstarch has thickened the juices). If needed, continue checking every 15 minutes. If the edges of the pie crust are becoming too dark before the pie is fully baked, cover them with aluminum foil.

When the pie is done, remove from the oven and place on a wire rack to cool at room temperature for at least 4 to 6 hours for the filling to set. Once baked, store, loosely covered, at room temperature or refrigerate, wrapped in plastic wrap, for up to 4 days.

Bluebarb Pie Variation: When making the fruit filling, substitute rhubarb, cut into ¼ in [6 mm] slices for about one-third of the blueberries. Proceed as directed for assembling, baking, and cooling the pie.

PEACH PIE

YIELDS ONE 10 IN [25 CM] TRADITIONAL ROUND PIE OR
ONE 9 BY 13 BY 1 IN [23 BY 33 BY 2.5 CM] RECTANGULAR SLAB PIE; 8 TO 10 SERVINGS

ROUND PIE

Chilled Einkorn Flaky Dough for Slab Pies rounds, each 12 in [30 cm] in diameter and 1/8 in [3 mm] thick (page 289)	2	
Granulated sugar	3/4 cup	150 g
Cornstarch	5 Tbsp	35 g
Ground cinnamon	1/2 tsp	
Salt	1/8 tsp	
Peaches or other stone fruit, such as plums, nectarines, or cherries, pitted and sliced into 1/4 in [6 mm] pieces	2 1/4 lb	1.1 kg
Lemon juice	1 1/2 tsp	
Large egg	1	
Coarse sugar for sprinkling (optional)		

SLAB PIE

Chilled Einkorn Flaky Dough for Slab Pies rectangles, each 11 by 15 in [28 by 38 cm] and 1/8 in [3 mm] thick (page 289)	2	
Granulated sugar	1 cup	200 g
Cornstarch	1/3 cup + 1 Tbsp	45 g
Ground cinnamon	3/4 tsp	
Salt	1/4 tsp	
Stone fruit, pitted and sliced into 1/4 in [6 mm] pieces	3 lb	1.4 kg
Lemon juice	2 tsp	
Large egg	1	
Coarse sugar for sprinkling (optional)		

I think of peach as a quintessentially Southern fruit, although in reality California produces almost half of all domestic crops, followed by South Carolina and Georgia. I've picked and eaten them straight off of the trees during hot Kentucky summers with my grandmother—who claims Kentucky has the best peaches—and it's easy to imagine how the first person to make a peach pie wanted to recreate that warm, sweet-tart juiciness in pie form.

All stone fruit work well here, but be sure to taste your fruit and adjust the sweetener as needed. Plums, for instance, can vary from very sweet to very tart.

Position the oven racks in the middle and lowest third of the oven. Preheat the oven to 400°F [200°C]. Butter a 10 in [25 cm] round pie dish or a 9 by 13 in [23 by 33 cm] rimmed baking sheet.

Gently fold one chilled flaky dough round or rectangle in half, then in half again, and place in the pie dish or baking sheet with its point at the center. Unfold the dough to cover the bottom of the dish or pan, carefully adjusting the dough into place, and pressing it lightly with your fingers, so as to not stretch or pull it. There will be about 1 in [2.5 cm] of dough hanging over the edge. Place in the refrigerator until ready to use.

In a small bowl, combine the granulated sugar, cornstarch, cinnamon, and salt and mix well with a spoon to combine. Place the fruit and lemon juice in a large bowl and fold gently to combine. Add the sugar-cornstarch mixture to the fruit, folding gently with a rubber spatula to coat the fruit filling. Remove the unbaked pie shell from the refrigerator and transfer the fruit to the shell. Arrange the filling in an even layer and smooth the surface by lightly pressing the fruit down with your fingers or a rubber spatula. (The more even the layer of fruit, the less likelihood an air gap will form between the fruit and crust in the baked pie.) Using a pastry brush or your finger, dampen the overhanging dough with water, to act as "glue" for the top crust. For a round pie, roll the second round of dough up around a rolling pin, and unroll it over the surface of the pie, gently repositioning if necessary. For a slab pie, drape the second rectangle of dough over the first, trimming the edges to line up with the edges of the bottom sheet of dough.

Press the top and bottom crusts together to seal the fruit inside. Using kitchen shears or a sharp paring knife, trim off the excess dough, using the edge of the dish as a guide. Evenly roll the dough edges away from the pie and tuck into the edge of the pie dish. Crimp the edges or press with the tines of a fork to create a decorative pattern. Then, place the pie in the freezer for 15 minutes to chill.

While the pie is chilling, prepare the egg wash by whisking the egg in a small bowl until the yolk and white are completely blended. Place the pie onto a baking sheet lined with parchment paper or aluminum foil. Brush the surface of the pie with the egg wash and sprinkle lightly with coarse sugar, if desired. Using a sharp paring knife, cut a few decorative slits in the top crust to create air vents to ensure a crisp crust.

Place the pie on the lowest oven rack and reduce the oven temperature to 350°F [180°C]. After 30 minutes, move the dish to the middle rack, and rotate it 180 degrees for even browning. Check the pie after another 45 minutes—when done it should be deep gold on top with the filling bubbling (visible through the vents, and a sign that the cornstarch has thickened the juices). If needed, continue checking every 15 minutes. If the edges of the pie crust are becoming too dark before the pie is fully baked, cover them with aluminum foil.

When the pie is done, remove it from the oven and place on a wire rack to cool at room temperature for at least 4 to 6 hours for the filling to set. Once baked, this pie can be stored, loosely covered, at room temperature or refrigerated, wrapped in plastic, for up to 4 days.

SHAKER LEMON PIE

YIELDS ONE 10 IN [25 CM] PIE; 8 TO 12 SERVINGS

Lemons	2	
Sugar	2 cups	400 g
Chilled Flaky Tart Dough rounds, each 12 in [30 cm] in diameter (page 286)	2	
Large eggs	4	
Salt	¼ tsp	

EGG WASH

Large egg yolk	1
Heavy cream	1 Tbsp

Coarse sugar for topping
Unsweetened, softly whipped cream for serving

This recipe perfectly demonstrates the simplicity, wholesomeness, and ingenuity of the Shakers, who were renowned bakers and responsible for many culinary inventions, including the mechanical apple peeler, the hand-crank egg beater, and the revolving oven, still used in many bakeries today. This is an elegantly easy pie to put together, combining eggs, sugar, and sliced whole lemons, rind and all, with a little salt—similar to the ingredients for lemon curd, but resulting in a tart, curd/marmalade mixture in flaky crust. The key to success is using a very sharp knife for slicing the lemons paper-thin; I've also had success using a mandoline, just make sure yours is knife-sharp.

I'm often tempted to cut back on sugar in recipes like this, but I would resist in this case. It may look like a lot, but I compensate by using a tart pan, rather than a pie pan or dish, for making this pie, which balances the quantity and intensity of the filling with more crust. You can use a range of sizes; 9 in [23 cm] to 11 in [28 cm] all work well here.

KITCHEN NOTES: Chilling the lemons in advance firms them up, making them easier to slice paper-thin. If you slice the lemon once lengthwise, you will have a flat surface to rest on the cutting board that allows you to slice the lemon more safely and evenly. Make sure not to use an aluminum bowl when making the filling. The lemons will react with the metal, giving the filling a metallic flavor.

Slice the lemons paper-thin, discarding the thicker stem end and any seeds. Put them in a nonreactive bowl (stainless steel or glass) and, using a spoon or your hands, toss with the sugar. Cover and let sit at room temperature for at least 3 hours or up to overnight. If any seeds are still left, they will usually float to the top, where they are easily fished out. If you are using the more tender-skinned Meyer lemons, you can skip this step, as the skins don't need the sugar to tenderize them.

Use one dough round to line a 10 in [25 cm] tart pan with a removable bottom, easing it into the bottom and sides and leaving a 1 in [2.5 cm] overhang. Set aside.

In a small bowl, whisk the eggs and salt together until blended. Add the eggs to the lemon mixture, mixing thoroughly. Pour the mixture into the pastry-lined tart pan. The mixture will be very liquidy, so you must evenly distribute the lemon pieces in the pan.

To make the egg wash, in a small bowl, whisk together the egg yolk and cream. Brush the rim of the dough with the egg wash to help the top round adhere. Lay the second dough round over the filling and trim the overhang for both rounds to ¼ in [6 mm]. Crimp the edge as you would for a pie, making sure you have a good seal. Brush the top of the pie with the egg wash and then sprinkle coarse sugar evenly over the top. Chill for about 30 minutes. (I chill this assembled pie, as I do nearly all pies and tarts, to firm up the pockets of butter in the dough, so that when the pie is put into the oven, the butter pockets will melt, creating the flaky texture you want in your finished crust.) While the pie is chilling, position a rack in the lower third of the oven and preheat the oven to 350°F [180°C].

Line a baking sheet with aluminum foil or parchment paper. Cut a few decorative slits in the top of the pie for air vents, and place the tart pan on the lined baking sheet. Bake the pie until it is deep gold on top and the filling is bubbling (visible through the vents), about 40 minutes. If the top is coloring too quickly, place a piece of foil or parchment loosely over the top. Let the pie cool completely before slicing to allow the filling to set properly. Serve at room temperature or slightly warmed with unsweet-ened, lightly whipped cream (though the pie needs to cool completely for the filling to set up, it can be warmed up a little in the oven before serving). The pie will keep in the refrigerator for up to 4 days.

FRUIT GALETTES

YIELDS 2 LARGE OR 12 SMALL GALETTES

DOUGH

Unsalted butter, very cold	2 cups	450 g
Water	1 cup	240 ml
Salt	1½ tsp	
Pastry flour	2¼ cups + 2 Tbsp	340 g
All-purpose flour	2⅔ cups	340 g

FILLING

Fruit, cut up or whole (see method), depending on type	2 lb	910 g
Granulated or brown sugar		
Lemon juice, if needed		

EGG WASH

Large egg yolks	2
Heavy cream	2 Tbsp

Granulated sugar for sprinkling	

This is a real baker's tart, very satisfying to make, and shows off a deft hand with dough—careful rolling will reward you with flaky layers. Free-form, these galettes are beautifully rustic, allowing you to make them as large or small as you wish. Apricots make a beautiful filling, with their cut tips blackening in the oven, but they also taste incredible because they contain less moisture than most fruits and thus develop a very concentrated flavor as they bake. I highly recommend yellow peaches or nectarines (the subtle flavor and low acid of white varietals are best enjoyed fresh, in my opinion). Berries are very good, either alone or combined with stone fruit—just make sure to mound them instead of placing them in an even layer since they lose so much volume when baked. In winter, use lightly sautéed apples or pears or poached quince. A little Frangipane Cream (page 304) spread on the bottom and topped with fruit is a classic and delicious pairing, and makes a more substantial pastry.

KITCHEN NOTES: If you have pastry flour, use half pastry and half all-purpose flour by weight. The blend makes the best crust. If you don't have pastry flour, the recipe is still excellent using entirely all-purpose flour. You'll notice that the recipe doesn't call for mixing all the fruit with the sugar en masse and then filling the galettes. Instead, each galette is sweetened individually. If you add sugar to the whole batch, you end up with lots of sweetened fruit juice in the bottom of the bowl. This way, you end up with a juicier pastry.

· · · · · ·

To make the dough, cut the butter into 1 in [2.5 cm] cubes and put them in the freezer. Measure the water, dissolve the salt into it, and put it in the freezer as well. Chill the butter and water for about 10 minutes.

Measure all of the flour onto your work surface. It is not necessary to mix the flours at this point, as they will become well mixed as the dough is being made. Spread the flour out into a rectangle about ⅓ in [8 mm] deep. Scatter the butter cubes over the flour. Toss a little of the flour over the butter so that your rolling pin won't stick and then begin rolling. When the butter starts flattening out into long, thin pieces, use a bench scraper to scoop up the sides of the rectangle so that it is again the size you started with.

continued

Repeat the rolling and scraping three or four times. Make a well in the center and pour all of the water into the well. Using the bench scraper, scoop the sides of the dough onto the center, cutting (mixing in with the bench scraper) the water into the dough. Keep scraping and cutting until the dough is a shaggy mass, and then shape the dough into a rectangle about 10 by 14 in [25 by 35 cm]. Lightly dust the top with flour. Roll out the rectangle until it is half again as large and then scrape the top, bottom, and sides together again to the original size and re-roll. Repeat three or four times until you have a smooth and cohesive dough. You should have a neat rectangle measuring about 10 by 14 in [25 by 35 cm]. Transfer the dough to a large baking sheet, cover with plastic wrap, and chill well, about 1 hour.

While the dough is chilling, prepare your fruit. Hull the berries if necessary; pit the peaches and cut them into eighths; pit the apricots and leave them in halves or quarter them. If using apples or pears, sauté and cool; pit the cherries; and so on.

Line two baking sheets with parchment paper. When you are ready to roll out the dough, divide it into two equal portions if making large galettes or into twelve equal portions if making individual galettes. To roll a circle from what is roughly a square for either small or large galettes, start out with the dough positioned as a diamond in front of you, with the handles of the pin at two points of the square. Roll from the center toward each end, only flattening the center, not the two points that are nearest to and farthest from you (at top and bottom); leave those two points thick. Now turn the dough so that the flattened-out corners are at the top and bottom. Again roll from the center toward the points nearest to and farthest from you, again stopping short of both the top and bottom. Now you should have a square that has little humps in between the pointy corners. Roll out the thicker areas and you will begin to see a circle forming. Keep rolling until the dough is a little more than $\frac{1}{8}$ in [3 mm] thick for large galettes (each circle should be about 14 in [35 cm] in diameter) and a little thinner for small galettes (each small circle should be 6 to 7 in [15 to 18 cm] in diameter). Fold the large circles into quarters, transfer each one to a prepared baking sheet, and unfold. Transfer the small circles to the prepared baking sheets. Chill the circles until firm, about 10 minutes.

Fill the center of each dough circle with fruit, leaving uncovered a border of 2 in [5 cm] on the large circles and 1 in [2.5 cm] on the small circles. Taste the fruit for sweetness to determine how much sugar you want to use to sweeten it. Then sprinkle with granulated or brown sugar, typically using 2 to 4 Tbsp [25 to 50 g] for each large galette or 1 to 2 tsp for each small galette. You may also want to add a squeeze of lemon juice to some fruits, such as blueberries, blackberries, or sautéed apples or pears. Fold in the sides of the circles to cover the fruit partially, being sure not to leave any valleys where the fruit juice can leak out. Chill until firm, about 10 minutes. While the galettes are chilling, position racks in the middle and lower third of the oven and preheat the oven to 375°F [190°C].

To make the egg wash, in a small bowl, whisk together the egg yolks and cream. Brush the egg wash over the pastry edges, and then sprinkle with granulated sugar. You can bake the galettes immediately or hold them, unwrapped, for a couple of hours in the refrigerator. (Or, you can skip the egg wash and sugar at this point, wrap the galettes airtight, and freeze them for up to 2 weeks. When ready to bake, remove from the freezer, brush with egg wash and sprinkle with sugar, and bake straightaway.)

Bake the galettes until the crust has visibly puffed and baked to dark brown and the juice from the fruit is bubbling inside, 45 to 60 minutes for large galettes and 40 to 50 minutes for small galettes. Rotate the baking sheets 180 degrees and switch the baking sheets between the racks at the midway point to ensure even browning. (If you are baking them straight from the freezer, add 10 minutes to the baking time.) If the pastry is browning too quickly, reduce the oven temperature to 350°F [180°C], or place aluminum foil over the tops of the galettes. Remove from the oven and serve hot, or let cool on a wire rack and serve warm or at room temperature.

Galettes will keep at room temperature for 2 days or refrigerated for up to 5 days. Re-crisp in a 400°F [200°C] oven for 5 minutes.

JAM TARTLETS

—

YIELDS SIXTEEN 3 IN [7.5 CM] TARTLETS

Rye Tart Dough (page 294), Matcha Tart Dough (page 296), or Chocolate Buckwheat Tart Dough (page 292) taken through the chilling phase	2 recipes	
Seasonal fruit jam	2 cups	560 g

These tartlets are a nice way to highlight a favorite batch of jam, and a quick, two-component recipe to put together with already-made dough, especially if you have some in the freezer. Carolyn paired the rye tart dough with our house-made jam to beautiful effect. They're a close cousin to the Linzer Torte (page 274), but earn a place in the book for their versatility, quick composition, and the sheer charm of their presentation. I like a jam with a little bit of chunk and character for this, such as apricot or raspberry, but any jam, marmalade, or preserve will work. You can mix and match flavor combinations, using different doughs from this book. Try Matcha Tart Dough with marmalade or Chocolate Buckwheat Tart Dough with strawberry or raspberry preserves.

KITCHEN NOTES: If your preserve is very thick, use a bit of water to thin it to the usual jam spreading consistency before filling the shells.

· · · · · ·

Preheat the oven to 350°F [180°C]. Line two baking sheets with parchment paper.

Using 1 recipe of Rye Tart Dough, follow the instructions on page 294 to roll, line pans, and partially bake the crusts. Set aside to cool before filling.

Following the directions on page 294, roll the remaining dough to a thickness of 1/8 in [3 mm]. Using a 1 in [2.5 cm] heart-shaped cookie cutter, cut sixteen hearts from the dough. Transfer to one of the prepared baking sheets, and bake until lightly colored and opaque, about 8 minutes.

Transfer the tart shells to the other prepared baking sheet. Fill each with 2 Tbsp of jam. Center the heart-shaped cutout on top of the jam. Bake until the jam just begins to bubble around the edges of the heart and rises to the edge of the tart shell, 12 to 15 minutes. Transfer the tarts to a wire rack to cool. The jam will still seem soft while hot and thicken once cool. The tarts will keep for 3 days in an airtight container at room temperature.

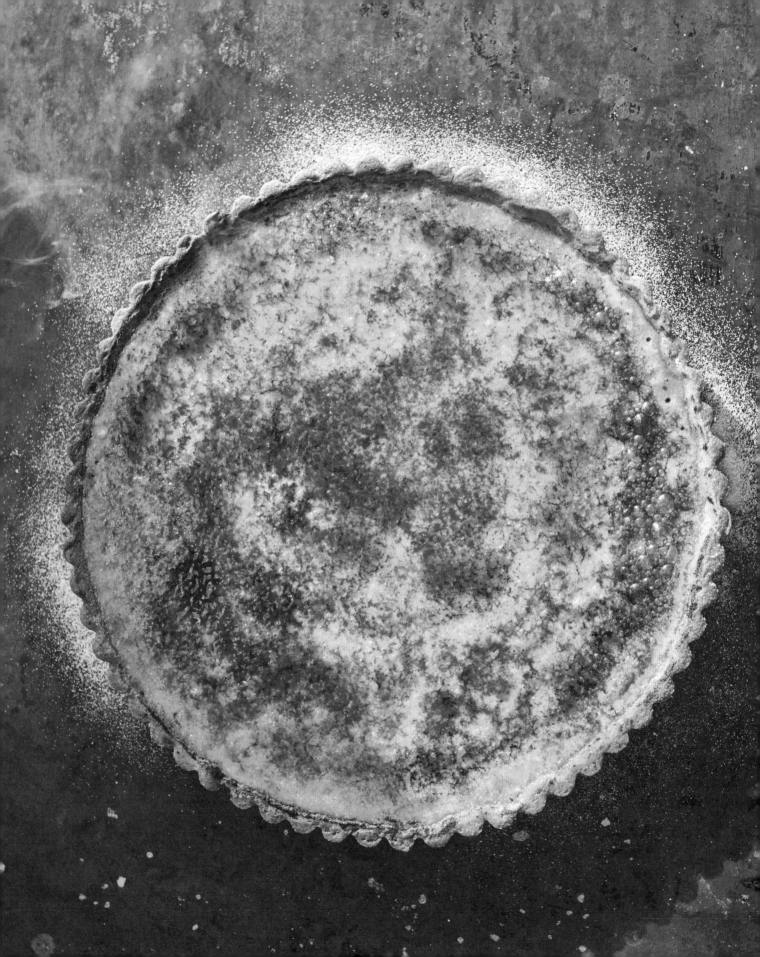

MATCHA CRÈME BRÛLÉE TART

Fully baked and cooled 5 in [12 cm] Matcha Tart Dough shells (page 296)	6	
Heavy cream, cold	2 cups + 2 Tbsp	530 ml
Sugar, plus more for topping	5 Tbsp	75 g
Large egg yolks	6	
Matcha powder, sifted	1 tsp	

This tart is based on classic crème brûlée but incorporates the distinct flavor of matcha to balance the richness of the filling. Carolyn Nugent developed this after we started working with Stonemill Matcha, a Japanese company specializing in this high-quality green tea. You could skip the tart shell and bake this filling in ramekins like a crème brûlée, sprinkling with sugar and torching the tops once they are cool. If you are new to custard-making, this is the ideal starting point, since all-cream custard bases won't curdle if slightly overcooked (as custard mixtures that contain milk do). This is a great make-ahead dessert; torch the top just before serving to add a bit of show. Granulated white sugar, with its uniform crystal size, works best.

KITCHEN NOTES: To make a brûlée tart without the matcha, simply omit the tea and add one scraped vanilla bean to the heated cream. Alternatively, add 1½ tsp of vanilla extract to the custard once it is strained.

Preheat the oven to 275°F [140°C] and position a rack in the middle of the oven. Have the tart shells ready for filling on a parchment-lined baking sheet. Have a large bowl ready for cooling the custard with a fine-mesh sieve resting on the rim.

To make the custard, combine half of the cream and half of the sugar in a heavy saucepan and heat over medium-high heat to just under a boil. Meanwhile, put the yolks in a small bowl. As the cream is heating, whisk together the egg yolks, remaining sugar, and sifted matcha powder. Once the cream-sugar mixture has come to a simmer, remove the pan from the heat, and slowly ladle about one-third of the hot cream into the egg mixture, whisking constantly. Pour the egg-cream mixture back into the hot cream and whisk to combine. Place the saucepan back over medium-low heat and stir with a rubber spatula along the bottom of the pan for 30 seconds. The matcha cream will thicken only slightly.

Remove from the heat and immediately pour the custard through the sieve into the bowl. (If the custard stays in the hot pot, it will continue to cook.) With a rubber spatula, press any remaining matcha powder through the sieve into the custard. Pour the remaining cream into the custard and stir to combine. The matcha custard is now ready to use or may be stored in the refrigerator for up to 5 days. To store, press a piece of plastic wrap on the surface of the custard so it does not form a skin.

continued

To make the tarts, fill the prepared tart shells three-quarters of the way full with matcha custard. Carefully put the tarts into the oven and top off each tart shell with more custard just to the rim. Bake the tarts until the custard is just set but still slightly wobbly in the center, about 1 hour, rotating the baking sheet halfway through baking (the filling will continue to set as it cools). Let the tarts cool on the sheet set on a wire rack for 15 minutes, then refrigerate them for at least 2 hours or until ready to serve.

To finish the tarts, using a small spoon, spread an even $\frac{1}{32}$ in [1 mm] thick layer of sugar on the surface of the custard. If the layer of sugar is too thin, the custard will burn, too thick and it will not caramelize evenly. Using a kitchen torch, caramelize the sugar, little by little, until it is deep amber, bubbling, and even in color. You may need to go back over the tarts a second time with the kitchen torch to create an evenly caramelized surface. Serve immediately; they are best eaten the same day.

MATCHA STREUSEL TART

YIELDS ONE 9 IN [23 CM] TART; 8 TO 12 SERVINGS

Unbaked 9 in [23 cm] Matcha Tart Dough shell (page 296)	1	

MATCHA STREUSEL

Unsalted butter, cold	5 Tbsp	75 g
Einkorn flour	½ cup + 2 Tbsp	75 g
Almond flour	3 Tbsp	20 g
Whole almonds	scant ½ cup	60 g
Granulated sugar	¼ cup	50 g
Matcha powder	1 tsp	
Salt	⅛ tsp	

Matcha Almond Cream (page 308)	1⅔ cups	400 ml
Sliced apricots, peaches, plums, or strawberries, or whole raspberries or blackberries	2 cups	300 g
Confectioners' sugar for dusting		

This tart is a beautiful contrast of colors and flavors, and one of the more unusual ones that we make. Our baker Carolyn developed this when we were experimenting with matcha tea in pastries, and found the pairing of the tea and fruit to marry beautifully. The filling bakes up very similar to the Frangipane Tart (page 107).

KITCHEN NOTES: The size of the streusel should match the size of the tart: pea-size or smaller for individual tarts.

Preheat the oven to 325°F [160°C]. Line a 9 in [23 cm] tart shell with parchment paper and fill with pie weights. Partially bake the crust for 15 minutes, remove from the oven, and carefully remove the weights and paper. Return the shell to the oven and bake until the surface looks dry but hasn't colored, 5 more minutes. Let cool in the pan (a wire rack is not necessary).

To make the matcha streusel, cut the cold butter into ½ in [12 mm] cubes. Refrigerate until ready to use. In the bowl of a food processor fitted with the steel blade, combine the einkorn flour, almond flour, whole almonds, granulated sugar, matcha powder, and salt. Process until the almonds are in small pieces, about the size of sunflower seeds. Transfer the dry ingredients and the butter to the bowl of a stand mixer fitted with the paddle attachment. Mix on low speed until the butter is incorporated and the mixture is crumbly. Alternatively, put the dry ingredients in a medium bowl and, using a pastry cutter or your fingers, cut the butter into the dry ingredients until no lumps remain, and the mixture is sandy and crumbly. The streusel should be pea-size. To achieve uniform texture, sand it between your palms, rubbing tablespoon-size amounts, using a back-and-forth rubbing motion, rolling and breaking it into smaller pieces.

continued

Store the streusel in an airtight container and refrigerate until ready to use. The streusel can be made in advance and frozen, in a well-sealed container, for up to 1 week.

To make the tart, spoon the Matcha Almond Cream into the cooled partially baked tart shell, smoothing the filling evenly to the edges of the shell with an offset spatula. Arrange the fruit over the cream and sprinkle the streusel evenly over the fruit.

Bake until the filling has risen slightly and the streusel has browned slightly, but is still green in color. 25 to 30 minutes. Remove from the oven and let cool to room temperature on a wire rack. Unmold and dust with confectioners' sugar before serving. If it sticks a bit, use the blade of a thin knife to release it when unmolding. This tart will keep, well wrapped, in the refrigerator for up to 4 days.

BUTTERSCOTCH TART

YIELDS ONE 9 IN [23 CM] TART; 8 TO 10 SERVINGS

Fully baked and cooled 9 in [23 cm] Rye Tart Dough shell (page 294)	1	

FILLING

Brown sugar, lightly packed	1 cup	180 g
Water	3 Tbsp	45 ml
Salt	3/4 tsp	
Heavy cream	1¼ cups	300 ml
Whole milk	1¼ cups	300 ml
Large eggs	3	
Cornstarch	5 Tbsp	35 g
White chocolate, melted	2 oz	60 g
Unsalted butter, at room temperature	2 Tbsp	
Scotch or dark rum (optional)	2 Tbsp	

CHOCOLATE CLUSTERS

Dark or milk chocolate	4 oz	110 g
Cornflakes or crisped rice cereal	1½ cups	110 g

Sweetened softly whipped cream	
Milk chocolate for making chocolate curls (optional, see page 96)	

I have wanted something butterscotch on the menu for a long time, but most butterscotches are too sweet, or not "butterscotch-y" enough. Our head of pastry, Lynn, worked on this to get just the right flavor by caramelizing the sugar, adding a little Scotch, and using a rye crust to create the best butterscotch dessert I have ever had. A pastry crust using rye flour sounds like it could be overwhelmingly strong with rye, but it is actually very mild and underscores the savoriness of the butterscotch.

KITCHEN NOTES: Have your ingredients measured and ready before beginning this recipe.

. . . . . .

Have your baked and cooled tart shell ready. Have a large bowl with a fine-mesh sieve resting on the rim ready for straining the butterscotch.

To make the filling, combine the brown sugar, water, and salt in a deep, heavy saucepan. Place the pan over medium-high heat and bring to a rapid boil for 2 minutes. Remove from the heat and immediately add the cream and milk. The caramel will seize at first, but whisk and it will come together. If necessary to smooth the mixture, return to low heat, stirring occasionally.

In a medium bowl, whisk the eggs and cornstarch together until smooth. Slowly ladle about one-third of the caramel into the egg mixture, whisking constantly. Pour the egg-caramel mixture into the rest of the caramel in the pan and continue whisking over medium heat until the custard is as thick as lightly whipped cream, about 2 minutes. In order for the cornstarch to cook and thicken fully, the mixture must come just to the boiling point. You want to see a few slow bubbles. Remove from the heat and immediately

continued

pour through the sieve into the bowl. Let cool for 20 minutes until it is warm to the touch but no longer hot, stirring occasionally to release the heat and prevent a skin from forming on top. When the butter is added, you want it to incorporate, not melt.

Add the white chocolate, softened butter, and Scotch, if using, to the butterscotch filling and whisk to combine. Continue whisking until the mixture is smooth and shiny, about 2 minutes. An immersion blender works here as well, if you have one. Pour the custard immediately into the fully baked pie shell. If the custard cooled too much, it will not fill the tart shell evenly and won't smooth out on top. Use an offset spatula to smooth the top of the tart. Transfer to the refrigerator to set for at least 6 hours, or overnight.

To make the chocolate clusters, line a baking sheet with parchment. Pour water to a depth of about 2 in [5 cm] into a saucepan, place over medium heat, and bring to a simmer. Put the chocolate into a large stainless-steel bowl that will rest securely on the rim of the pan and place it over, but not touching, the water. Heat, stirring occasionally with a rubber spatula, just until the chocolate melts and is smooth. Remove from the heat and stir in the corn-flakes until evenly coated. Spread the mixture on the prepared baking sheet and set aside to cool, 1 hour. Store in an airtight container at room temperature for up to 5 days.

To finish the tart, top with the chocolate clusters, whipped cream, and chocolate curls, if using. Serve cold. The tart will keep in the refrigerator for up to 2 days.

JAMS & PRESERVES

This is a short recipe section, with a wide variety between very simple preserves (Raspberry), more involved (Apple Butter), and very involved (Orange Passion Fruit). I generally like to distill a recipe to its core, without taking more steps than necessary to get to the desired result. Preserve-making is like this for me: it's quick, delicious, and straightforward. Preserves almost always set at the same temperature and there are some easy-to-remember sugar-to-fruit ratios, so one never needs to rely on a recipe.

Here is preserve-making distilled to its basics: 1 part fruit, slightly more than ½ part sugar, and some acid.

The fruit part needs to include some underripe fruit, as it contains more natural pectin. The sugar part needs to be at least 55 percent of the fruit weight or it won't activate the pectin. You can use a ratio of 1:1, but that's an awful lot of sugar, and you get less fruit per spoonful. It's easiest to use grams for weighing, and I like a ratio of 1,000 g fruit to 600 g sugar. For that 1,000 g of fruit, I'd use about 4 lemons, depending on how juicy they are. The acid in the lemons activates the pectin.

Cook the preserves to 221°F [105°C], and that's it.

There are many different ways to treat the fruit before cooking it, such as letting it macerate overnight or bringing it to a boil before letting it sit overnight. These various methods result in different textures. Boiling or soaking overnight preserves the integrity of the fruit. Peeling, not peeling, leaving fruit whole, or cutting it into small chunks also will yield different results, but these basics are all based on the same theory of heat, pectin activation, and setting.

The Orange Passion Fruit Preserves recipe is one I developed in the winter, when California has lots of beautiful citrus but not much else. Passion fruit's pronounced flavor marries well with citrus, discernible even in smaller amounts. However, unless you lived in Hawaii with unlimited amounts of passion fruit (it's called *lilikoi* there) at your disposal, it would be prohibitively expensive to make into preserves. I wanted to create something different in texture from classic marmalade, so I came up with this recipe (which admittedly has many steps), and the result is a very soft, smooth, flavorful preserve, beautifully bright with spots of passion fruit seeds (if you opt to use them).

Carolyn Nugent created the Apple Butter recipe, which is among the best I've had and will leave you licking the pot. It's warmly spiced, with a beautiful color and silken, spreadable texture you'll want to use on everything. Try it in the Rugelach (page 222) or as an alternative filling in Linzer Torte (page 274).

For the best flavor and texture, I make sure to use a variety of apples. I like the acidity of Granny Smith, Honeycrisp, and Pippin, mixing them with Pink Lady and McIntosh (both have a balance of sweet and tart), and the sweeter Gala, Golden Delicious, Fuji, and Braeburn. There are more varieties of apple than I could list here, but if you buy a mixture at market, you'll get a better flavor in your apple butter.

At the other end of the preserve-making spectrum is my Raspberry Preserves. You'll be shocked at how quickly you can go from fruit-in-pot to jar-filling. The same ratio can be used for blueberries, blackberries, and strawberries, making sure to use a portion of underripe fruit (especially in the case of strawberries, which have less natural pectin) to ensure a good set; the riper a fruit is, the less pectin it contains.

RASPBERRY PRESERVES

———

YIELDS ABOUT 2½ CUPS [700 G] SMALL-BATCH PRESERVES, OR 10 CUPS [2.8 KG] LARGE-BATCH PRESERVES

SMALL BATCH

Raspberries	1 lb ½ oz	500 g
Sugar	1½ cups	300 g
Lemon juice	from 1 lemon	

LARGE BATCH

Raspberries	4½ lb	2 kg
Sugar	6 cups	1.2 kg
Lemon juice	from 2 lemons	

KITCHEN NOTES: I like a seedy jam, but raspberries can sometimes be overwhelmingly so. I strain half of the raspberry preserves, and when mixed with the rest of the batch it has a perfect amount. If the seeds don't bother you, you will get a slightly higher yield.

· · · · · ·

Have sterilized jars, a funnel (if using), a ladle, a bowl for the foam that you will skim, and a thermometer ready.

Place all the ingredients in a heavy-bottomed pot so that there is at least two-thirds the amount of headroom as fruit. With a potato masher or the back of a wooden spoon, mash the ingredients together until the juices run from the raspberries. Bring to a boil over high heat. Let the mixture cook, stirring with a wooden spoon, and skimming off and discarding the foam as it rises to the top with a ladle, until the mixture reaches 221°F [105°C] on a thermometer. If you are straining out the seeds, remove from the heat and pour as much as you want to strain through a clean fine-mesh strainer set over a heatproof bowl. Return the strained jam back to the pot with the unstrained jam, set over high heat, and quickly return to a boil to sterilize. Remove from the heat. Pour into jars, leaving ⅛ to ¼ in [4 to 6 mm] of headroom, put the lids on, and process according to the manufacturer's instructions. Processed preserves will keep at room temperature for up to 1 year. Alternatively, for short-term use, skip the processing step, let the preserves cool in the jars, and store the jars in the refrigerator for up to 10 days or freeze for up to 1 month.

ORANGE PASSION FRUIT PRESERVES

YIELDS ABOUT 9 CUPS [2.7 KG]

PECTIN

Apples, with peel and core, each cut into eight pieces	2¼ lb	1 kg
Water	4 cups	1 L

SLICED ORANGE

Oranges, ends removed, quartered, and thinly sliced	about 4	835 g
Water	1⅓ cups	330 ml
Sugar	scant 1¾ cups	340 g

ORANGE-PASSION FRUIT PULP

Oranges	6 to 8	
Sugar	10 cups	1 kg
Passion fruit pulp, from fresh or frozen fruits	1 cup + 3 Tbsp	285 ml

KITCHEN NOTES: If using fresh passion fruit, remove some or all of the seeds unless you like a very crunchy preserve.

. . . . . .

Begin by making apple pectin. Cook the whole apple chunks with the water for 30 minutes. The water should remain at a constant simmer throughout cooking. Strain through a fine-mesh sieve into a bowl, pushing down gently on the solids to extract as much juice as possible, or let hang in cheesecloth for a few hours, gently squeezing at the end. Discard the cooked apple.

Meanwhile, to make the sliced orange mixture, simmer the sliced oranges, water, and sugar until the oranges are soft and translucent, about 30 minutes.

Next, cut the remaining oranges into supremes. Slice off the ends of an orange. Placing the flat side down on the cutting board, use a very sharp paring knife to slice off the peel and white pith in strips, following the shape of the orange, until it is all removed. Cut into the center along the membrane, releasing each segment from between two membranes. Place in a bowl. Repeat with the remaining oranges, then squeeze the juice into the bowl with the segments before discarding the peels. You need enough to equal 680 g [approximately 3 cups] of supremes.

In a large saucepan, combine the apple pectin, the sliced orange mixture, the supremes, the sugar, and the passion fruit pulp. Cook over medium heat until the mixture reaches 221°F [105°C], stirring with a wooden spoon and skimming off and discarding the foam as it rises to the top with a ladle.

Spoon into jars, leaving ⅛ to ¼ in [4 to 6 mm] of headroom, put the lids on, and process according to the manufacturer's instructions. Processed preserves will keep at room temperature for up to 1 year. Alternatively, for short-term use, skip the processing step, let the preserves cool in the jars, and store the jars in the refrigerator for up to 10 days or in the freezer for up to 1 month.

APPLE BUTTER

YIELDS 2 CUPS [480 G]

Apples (6 to 7 medium)	2 lb	910 g
Sugar	1¼ cups	250 g
Cinnamon stick, or Ground cinnamon	1 stick, or ¼ tsp	
Ground nutmeg	½ tsp	
Ground cloves	¼ tsp	
Ground allspice	⅛ tsp	
Star anise pod	1	
Vanilla bean, split and scraped	1	
Apple cider	1 cup	240 ml
Apple cider vinegar	2 Tbsp	
Salt	⅛ tsp	

Preheat the oven to 300°F [150°C]. Cut the apples into eighths (retaining the core and seeds), and place in a large bowl. Add the sugar, cinnamon, nutmeg, cloves, allspice, star anise, and vanilla bean pod and seeds and mix well. Add the cider, vinegar, and salt, and mix to incorporate. Transfer the apple mixture to a 9 by 13 in [23 by 33 cm] pan, cover with parchment paper cut to fit the pan, and cover the pan with aluminum foil.

Bake 3½ hours, removing the pan from the oven every 45 minutes to stir the mixture. When the liquid has reduced by three-quarters and the apples are very soft, remove the pan from the oven, uncover, and allow to cool.

Set a food mill over a large bowl and process the apple mixture. Be sure to scrape the bottom plate and sides with a rubber spatula to collect all of the apple butter on the underside of the food mill. Transfer the apple butter to a lidded storage container. It will keep for up to 2 weeks in the refrigerator.

CHAPTER THREE

CAKES

LEMON MERINGUE CAKE

YIELDS ONE 10 IN [25 CM] CAKE; 12 TO 16 SERVINGS

10 in [25 cm] Génoise (page 312), split into 4 layers	1	
Caramel Sauce (page 309)	1 cup	240 ml
Lemon Cream (page 306)	2 2/3 cups	625 ml

LEMON SYRUP

Water	5 Tbsp	75 ml
Sugar	1/3 cup	70 g
Lemon juice	5 Tbsp	75 ml

ITALIAN MERINGUE

Large egg whites	1 cup (about 7)	240 ml
Sugar	1 3/4 cups	350 g
Salt	pinch	

This is by far the most popular cake at Tartine, requested for special occasions and many weddings. It is also our sweetest cake—or was. Over the years, we've decreased the level of sweetness in the syrup that soaks the cake to reflect our preference for less-sweet desserts. It's easily adjusted, and if you like the original, I've included that higher amount of lemon syrup.

KITCHEN NOTES: For more flavor and less sweetness in the final caramel sauce, make sure to take the sugar to a deep brown for the caramel layer. As with most cream-filled cakes, you must give the cream filling time to set up before slicing, at least a few hours but preferably overnight.

• • • • • •

Have the cake, caramel, and lemon cream ready.

To make the lemon syrup, combine the water and sugar in a small, heavy saucepan and bring to a boil over medium heat, stirring with a wooden spoon. When the sugar has dissolved, remove the pan from the heat, let cool for a few minutes, and then chill until cool to the touch, about 30 minutes. Whisk the lemon juice into the syrup.

Line the sides of a 10 in [25 cm] springform pan with plastic wrap, allowing enough overhang to cover the top of the cake completely when it is assembled. Leave the bottom of the pan unlined. Fit one cake layer into the bottom of the pan. Using a pastry brush, moisten the layer evenly with one-quarter of the lemon syrup. Using an offset spatula, spread one-third of the caramel over the cake, and then spread with one-third of the lemon cream. Repeat with two more layers, using up the remaining caramel and lemon cream. Top with the fourth cake layer and moisten with the remaining lemon syrup. Fold the overhanging plastic wrap over the top of the cake, covering completely, and refrigerate for at least 4 hours or up to overnight.

continued

When you are ready to finish the cake, make the meringue. Pour water to a depth of about 2 in [5 cm] into a saucepan, place over medium heat, and bring to a simmer. Combine the egg whites, sugar, and salt in the bowl of a stand mixer. Whisk together and then place over the saucepan and continue to whisk until the whites are hot to the touch (120°F [50°C]), about 5 minutes or so. Remove the bowl from over the water and place on the mixer stand fitted with the whisk attachment and mix on high speed until the mixture is very thick and holds glossy, stiff peaks when you lift the beater.

Take the cake out of the refrigerator. Release and lift off the pan sides and peel away the plastic wrap. Using a wide metal spatula, transfer the cake to a serving plate, if using, or leave it on the pan base. Using the offset spatula, immediately frost the top and sides of the cake with the meringue, creating swoops and peaks. Using a kitchen torch, lightly brown the meringue. The cake can be served immediately or kept cold in the refrigerator until ready to serve. It will keep for up to 1 week.

Variation for a Rectangular Cake: For a rectangular cake (as pictured), use a 13 by 18 in [33 by 46 cm] half-sheet pan lined with parchment paper to bake one recipe of Génoise (page 312). It will bake in 15 to 20 minutes; test the cake for doneness after 12 minutes.

When cool, loosen the cake from the sides of the pan with a thin knife and peel the paper from the bottom. Cut into four equal lengths of approximately 4½ by 13 in [11 by 33 cm]. To make the most even cake, use a ruler and cut the cake in half, stack the halves, and cut in half again. Proceed as directed.

DEVIL'S FOOD LAYER CAKE

YIELDS ONE 9 IN [23 CM] CAKE; 12 TO 16 SERVINGS

CAKE LAYERS

Cocoa powder	1¼ cups	115 g
All-purpose flour	¾ cup + 2 Tbsp	115 g
Einkorn flour	¾ cup	100 g
Dark rye flour	½ cup	70 g
Baking powder	1 tsp	
Baking soda	¼ tsp	
Unsalted butter, at cool room temperature	¾ cup	170 g
Sugar	2¾ cups	550 g
Salt	1 tsp	
Olive oil	3 Tbsp	45 ml
Large eggs	5	
Large egg yolks	2	
Buttermilk	1¼ cups	300 ml
Coffee, cooled	1¼ cups	300 ml

CHOCOLATE FILLING

Bittersweet chocolate	5 oz	140 g
Cream	1 cup + 2 Tbsp	270 ml
Whole milk	1 cup + 1 Tbsp	255 ml
Sugar	¾ cup	150 g
Cocoa powder	¼ cup	25 g
Cornstarch	2 Tbsp	
Salt	¼ tsp	
Unsalted butter, cubed, at room temperature	¼ cup	60 g

CHOCOLATE GANACHE FROSTING

Bittersweet chocolate	8 oz	225 g
Heavy cream	1 cup	240 ml
Sugar	½ cup	100 g
Unsalted butter, at room temperature	10 Tbsp	140 g
Caramel Sauce (page 309)	½ cup + 1 Tbsp	130 g

This is a rich, dark, very chocolaty chocolate cake that has gone through several iterations since we first made it in 2002. I originally wanted a cake that reminded me of one from my Brooklyn childhood, the Blackout Cake from Ebinger's on Flatbush that my parents would occasionally bring home. Because we are always evolving ideas and trying out different flours, it's become what it is today: a dark, four-layer cake, filled with chocolate ganache and caramel. Lynn developed the layers to have a boost of flavor from rye flour as well as a good amount of coffee, both working really well with the chocolate flavors.

· · · · · ·

continued

Preheat the oven to 350°F [180°C]. Butter and lightly flour the sides of two 9 in [23 cm] cake pans, knocking out the excess flour. Line the bottom of each pan with parchment paper cut to fit exactly.

To make the cake layers, sift together the cocoa powder, flours, baking powder, and baking soda into a bowl and set aside. In the bowl of a stand mixer fitted with the paddle attachment, beat the butter, sugar, and salt on medium speed for 1 minute. Slowly add the olive oil and continue to beat until incorporated. Add the eggs and yolks, one at a time, mixing well after each addition. Stop the mixer and scrape down the sides of the bowl with a rubber spatula. With the mixer on low speed, add the flour mixture in three equal batches, alternating with the buttermilk in two batches, beginning and ending with the flour mixture. Stop the mixer; scrape down the sides of the bowl. Turn the mixer back on low speed, add the cooled coffee, and mix for another few seconds.

Divide the cake batter evenly between the prepared cake pans. Bake until the top springs back when lightly touched or a cake tester inserted into the center comes out clean, about 45 minutes. Let the cakes cool completely in the pans on a wire rack.

To make the chocolate filling, rest a fine-mesh sieve over a heatproof bowl and set aside.

Pour water to a depth of about 2 in [5 cm] into a saucepan, place over medium heat, and bring to a simmer. Put the chocolate into a stainless-steel bowl that will rest securely on the rim of the pan and place it over, but not touching, the water. Stir the chocolate with a rubber spatula and heat just until the chocolate is melted. Set aside.

Heat the cream and milk in a medium saucepan over medium heat. In a medium bowl, whisk together the sugar, cocoa powder, cornstarch, and salt. When the milk and cream are just under a boil, remove from the heat. Pour half of the milk mixture into the sugar mixture, and whisk until smooth. Pour the sugar mixture back into the milk mixture and cook over medium heat, whisking constantly, until the mixture thickens and boils, 3 minutes.

Immediately pour the mixture through the sieve into the heatproof bowl. Once the mixture has cooled, but is still warm, about 20 minutes, whisk the melted chocolate into the cooled filling. Whisk in the softened butter. Cover and refrigerate for at least 2 hours until cool and set.

To make the ganache frosting, pour water to a depth of about 2 in [5 cm] into a saucepan, place over medium heat, and bring to a simmer. Put the chocolate into a stainless-steel bowl that will rest securely on the rim of the pan and place it over, but not touching, the water. Stir the chocolate with a rubber spatula and heat just until the chocolate is melted. Heat the cream and sugar in a small saucepan until hot to the touch (120°F [50°C]). Pour half of the cream mixture over the melted chocolate and whisk to combine. Pour in the remaining cream mixture and whisk vigorously to combine. Add the butter and whisk for 1 more minute to emulsify the ganache and to be sure all the butter is combined. Transfer the frosting to an airtight container or cover with plastic wrap. Let it sit at cool room temperature for 6 hours or overnight.

continued

When the cakes are cool, turn them out by inverting the pans, and then turn the cakes upright. Using a serrated knife, slice off the domed portion from the top of each cake to make the tops flat. Slice each cake in half to create four equal layers.

To assemble the cake, transfer one layer to a serving plate. Using an offset spatula, spread 3 Tbsp of the caramel evenly over the cake layer. Spread a thin layer of chocolate filling (about ¼ in [6 mm]) over the caramel. Top with a second cake layer, and again spread with 3 Tbsp caramel and a thin layer of chocolate filling. Repeat with the third cake layer, spreading with 3 Tbsp caramel and a thin layer of chocolate filling. Top with the fourth cake layer. Refrigerate the cake until the center is firm, 1 to 2 hours.

Remove the cake from the refrigerator. Frost the top and sides of the cake with the ganache, using an offset spatula.

Serve the cake at room temperature. To store, cover tightly and keep in a cool place for up to 4 days. It is not necessary to store this cake in the refrigerator.

CHOCOLATE SOUFFLÉ

YIELDS ONE 10 IN [25 CM] CAKE; 12 TO 16 SERVINGS

CAKE BASE

Oat flour	¾ cup	85 g
Rice flour	⅓ cup	40 g
Cocoa powder	½ cup	55 g
Cornstarch	2 Tbsp	
Baking powder	½ tsp	
Baking soda	⅛ tsp	
Unsalted butter, at room temperature	6 Tbsp	85 g
Sugar	1⅓ cups	265 g
Salt	½ tsp	
Olive oil	1½ Tbsp	
Large eggs	2	
Large egg yolk	1	
Buttermilk	⅔ cup	160 g
Coffee, cooled	⅔ cup	160 g

OR

NUT BASE

Walnuts or pecans, lightly toasted and finely chopped	1 cup	90 g

FILLING

Unsalted butter	¾ cup + 1 Tbsp	185 g
Bittersweet chocolate, chopped	14 oz	395 g
Large eggs	7	
Sugar	¾ cup + 2 Tbsp	175 g
Salt	¼ tsp	

GANACHE TOPPING (OPTIONAL)

Bittersweet chocolate, chopped	4 oz		115 g
Heavy cream		½ cup	120 ml

This rich cake, made without flour but with a good amount of butter and chocolate, is not dense in the way most flourless cakes are because the yolks and whites are beaten separately and then combined with the chocolate and butter. Its character changes depending on whether you serve it at room temperature or cold. At room temperature, the chocolate and butter soften and the cake becomes mousse-like, more easily scooped than sliced. When cold, it is sliceable and light but firm. This cake is perfect for Passover—and gluten free—if you make it with the nuts rather than the chocolate cake base. Or you can omit the base altogether (you'll still need to line the pan with parchment).

KITCHEN NOTES: The success of this cake depends on two things. First, you must incorporate air into the egg-sugar mixture, whipping it to a thick ribbon, or the cake will not have the correct, light texture. Second, you must not overbake the cake, or it will turn out dry. Many cooks are inclined to turn the mixer to high speed for whipping egg whites until they hold stiff peaks. But you will find that if you whip whites on medium speed and take a little longer, the whites will have a tighter, more stable structure and fewer irregular air pockets.

. . . . . .

continued

Preheat the oven to 350°F [180°C]. Butter and lightly flour a 10 in [25 cm] cake pan with oat flour, knocking out the excess flour. Line the bottom of the pan with parchment paper cut to fit exactly.

If using the chocolate base layer, mix the cake as directed in the Devil's Food Layer Cake recipe (page 157). Pour into the prepared pan, and bake for about 1 hour. When tested with a paring knife inserted into the center of the cake, the knife should come out clean, and the cake should feel firm in the center when gently pressed with your fingers. Allow the cake to cool completely before removing from the pan. Chill the cake for at least 3 hours before slicing a ¼ in [6 mm] thick layer of cake for the base.

If using nuts, evenly distribute them over the bottom of the pan, then gently shake it back and forth to fill in any gaps.

In a small saucepan, melt the butter over medium heat and then add the chocolate. Stir as the chocolate melts, blending it with the butter. Remove from the heat and set aside.

Separate the eggs, placing the yolks and whites in separate mixing bowls. Add half of the sugar to the egg yolks. Using a mixer fitted with the paddle attachment, beat the yolk mixture on high speed until it is light, fluffy, and tripled in volume, and falls off the beater in a wide ribbon that folds back on itself and slowly dissolves, 4 to 5 minutes. Using a rubber spatula, fold the chocolate mixture into the egg yolks. Don't worry about the mixture being perfectly blended at this point because you will be folding in the whites next.

Using the mixer, beat the egg whites on medium speed until soft peaks form. Add the rest of the sugar and the salt and beat until the whites hold glossy, medium-stiff peaks. Stir one-third of the whites into the chocolate-yolk mixture to lighten it, and then gently fold in the remaining whites just until no white streaks are visible. Immediately turn the batter into the prepared pan.

Bake until the top of the cake is no longer shiny, being careful not to let it "soufflé" (puff up and expand beyond its original volume), 30 to 40 minutes. Let cool completely in the pan on a wire rack. As the cake cools, it will become firmer. Cover and refrigerate until well chilled, at least 3 hours and up to overnight.

To make the ganache topping, if using, remove the cake from the refrigerator, uncover it, and let it sit at room temperature for about 15 minutes to warm up a bit before you top it. Place the chocolate in a heatproof bowl. Heat the cream in a small saucepan and bring to just under a boil. Pour the cream over the chocolate. Let the mixture sit for about 2 minutes without stirring, until the chocolate melts, and then stir gently with a rubber spatula until smooth, incorporating as little air as possible. Pour the ganache over the cake, and tilt and turn the cake to cover the top evenly. The cold temperature of the cake will help the ganache set.

When the chocolate is set, after about 20 minutes, run a thin knife around the inside edge of the pan to loosen the cake. Release and lift the pan sides. Using a wide metal spatula, transfer the cake to a serving plate, if using, or leave it on the pan base.

Serve the cake cold or at room temperature. If served cold, slice the cake with a warm knife (have a tall container filled with very hot water for dipping the knife before each cut and a towel to wipe the knife clean after each cut). It will keep, well wrapped, in the refrigerator for up to 1 week.

VICTORIA SPONGE

YIELDS ONE 8 IN [20 CM] CAKE; 8 TO 10 SERVINGS

CAKE

Unsalted butter, at room temperature	1 cup + 1 Tbsp	240 g
Superfine sugar	1 cup + 3 Tbsp	240 g
Salt	½ tsp	
Pastry flour	1¾ cups	240 g
Baking powder	¼ tsp	
Crème fraîche	¼ cup	60 g
Vanilla extract	2 tsp	
Large eggs, at room temperature	4	

FILLING

Heavy cream	1 cup	240 ml
Granulated sugar	2 Tbsp	
Raspberry Preserves (page 146)	½ cup	140 g
Confectioners' sugar for dusting		

Victoria Sponge—two simple sponge cake layers sandwiched with raspberry jam and whipped cream and topped with a dusting of confectioners' sugar—has been a staple of tea time in the United Kingdom since the early 1800s, when it was introduced to and named after Queen Victoria by its creator, Anna Maria, Duchess of Bedford.

When considering what cakes to add to our repertoire, I landed on Victoria Sponge because it brings together many elements of what I consider classic to Tartine's baking ethos: freshly made and served right away, showcasing our fruit, and simplicity of presentation. Victoria Sponge is eaten not long after making; the cake isn't encased in buttercream to keep it fresh for days. Like the Shaker Lemon Pie (page 124), pound cake, or pie dough, there really isn't a proprietary recipe for it, although we tried over a dozen versions before landing back at square one, with one little variation that we thought was a bit of an improvement over the original. This small, but I think important, detail is that our baker, Kelsey, experimented with incorporating a small amount of crème fraîche, which adds more moisture and a little more luxurious texture to the crumb. Similar to the way an omelet showcases a chef's skill, Victoria Sponge, too, shows itself plainly without embellishments to cover up mistakes.

KITCHEN NOTES: All early recipes for Victoria Sponge (pre-1843) only call for equal parts eggs, sugar, flour, and butter. Once baking powder was invented in the 1840s, it was used in cakes to ensure a lighter crumb. Superfine sugar is traditional, although granulated sugar will work. Raspberry is the traditional jam filling, but any preserve will be delicious, especially if it has a bit of body to it to make a proper layer.

······

continued

Preheat the oven to 325°F [160°C]. Line the bottom of an 8 in [20 cm] cake pan with parchment paper cut to fit exactly.

In the bowl of a stand mixer fitted with the paddle attachment, combine the butter, superfine sugar, and salt. Cream on medium speed for 10 minutes until light and fluffy, stopping occasionally to scrape down the sides of the bowl with a spatula to ensure all the butter is well incorporated.

Meanwhile, sift together the pastry flour and baking powder in a medium bowl. Sift three more times and set aside. In a small bowl, combine the crème fraîche and vanilla extract. Set aside.

Add the eggs, one at a time, to the butter mixture, scraping down the mixing bowl after each addition and mixing until smooth. Add the crème fraîche and vanilla and mix well.

Remove the bowl from the mixer and add the sifted flour mixture. Fold by hand with a rubber spatula until the batter comes together and no loose flour remains. Be sure not to overmix.

Pour into the prepared pan and bake until golden brown and the top of the cake springs back when lightly touched, 55 to 60 minutes. Allow to cool in the pan on a wire rack. To unmold, run a small, thin knife around the sides of the pan to loosen the cake and then gently invert the pan. Peel off the parchment from the bottom of the cake and turn the cake right-side up.

To assemble, place the cake on a flat surface and mark half the thickness all the way around the cake using a long, thin serrated knife. Holding the knife parallel to the work surface and using a sawing motion, cut through the cake, ensuring that the tip end and handle of the knife are level and slicing where you marked. Separate the two layers.

In the bowl of a stand mixer fitted with the whisk attachment, or by hand with a whisk, whip the heavy cream and granulated sugar until pillowy, soft peaks form. Spread the raspberry preserves onto the bottom cake layer, cut-side up, and smooth to the edge with an offset spatula. Top with the sweetened whipped cream and gently sandwich the two cake layers together. Dust liberally with confectioners' sugar and serve immediately.

The cake keeps, tightly wrapped and refrigerated, for up to 2 days.

SUMMER FRUIT BAVARIAN

YIELDS ONE 10 IN [25 CM] CAKE; 12 TO 16 SERVINGS

10 in [25 cm] Génoise (page 312), split into 2 layers each about ½ in [12 mm]	1	

FRUIT PURÉE (see Variation, page 169)

Berries	1¼ cups	180 g
Sugar	¼ cup	50 g
Salt	pinch	

FILLING

Gelatin (½ envelope)	1½ tsp	
Water	1 Tbsp	
Pastry Cream (page 300), cold	2½ cups	600 ml
Heavy cream, very cold	2 cups + 1 Tbsp	500 ml

FRESH FRUIT (ONE TYPE OR A MIXTURE)

Berries or cherries, pitted, or sliced peaches, apricots, or nectarines	4 cups	600 g

TOPPING

Heavy cream, very cold	1¼ cups	300 ml
Sugar	4 tsp	

This recipe makes a light, soft, mousse-like filling that goes well with most summer fruits. Generally when we make this type of filling at the bakery, we use cake layers on the top and bottom only, and wrap a clear cake band around the sides so that the beautiful layers of fruit, cake, and filling are all visible.

KITCHEN NOTES: The thing to remember when combining the pastry cream, whipped cream, and gelatin (or anything that contains gelatin) is that when you add gelatin to any cold mixture, its setting action begins immediately. Because of this you have to (1) make sure that the mixture the gelatin is going into isn't stone cold, and (2) add the gelatin first to a small amount of the base and then whisk that smaller amount into the remainder.

. . . . . .

Line the sides of a 10 in [25 cm] springform pan with 3 in [7.5 cm] sides with plastic wrap, allowing enough overhang to cover the top of the cake completely when it is assembled. Leave the bottom of the pan unlined. Have the cake layers ready.

To make the fruit purée, combine the berries, sugar, and salt in a blender and process on high speed until smooth.

To make the filling, in a small bowl, sprinkle the gelatin over the water and let stand for a few minutes to soften. Pour water to a depth of about 2 in [5 cm] into a saucepan, place over medium heat, and bring to a simmer. Place ½ cup [120 ml] of the pastry cream in a stainless-steel bowl that will rest securely on the rim of the saucepan over, but not touching, the water. Heat the pastry cream, whisking constantly, until hot to the touch (120°F [50°C]), about 5 minutes. Add the softened gelatin and whisk until smooth. Remove from the double boiler. Whisk half of the remaining cold pastry cream into the hot mixture, then whisk in the rest.

continued

In a bowl, using a mixer fitted with the whisk attachment or a whisk, whip the cream until it holds medium-stiff peaks. Immediately and gently fold the whipped cream into the pastry cream with a rubber spatula.

Fit one cake layer into the bottom of the prepared springform pan. Using a pastry brush, moisten the layer evenly with half of the fruit purée. Spoon half of the filling onto the layer, add the fruit (if using strawberries, directions follow), and spoon the rest of the filling over the fruit. Smooth the surface with an offset spatula. If using strawberries, spoon only enough of the filling onto the cake to create a layer 1/4 in [6 mm] thick and stand the strawberries upright, pointed end up, pushing them into the cream. Quickly pour the remaining filling onto the fruit, lightly pressing down with the back of a large spoon to fill in any air pockets. Place the second cake layer on top and moisten it with the rest of the fruit purée. Fold the overhanging plastic wrap over the top of the cake, covering completely, and then gently press down on the plastic to distribute the cream evenly (don't use too much pressure). Refrigerate for at least 4 hours or preferably overnight.

When you are ready to finish the cake, release and lift off the pan sides and peel away the plastic wrap. Using a wide metal spatula, transfer the cake to a serving plate, if using, or leave it on the cake pan base.

To make the topping, using the mixer or a whisk, whip the cream until thickened. Add the sugar and whip until the cream holds soft peaks. Using an offset spatula, frost the top of the cake. The cake can be served immediately or kept cold in the refrigerator until ready to serve. It will keep for up to 3 days.

Variation: You can make a liqueur-flavored sugar syrup in place of the fruit purée for moistening the cake layers. In a small, heavy saucepan, combine 1 cup minus 2 Tbsp [170 g] of sugar and 1/2 cup [120 ml] of water and bring to a boil, stirring to dissolve the sugar. When the sugar has dissolved, remove the pan from the heat and refrigerate until cold. Select a liqueur or other spirit, such as Cointreau, Grand Marnier, Chambord, brandy, or Armagnac, that complements the fruit you are using, and whisk 2 to 4 Tbsp [30 to 60 ml]—the amount depends on how strong you want your syrup to taste—into the sugar syrup.

PASSION FRUIT AND LIME BAVARIAN

YIELDS ONE 10 IN [25 CM] CAKE; 12 TO 16 SERVINGS

10 in [25 cm] Génoise (page 312), split into 4 layers	1 recipe	

LIME SYRUP

Sugar	1/2 cup	100 g
Water	1/2 cup	120 ml
Lime juice	5 Tbsp	75 ml
Lime zest	from 2 limes	

BAVARIAN CREAM

Passion fruit pulp, from fresh or frozen (about 12 fruits)	1/2 cup + 2 Tbsp	150 ml
Large egg yolks	2	
Sugar	1/3 cup	70 g
Salt	pinch	
Unflavored gelatin (1/2 envelope)	1 1/2 tsp	
Water	2 Tbsp	
Heavy cream, very cold	1 1/2 cups	360 ml

TOPPING

Heavy cream, very cold	1 1/2 cups	360 ml
Sugar	3 Tbsp	40 g
Unsweetened large-flake dried coconut	1 cup	60 g

We almost always make this cake with passion fruit. It started out as a fall and winter cake, when passion fruits are easy to get, but it became so popular that we now sell it almost year-round. We usually make some small changes along the way, such as altering the flavor of the moistening syrup or adding tangelo zest to the filling. Whatever flavors we use, the outside is always covered with wide shavings of dried coconut that turn soft from the barely whipped cream, which makes them taste as if they were freshly shaved from young, soft coconuts.

KITCHEN NOTES: The thickening power of gelatin continues after the first day the cake has set up. You will notice that on the second and even third days you serve the cake that the filling will be a bit stiffer. If you have difficulty finding passion fruits, some high-quality companies sell the pulp frozen. If you do add zest to the filling as suggested in the headnote, add it after the fruit-yolk mixture has cooled, or the zest will toughen.

. . . . . .

Wrap one cake layer in plastic wrap and reserve for another use. Have the remaining three layers ready.

To make the lime syrup, combine the sugar and water in a small, heavy saucepan and bring to a boil over medium heat, stirring with a wooden spoon. When the sugar has dissolved, remove the pan from the heat and chill until cool to the touch, about 30 minutes. Whisk the lime juice and zest into the syrup.

Line the sides of a 10 in [25 cm] springform pan with 3 in [7.5 cm] sides with plastic wrap, allowing enough overhang to cover the top of the cake completely when it is assembled. Leave the bottom of the pan unlined. Fit one cake layer into the bottom of the pan. Using a pastry brush, moisten the layer evenly with one-third of the lime syrup.

To make the Bavarian cream, pass the passion fruit pulp through a fine-mesh sieve placed over a small bowl and discard the seeds. Prepare an ice bath, using both ice and water, in a large bowl. Pour water to a depth of about 2 in [5 cm] into a saucepan, place over medium heat, and bring to a simmer. Combine the egg yolks, sugar, passion fruit juice, and salt in a stainless-steel bowl that will rest securely on the rim of the saucepan over, but not touching, the water. Whisk together and then place over the saucepan and continue to whisk until the whites are hot to the touch (120°F [50°C]), about 7 minutes. This is the bombe.

Meanwhile, in a small bowl, sprinkle the gelatin over the water and let stand for a few minutes to soften. When the bombe is ready, add the softened gelatin and whisk well to dissolve. Remove the bowl from over the hot water and nest the bowl in the ice bath just until slightly cool to the touch, whisking to cool the mixture evenly.

In a mixing bowl, whip the cream with a whisk or a stand mixer fitted with the whisk attachment until it holds medium-stiff peaks. Scoop about one-third of the cream into the bombe and whisk together to lighten the bombe. Gently fold in the rest of the whipped cream with a rubber spatula.

Working quickly, pour half of the mixture onto the first layer of cake. Top with the second layer, being careful as the filling is very liquid. Brush this layer with half of the remaining lime syrup and then immediately pour the remaining Bavarian cream over it. Carefully top with the last cake layer and moisten it with the remaining lime syrup. Fold the overhanging plastic wrap over the top of the cake, covering completely, and refrigerate overnight.

When you are ready to finish the cake, release and lift off the pan sides and peel away the plastic wrap. Using a wide metal spatula, transfer the cake to a serving plate, if using, or leave it on the cake pan base.

To make the topping, using the stand mixer or a whisk, whip the cream until thickened. Add the sugar and whip until the cream holds soft peaks. Using an offset spatula, frost the top and sides of the cake with the whipped cream, and then sprinkle the top and sides with the coconut. Return the cake to the refrigerator for about 2 hours before serving to allow the coconut flakes to absorb the moisture from the cream and soften.

Serve the cake cold. It will keep in the refrigerator for up to 1 week.

FROMAGE BLANC BAVARIAN

YIELDS ONE 10 IN [25 CM] CAKE; 12 TO 16 SERVINGS

CAKE BASE

10 in [25 cm] Génoise cake layer, ½ in [12 mm] thick (page 312)	1	
Water	¼ cup	60 ml
Lemon juice	1 Tbsp	
Sugar	3 Tbsp	

OR

NUT BASE

Pistachios, finely chopped	⅔ cup	90 g

FILLING

Water	¾ cup	180 ml
Sugar	½ cup	100 g
Large egg yolks	8	
Unflavored gelatin	4½ tsp	
Fromage blanc	3 cups	600 g
Heavy cream	3 cups	720 ml
Lemon juice	4 tsp	
Lemon zest	from 1 small lemon	
Orange zest	from ½ small orange	

GLAZE (OPTIONAL)

Apricot jam	¾ cup	210 g

Fromage blanc is a fresh cow's milk cheese made from skim milk (there is plenty of cream added to the Bavarian, so it actually ends up being a rich cake in spite of the low-fat cheese). The flavor of the cheese is slightly tart and the texture is smooth yet crumbly, similar to fresh goat cheese. If you are a fan of goat cheese, you can substitute it for the fromage blanc. The texture of the Bavarian is light and just barely set. I'm from Brooklyn and love a good New York–style cheesecake from time to time, but I find this much lighter, velvety version, with its slight acidity, to be more in tune with what I want after a meal, and the apricot glaze goes beautifully with the flavor of the fromage blanc (or with the other cheeses suggested in the Kitchen Notes). For fruit accompaniments, apricots and plums are on the top of my list in the summertime, followed by any other stone fruit. In the winter, candied quince or sautéed apples are good choices, as is any type of candied citrus peel or tropical fruit, such as sautéed banana or pineapple.

KITCHEN NOTES: You can use any soft fresh cheese in this Bavarian. Soft goat cheese and ricotta cheese work well, as does quark, a low-fat cheese similar to fromage blanc. Make sure that if you are using a cake base, it is ready and waiting, as the filling will begin to set up once the gelatin is added. Also, don't let the egg yolks come into contact with the sugar syrup before you are ready to whisk them together over the heat; if they sit, the sugar will coagulate the yolks, turning them irretrievably grainy.

. . . . . .

Line the sides of a 10 in [25 cm] springform pan with 3 in [7.5 cm] sides with plastic wrap, allowing a little overhang. Leave the bottom of the pan unlined.

To prepare the Bavarian using the cake base: Have the cake ready. In a small saucepan, stir together the water, lemon juice, and sugar over low heat just until the sugar dissolves. Remove from the heat and let cool to room temperature. Place the cake layer in the bottom of the prepared springform pan. Using a pastry brush, moisten the layer evenly with the syrup.

To prepare the Bavarian using the nut base: Evenly distribute the chopped nuts over the bottom of the springform pan. Gently shake the pan back and forth to fill in any gaps. It is not necessary to grease or otherwise prepare the bottom of the pan.

To make the filling, combine ½ cup [120 ml] of the water and all of the sugar in a small saucepan over medium heat and bring to a boil, stirring to dissolve the sugar. When the sugar has dissolved, remove from the heat and let cool until warm to the touch.

Pour water to a depth of about 2 in [5 cm] into a saucepan, place over medium heat, and bring to a simmer. Combine the sugar syrup and egg yolks in a stainless-steel bowl that will rest securely on the rim of the saucepan over, but not touching, the water. Heat the mixture, whisking often, until it thickens and registers 180°F [82°C] on a thermometer, 5 to 10 minutes.

Meanwhile, in a small dish, sprinkle the gelatin over the remaining ¼ cup [60 ml] water and let stand for a few minutes to soften. When the egg yolk mixture is ready, remove from the double boiler, add the softened gelatin, and whisk until smooth. The mixture must now be cool to the touch. You can cool it by nesting it in a larger bowl filled with ice and water or by putting it in the refrigerator. In either case, you must stir it with a rubber spatula or whisk so that the gelatin does not begin to set up unevenly.

In a large bowl, combine the fromage blanc and ½ cup [120 ml] of the cream and stir to break up and soften the cheese. Using a stand mixer fitted with the whisk attachment or a whisk, whip the remaining cream in a separate bowl until it holds soft peaks. Using a rubber spatula, fold the egg yolk mixture into the cheese, and then fold in the lemon juice and the lemon and orange zests. Finally, fold in one-third of the whipped cream to lighten the mixture, and then gently fold in the remaining whipped cream until it is fully incorporated and the mixture is smooth.

Transfer the filling to the springform pan, smoothing the top with the spatula. Cover the Bavarian with a sheet of plastic wrap, being careful that it does not touch the surface. Refrigerate for at least 4 hours or preferably overnight.

continued

You can serve the cake with or without a glaze. To serve without a glaze, release and lift off the pan sides and peel away the plastic wrap. Using a wide metal spatula, transfer the cake to a serving plate, if using, or leave it on the cake pan base.

To glaze the cake, keep the cake in the refrigerator until the moment you are going to glaze the top. Put the jam in a small saucepan over medium heat. Depending on how thick it is, you may need to thin it with a little water. I suggest starting with 1 Tbsp of water and stirring with a spoon or small whisk to break up any lumps. Be careful not to add too much water, as you want the jam to set back up again once it is poured onto the cake and allowed to cool.

Remove the jam from the heat, pour it through a medium-mesh sieve, and let cool until it is still liquid and warm. It must not be too hot to the touch, or it will melt the surface of the cake when you pour it on. Take the cake out of the refrigerator and lift away the plastic wrap. Working quickly, pour the warm jam on top of the cake and turn and slightly tip the cake so that the glaze spreads evenly to the sides. Return the cake to the refrigerator until the top has set, about 30 minutes, then remove from the pan and serve as directed above.

Serve the cake cold. It will keep in the refrigerator for up to 1 week.

CREAMY CHEESECAKE

YIELDS ONE 9 OR 10 IN [23 OR 25 CM] CAKE; 12 TO 14 SERVINGS

DIGESTIVE BISCUIT CRUST

½ recipe fully baked Oat Digestive Biscuits (page 208) or about 10 graham crackers		150 g
Unsalted butter, melted	4 Tbsp	60 g
Granulated sugar	1 Tbsp + 1½ tsp	
Salt	⅛ tsp	

CHEESECAKE FILLING

Cream cheese, at room temperature	4 cups	900 g
Granulated sugar	1¼ cups	250 g
Salt	¼ tsp	
Vanilla extract	2 tsp	
Lemon juice	2 Tbsp	
Lemon zest	2 tsp	
Large eggs	4	
Large egg yolks	2	
Crème fraîche	1⅓ cups	320 g

TOPPING

Crème fraîche	1½ cups	360 g
Confectioners' sugar, sifted	3 Tbsp	
Vanilla bean, split and scraped	½ bean	

I grew up in Brooklyn and have a soft spot for the dense cheesecake and classic graham crust that diners serve in all the boroughs. In fact, I love any kind of cheesecake, from the Italian ricotta version to Sara Lee. They're all good, but this one hits the mark for me due to its light, smooth texture and slight lemon tang. Baker Alexa Prendergast took my notes for a perfect cake and struck just the right balance here, even incorporating a gluten-free crumb crust made from our Oat Digestive Biscuits (page 208). Serve with fresh fruit or fruit purée.

KITCHEN NOTES: If you don't have a springform pan, a high-sided 9 in [23 cm] cake pan will work in a pinch. Simply line the bottom of the cake pan with a 9 in [23 cm] round of parchment paper and continue with the recipe, omitting the use of aluminum foil during the double boiler. When ready to serve, run a knife around the cake's edge, flip the cake pan over onto a plate, and quickly torch or blow dry the bottom surface of the pan to gently release the cheesecake. Give it a couple gentle taps if necessary. Remove the cake pan and flip the cake onto a serving platter.

. . . . . .

Position a rack in the middle of the oven. Preheat the oven to 350°F [180°C]. Prepare a 9 or 10 in [23 or 25 cm] springform pan by gently wrapping three layers of heavy-duty aluminum foil securely around the outside of the pan, making sure to press the foil against the side of the pan and gently crimping the top around the rim. Check that there are no holes or gaps for water to leak through. Have the biscuits ready.

To make the biscuit crust, place the biscuits in the bowl of a food processor fitted with the steel blade and process until the biscuits are finely ground and sandy. You need 1½ cups [150 g]. Alternatively,

continued

place the biscuits in a sealed bag and crush them with a rolling pin. Add the melted butter, granulated sugar, and salt to the food processor and pulse four times, or until the mixture looks slightly damp and will hold together when a small amount is squeezed in your palm. Spoon the crumb mixture into the springform pan and flatten into an even layer with your hands. Bake the crust until golden brown, about 10 minutes. Set aside and let cool while you prepare the filling. Reduce the oven temperature to 325°F [160°C].

To make the filling, cut the softened cream cheese into cubes and place in the bowl of a stand mixer fitted with the paddle attachment. Beat on medium speed for 4 minutes until smooth and creamy. Scrape down the sides and bottom of the bowl with a rubber spatula. Add the granulated sugar and salt and continue mixing on medium speed for an additional 4 minutes, scraping down the sides and bottom of the bowl after 2 minutes. Add the vanilla extract, lemon juice, and lemon zest and mix until combined. Place the whole eggs and yolks in a pourable container. Reduce the mixer speed to low and add the eggs and yolks, one at a time, to the cream cheese mixture, scraping the bowl after each addition and fully incorporating each before adding another. Be careful not to overmix or aerate the batter at this point; air bubbles will cause the cheesecake to crack. Give the crème fraîche a few stirs to smooth out any lumps. With the mixer on low, add the crème fraîche to the egg–cream cheese mixture and mix until the batter is smooth, creamy, and homogenous, about 1 minute. Give the mixture a final stir by hand, scraping the bottom and sides of the bowl well. Pour the batter into the prepared springform pan and smooth the surface with the back of a spoon or small spatula.

Bring a large pot of water to a boil. Place the springform pan in the center of a large roasting pan with tall sides, and gently place the pan on the middle rack of the preheated oven (have the oven rack pulled out slightly to make it easier to add the boiling water to the pan). Carefully pour enough boiling water into the roasting pan so it reaches halfway up the sides of the springform pan (be sure not to exceed the level of the foil). Very gently, slide the oven rack back in place. Bake the cheesecake for 1 hour and check for doneness. When done, the cheesecake will be jiggly in the center if given a gentle nudge, with the outer edge set. If it is still very loose and liquidy, continue baking up to 30 minutes more, checking every 10 minutes. Cool in the roasting pan for 1 hour. Remove the cheesecake from the double boiler and let it cool at room temperature for 1 more hour. At this point, the surface will still have a slight jiggle to it. Remove the foil wrap from the springform pan.

To prepare the topping, in a small bowl, whisk together the crème fraîche, confectioners' sugar, and vanilla bean seeds until smooth and creamy. Spread evenly on the surface of the cheesecake. Loosely cover the top of the pan with a fresh sheet of foil and chill in the refrigerator for a minimum of 4 hours, or overnight. This gentle cooling helps produce a smooth-surfaced cheesecake with no cracks.

To serve, loosen the cheesecake from the pan by running a small knife with a thin blade around the edge. Release and lift off the pan sides. Using a wide metal spatula, transfer the cake to a serving plate, if using, or leave it on the cake pan base. To serve, dip your knife in warm water, wipe dry, then cut firmly, especially through the crust, which takes a little extra pressure. Wipe the blade between slices. The cheesecake will keep in the refrigerator, well wrapped, for up to 1 week.

PASTEL DE TRES LECHES

––––––––––

YIELDS ONE 10 IN [25 CM] CAKE; 12 TO 16 SERVINGS

10 in [25 cm] Génoise (page 312), split into 3 layers	1	

COCONUT SYRUP

Unsweetened coconut milk	1 cup	240 ml
Sugar	6 Tbsp	75 g
Vanilla extract	1 tsp	
Salt	pinch	

FILLING

Unflavored gelatin (½ envelope)	1½ tsp	
Water	2 Tbsp	
Pastry Cream (page 300)	2½ cups	600 ml
Heavy cream, very cold	1 cup	240 ml
Caramel Sauce (page 309)	½ cup	120 ml

TOPPING

Heavy cream, very cold	1¼ cups	300 ml
Sugar	4 tsp	

The Mission District of San Francisco, where Tartine is located, is home to a large, long-established Latin community, evident in the neighborhood's many Salvadoran, Mexican, and Guatemalan restaurants. A slice of *pastel de tres leches* (three milks cake) makes complete sense after eating an especially spicy meal: it's the horchata of desserts—or the flan of cakes—the perfect way to put out the fire in your mouth. The cake is soft, moist, and delicately flavored, here with coconut milk, pastry cream lightened with whipped cream, and a lightly sweetened whipped cream frosting. It's a little like Boston cream pie, but without the strong flavor of chocolate. I would definitely serve this with tropical fruits, such as freshly scooped passion fruit pulp; a compote of orange, lime, and grapefruit; or pineapple. You often see this cake with caramel spread on the cake layers, which is delicious as well.

KITCHEN NOTES: There are different types of coconut milk and coconut cream on the market, many of them sweetened. You will need unsweetened coconut milk for this recipe. When whisking anything in a stainless-steel bowl, especially one that has been used to heat ingredients over a double boiler and is hot to handle and wet on the bottom, have a folded, lightly dampened kitchen towel ready to put the bowl on. The towel will keep the bowl steady as you whisk. The cold cream will make the gelatin begin to set up quickly, so be sure you have all of your cake components—moistening syrup, caramel, if using, and cake layers—and tools ready.

· · · · · ·

Line the sides of a 10 in [25 cm] springform pan with 3 in [7.5 cm] sides with plastic wrap, allowing enough overhang to cover the top of the cake completely when it is assembled. Leave the bottom of the pan unlined. Have the cake layers ready.

To make the coconut syrup, in a small bowl, stir together the coconut milk, sugar, vanilla, and salt until the sugar dissolves. Set aside.

To make the filling, sprinkle the gelatin over the water in a small bowl and let stand for a few minutes to

continued

soften. If using freshly made pastry cream and it is still hot, whisk the gelatin into the entire amount, then place the bowl in an ice bath (a large bowl filled with ice cubes and water) and let the pastry cream cool before continuing. If using pastry cream that is cold, pour water to a depth of about 2 in [5 cm] into a saucepan, place over medium heat, and bring to a simmer. Place ½ cup [120 ml] of the pastry cream in a stainless-steel bowl that will rest securely on the rim of the saucepan over, but not touching, the water. Heat the pastry cream, whisking often, until it is very hot to the touch, 4 to 5 minutes. Whisk in the softened gelatin until smooth. Remove from the double boiler. Whisk half of the remaining cold pastry cream into the hot mixture, then whisk in the rest.

Using a stand mixer fitted with the whisk attachment or a whisk, whip the cream until it holds medium-soft peaks. Working quickly, gently fold the whipped cream into the pastry cream mixture with a rubber spatula.

Place one cake layer in the bottom of the prepared springform pan. Using a pastry brush, moisten the layer evenly with one-third of the coconut syrup. Drizzle half of the caramel over the cake layer. Pour half of the filling over the layer and spread it evenly (the back of a large spoon works well).

Place the second cake layer over the filling, pressing down gently with even pressure. Moisten this layer with half of the remaining coconut syrup, and then drizzle over the remaining caramel. Pour the remaining filling over the second layer. Place the third cake layer on top and moisten it with the rest of the coconut syrup. The top layer should come right up to the rim of the cake pan or go a little over. Fold the overhanging plastic wrap over the top of the cake, covering it completely. Place something flat, such as a flat plate or a baking sheet, over the cake, and press down gently to level the cake layers. Refrigerate for at least 4 hours or preferably overnight.

When you are ready to finish the cake, release and lift off the pan sides and peel away the plastic wrap. Using a wide metal spatula, transfer the cake to a serving plate, if using, or leave it on the cake pan base.

To make the topping, using the mixer or a whisk, whip the cream until thickened. Add the sugar and whip until the cream holds soft peaks. Using an offset spatula, frost the top of the cake. The cake can be served immediately or kept cold in the refrigerator until ready to serve. It will keep for up to 5 days.

BANANA-DATE TEA CAKE

─────────

YIELDS ONE 9 BY 5 IN [23 BY 12 CM] LOAF; 6 TO 8 SERVINGS

All-purpose flour	1 cup + 2 Tbsp	155 g
Cornstarch	2 Tbsp	
Baking powder	2 tsp	
Baking soda	1 tsp	
Ground cinnamon	1 tsp	
Bananas, very ripe	3 medium	
Large eggs	2	
Vanilla extract	1½ tsp	
Salt	½ tsp	
Unsalted butter, at room temperature	6 Tbsp	85 g
Sugar	¾ cup + 2 Tbsp	175 g
Dates, pitted and coarsely chopped	1 cup	220 g
Walnuts, lightly toasted and coarsely chopped	1 cup	115 g

TOPPING

Banana	1 medium	
Sugar	2 Tbsp	

The texture and flavor of dates go wonderfully with banana in this moist tea cake, with its delicate buttery crumb. This versatile recipe takes well to a number of additions; dark chocolate chips go particularly well with the date/banana/walnut combination, or try using peanuts or pecans.

KITCHEN NOTES: Use very ripe bananas in this recipe. I keep a resealable plastic bag of bruised and too-soft-for-eating bananas in my freezer, so there is never a wasted piece of fruit.

Preheat the oven to 325°F [160°C]. Lightly butter the bottom and sides of a 9 by 5 in [23 by 12 cm] loaf pan.

In a bowl, combine the flour, cornstarch, baking powder, baking soda, and cinnamon. Set aside. Peel the bananas and place in a second bowl. Mash with a fork until you have a chunky purée. Add the eggs, vanilla, and salt and stir to mix well. Set aside.

In a third bowl, beat the butter until light and creamy, about 2 minutes. Slowly add the sugar and beat until light in color and fluffy, about 2 minutes. Scrape down the sides of the bowl with a rubber spatula. Slowly add the banana mixture and beat until incorporated. Again, scrape down the sides of the bowl, and then mix for another 30 seconds to make sure all the ingredients are incorporated.

Using the rubber spatula, fold the dry ingredients into the banana mixture. Then fold in the dates and nuts. Scrape down the sides of the bowl and mix again, making sure all the ingredients are fully incorporated.

Transfer the batter to the prepared loaf pan and smooth the surface with an offset spatula. To top the cake, peel the banana and cut into quarters lengthwise. Lay the slices on top of the batter. Sprinkle with the sugar.

Bake until a cake tester inserted into the center comes out clean, about 1 hour. Let cool in the pan or on a wire rack for about 20 minutes, and then invert onto the rack, turn right side up, and let cool completely. Serve the cake at room temperature. It will keep, well wrapped, at room temperature for 2 days or in the refrigerator for about 1 week.

······

ALMOND-LEMON TEA CAKE

YIELDS ONE 8½ IN [21.5 CM] TUBE PAN OR 9 BY 5 IN [23 BY 12 CM] LOAF; 8 TO 10 SERVINGS

Pastry flour	¾ cup + 2 Tbsp	95 g
Baking powder	½ tsp	
Salt	⅛ tsp	
Large eggs	5	
Vanilla extract	1 tsp	
Almond paste, at room temperature	¾ cup	200 g
Granulated sugar	1 cup	200 g
Unsalted butter, at room temperature	1 cup	225 g
Poppy seeds	2 Tbsp	
Lemon zest	1 tsp	
Orange zest	1 tsp	

CITRUS GLAZE

Lemon juice	3 Tbsp	45 ml
Orange juice	3 Tbsp	45 ml
Confectioners' sugar	¾ cup	150 g

This tea cake is from our late friend and accomplished baker Flo Braker, author of *The Simple Art of Perfect Baking*, among other books, and it is one of the most perfectly textured, moist, and flavorful cakes that I have come across. It is rich with almond paste, and glazed with a mixture of lemon and orange juices and sugar, which crystalizes to create a perfect citrusy-tart contrast to the rich almond cake, and helps seal in moisture.

KITCHEN NOTES: The key to making this cake batter smooth is incorporating the almond paste completely before the eggs are added. And the pretty, crystallized look and proper set of the glaze is dependent on two things: it must be made just before it is brushed on the cake, and the cake must be warm from the oven so that the sugar and juices can penetrate it properly and form crystals.

Position a rack in the lower third of the oven and preheat the oven to 350°F [180°C]. Lightly butter and flour an 8½ in [21.5 cm] tube pan or a 9 by 5 in [23 by 12 cm] loaf pan, knocking out the excess flour.

To make the cake, sift together the flour, baking powder, and salt twice. Set aside. In a small bowl, combine the eggs and vanilla and whisk together just to combine. In the bowl of a stand mixer fitted with the paddle attachment, beat the almond paste on low speed until it breaks up. Slowly add the granulated sugar in a steady stream, beating until incorporated. If you add the sugar too quickly, the paste won't break up as well.

Cut the butter into 1 Tbsp pieces. Continue mixing on low speed while adding the butter, 1 Tbsp at a time, for about 1 minute. Stop the mixer and scrape down the sides of the bowl with a rubber spatula. Then turn on the mixer to medium speed and beat until the mixture is light in color and fluffy, 3 to 4 minutes. With the mixer still on medium speed, add the egg mixture in a very slow, steady stream and mix until

continued

incorporated. Stop the mixer and again scrape down the sides of the bowl. Turn on the mixer again to medium speed and mix for another 30 seconds. Add the poppy seeds and citrus zests and mix with a wooden spoon. Finally, add the flour mixture in two batches, stirring after each addition until incorporated. Scrape down the sides of the bowl one last time, and then spoon the batter into the prepared pan and smooth the surface with an offset spatula.

Bake until the top springs back when lightly touched and a cake tester inserted into the center comes out clean, 45 to 50 minutes. Let cool in the pan on a wire rack for 5 to 7 minutes while you make the glaze.

To make the glaze, stir together the lemon and orange juices and the confectioners' sugar in a small bowl. Place the wire rack holding the cake over a sheet of waxed paper or aluminum foil to catch any drips of glaze, and invert the cake onto the rack. If the cake does not want to release from the pan, run the tip of a small knife around the edge to loosen it. Brush the entire warm cake with the glaze, then let the cake cool completely on the rack. The cake breaks apart easily when warm, so don't attempt to move it.

When the cake is cool, transfer it to a serving plate, using two crisscrossed icing spatulas or the base of a two-part tart pan to lift it. Serve at room temperature. The cake will keep, well wrapped, for 1 week in the refrigerator.

TEFF CARROT CAKE

YIELDS ONE 9 IN [23 CM] CAKE; 8 TO 10 SERVINGS

CAKE

Raisins	1¾ cups	250 g
Granulated sugar	1 cup	200 g
Coconut or brown sugar	1 cup	180 g
Large eggs	4	
Carrots, grated	1 lb	450 g
Milk	1 cup	240 ml
Olive oil	¾ cup	180 ml
Orange zest	2 tsp	
Teff flour	1 cup + 2 Tbsp	150 g
Rice flour	½ cup	70 g
Potato starch	⅔ cup	70 g
Ground cinnamon	2½ tsp	
Ground nutmeg	½ tsp	
Ground cloves	½ tsp	
Baking soda	2 tsp	
Baking powder	1 tsp	
Salt	1 tsp	
Walnuts, toasted	heaping 1½ cups	200 g
Unsweetened shredded coconut	½ cup	40 g

CREAM CHEESE FROSTING

Cream cheese, at room temperature	1 cup	225 g
Unsalted butter, at room temperature	6 Tbsp	85 g
Confectioners' sugar, sifted	3 cups	375 g
Lemon juice	1 Tbsp	
Salt	¼ tsp	

This is a cake with a lot of character, and hits every note I like in a carrot cake square-on: plenty of texture from coconut and walnuts, moisture from applesauce and freshly grated carrots, and well spiced with a little added savoriness from teff flour. The cake is sandwiched with the classic accompaniment of cream cheese frosting, which I like on the tangy side. In America we tend to go for yellow or chocolate cakes for celebrations, while in much of Europe, including Switzerland, the United Kingdom, Germany, and France, carrot cake is the most popular. Carrot cake has been made for centuries; a recipe for it dates back to *A Booke of Cookrye*, published in 1591, where it was more like a pudding.

KITCHEN NOTES: You can split the layers, as in the photo on page 186, or make a two-layer cake. To make a four-layer cake, you will need to double the frosting recipe.

• • • • • •

Preheat the oven to 350°F [180°C]. Butter the bottom and sides of two 9 in [23 cm] round cake pans with unsalted butter and line the bottoms with parchment paper circles. In a small bowl, cover the raisins with hot water. Plump for 10 minutes, then drain and set aside. **continued**

To make the cake, in a large bowl using a handheld mixer or a stand mixer fitted with the whisk attachment, and on medium speed, whip the granulated sugar, coconut sugar, and eggs until thick and light in color, 4 minutes. When you lift up the whisk, the beaten egg mixture should fall back into the bowl in ribbons. Add the carrots, milk, olive oil, and zest, and mix well to combine.

In a separate bowl, stir together the teff flour, rice flour, potato starch, cinnamon, nutmeg, cloves, baking soda, baking powder, and salt. Add to the egg mixture and, using a rubber spatula, fold just until combined. Fold in the raisins, walnuts, and coconut.

Divide the batter evenly between the prepared pans. Bake until a knife inserted into the centers comes out clean, 35 to 40 minutes. Let the cakes cool in the pans on a wire rack for about 10 minutes. To unmold, run a small knife around the edges of the pan, and then invert the cake onto the wire rack and turn right-side up. Let cool completely, then transfer the layers to the refrigerator and chill for at least 30 minutes before frosting.

To make the frosting, using a stand mixer fitted with the paddle attachment, beat the cream cheese and butter on medium-high speed until fluffy and light, 3 minutes. Add the confectioners' sugar, lemon juice, and salt and mix until smooth.

Spread half of the icing on top of one of the cake layers, cover with the second layer, and smooth the remainder of the icing over the top. Serve at room temperature and store, covered, in the refrigerator for up to 3 days.

HONEY SPICE CAKE

MAKES ONE 9 BY 5 IN [23 BY 12 CM] LOAF OR ONE 8 IN [20 CM] ROUND; 6 TO 8 SERVINGS

Gluten-free flour blend	1²/₃ cups	200 g
OR		
Oat flour	1¹/₃ cups	140 g
Cornstarch	¹/₃ cup + 1 Tbsp	45 g
Almond flour	1¹/₄ cups	120 g
Baking soda	1 tsp	
Salt	¹/₂ tsp	
Ground cinnamon	2 tsp	
Ground allspice	¹/₄ tsp	
Ground nutmeg	¹/₄ tsp	
Neutral oil, such as canola	¹/₂ cup	120 ml
Honey	¹/₂ cup	170 g
Brown sugar, packed	¹/₂ cup	90 g
Large eggs	2	
Vanilla extract	1 tsp	
Strong black tea, at room temperature	¹/₂ cup	120 ml
Greek or plain full-fat yogurt	¹/₃ cup	95 g
Fresh ginger, grated	1¹/₂ tsp	

KITCHEN NOTES: To make this nondairy for Rosh Hashanah, you can substitute almond or cashew yogurt.

• • • • • •

Preheat the oven to 325°F [160°C]. Butter the sides of a 9 by 5 in [23 by 12 cm] loaf pan or 8 in [20 cm] round cake pan and fit parchment paper into the bottom.

In a large bowl, combine the gluten-free flour, almond flour, baking soda, salt, cinnamon, allspice, and nutmeg. In a medium bowl, whisk together the oil, honey, brown sugar, eggs, vanilla, tea, yogurt, and ginger. Quickly whisk the wet ingredients into the dry ingredients and transfer the batter to the prepared loaf pan.

Bake for 1 hour, or until a knife inserted into the center comes out clean. Cool in the pan on a wire rack for 30 minutes. Loosen the sides with a small knife, and turn out onto a wire rack to finish cooling.

Store the cake in an airtight container or tightly wrapped for up to 4 days at room temperature or in the refrigerator for 1 week.

This is a quick, fragrant, and satisfying cake to make, filling your kitchen with a spiced honey scent. It will last for days at room temperature, improving over time. I was inspired by both the honey cakes traditionally served at Rosh Hashanah, the Jewish New Year, as well as *pain d'épice*, the spiced honey cake made in the south of France. I like this right from the oven or toaster served with cold salted butter or at room temperature with softened cream cheese.

MARBLED POUND CAKE

YIELDS ONE 9 BY 5 IN [23 BY 12 CM] LOAF; 6 TO 8 SERVINGS

All-purpose flour	1⅓ cups + 1 Tbsp	185 g
Baking powder	¾ tsp	
Unsalted butter, at room temperature	¾ cup + 2 Tbsp	200 g
Granulated sugar	1 cup	200 g
Salt	½ tsp	
Large eggs, at room temperature	3	
Large egg yolk	1	
Sour cream	½ cup	120 g
Vanilla extract	1 Tbsp	

MATCHA MARBLE VARIATION

Matcha powder	1 Tbsp	

CHOCOLATE MARBLE VARIATION

Cocoa powder	3 Tbsp	15 g
Coffee, cooled, or water	1 Tbsp	

GLAZED LEMON VARIATION

Lemon zest	2 tsp	
Lemon juice	1½ Tbsp	
Confectioners' sugar	1 cup	125 g

Pound cake is simple—traditionally equal parts sugar, eggs, butter, and flour—but also easily transformed by simple changes in technique or variations in the proportions of ingredients. Even though it's such a bakery shop mainstay, we've never served one before. When talking about how we wanted this book to evolve

and the new things we wanted to include, we thought it a good opportunity to come up with our definitive pound cake. What they all have in common is a tight, even crumb structure, golden brown crust, and satisfying toothsomeness. Our baker Lynn developed this recipe to include a beautiful swirl of matcha or cocoa. You can also make it plain and simple, or with lemon. This recipe contains sour cream, which gives it a very slight tang and delightful scent.

KITCHEN NOTES: Crème fraîche, with its significantly higher fat percentage, does not produce a light crumb as sour cream does, so it's not a substitute here.

Preheat the oven to 350°F [180°C]. Lightly butter a 9 by 5 in [23 by 12 cm] loaf pan.

In a small bowl, sift the flour and baking powder together, and set aside.

In the bowl of a stand mixer fitted with a paddle attachment, beat the butter, granulated sugar, and salt on medium speed until combined and lighter in color, about 1 minute. Add the eggs and egg yolk one at a time, mixing well after each addition until incorporated before adding the next. Stop the mixer and scrape down the sides and bottom of the mixing bowl with a rubber spatula. With the mixer on medium speed, add the sour cream and vanilla extract. With the mixer on low speed, add half of the flour mixture. Once it's mostly combined, add the remaining flour mixture, and mix until fully incorporated.

continued

Matcha Marble Variation: Spoon two-thirds of the batter into the prepared pan, reserving one-third in the bowl. Using a rubber spatula, mix the sifted matcha powder into the reserved batter until smooth. Spoon the matcha batter on top of the batter in the pan. Marble the two cake batters together slightly using an offset spatula. Bake as directed.

Glazed Lemon Variation: Mix the lemon zest into the cake batter. Pour the batter into the prepared pan. Smooth the top of the cake batter with an offset spatula. Bake as directed. Once the cake has cooled, whisk the lemon juice and confectioners' sugar together until smooth. Pour the glaze over the top of the cake. Using a spatula, push the glaze out to the edges to cover the top of the cake. Allow the glaze to spill down the sides. Let the glaze set, about 30 minutes.

Chocolate Marble Variation: Spoon two-thirds of the batter into the prepared pan, reserving one-third in the bowl. Using a rubber spatula, mix the sifted cocoa powder and coffee into the reserved batter. Spoon the chocolate batter on top of the batter in the pan. Marble the two cake batters together slightly using an offset spatula. Bake as directed.

For each variation, bake until the center of the cake is set, and a knife inserted into the center comes out clean. Transfer the cake to a wire rack and let cool completely. Once cool, turn out the cake from the pan and return the cake right side up. Store the cake in an airtight container for 3 to 4 days at room temperature or in the refrigerator for 1 week.

CRANBERRY UPSIDE-DOWN CAKE

YIELDS ONE 10 BY 5 IN [25 BY 12 CM] LOAF; 8 TO 10 SERVINGS

FRUIT LAYER

Fresh or frozen cranberries	2¾ cups	275 g
Brown sugar	1 Tbsp	
Orange zest	2 tsp	

CARAMEL

Brown sugar, packed	¾ cup	135 g
Unsalted butter	3 Tbsp	45 g

CAKE

All-purpose flour	2 cups	260 g
Baking powder	1½ tsp	
Baking soda	½ tsp	
Granulated sugar	1⅓ cups	265 g
Salt	½ tsp	
Large eggs, at room temperature	2	
Crème fraîche	1 cup + 3 Tbsp	280 g
Vanilla extract	1 Tbsp	
Unsalted butter, at room temperature	6 Tbsp	85 g

Our baker Carolyn has transformed what is usually a sweet summertime cake made with peaches or pineapple into a beautiful winter version using caramel-coated cranberries, which turn out of their baking mold perfectly juicy and glazed, ready to serve. The cake is tender and moist, and ideal with tart fruit.

. . . . . .

Preheat the oven to 325°F [160°C]. Butter a 10 by 5 in [25 by 12 cm] loaf pan and line with parchment paper, leaving a few inches of overhang on each side.

To prepare the fruit layer, combine the cranberries, brown sugar, and orange zest in a bowl and gently mix with your hands or a rubber spatula to coat the cranberries and evenly distribute the sugar and zest. With a spoon, transfer the fruit from the bowl to the prepared pan, keeping in mind that there will be more fruit than the bottom of the pan can accommodate. The cranberries will shrink during baking so the fruit settles into an even layer.

To prepare the caramel, stir together the brown sugar and butter in a small, heavy saucepan; bring the mixture just to a boil over medium-low heat, stirring to combine with a rubber spatula, so the sugar doesn't burn before the butter is fully melted. When the caramel has softened and begun to boil, remove the pan from the heat. Immediately pour the caramel evenly over the fruit mixture in the loaf pan and set aside to cool and set without agitating the mixture.

To make the cake, sift the flour, baking powder, and baking soda into the bowl of a stand mixer fitted with the paddle attachment. Add the granulated sugar and salt and stir to combine. In a small bowl, whisk together the eggs, crème fraîche, and vanilla extract. Add the softened butter to the dry ingredients in the mixer bowl. Mix on low speed until the mixture is sandy and the butter can no longer be seen. Add the egg mixture, and then beat thoroughly on medium speed until the batter is smooth, about 1 minute, stopping the mixer halfway through to scrape down the sides of the bowl with a rubber spatula.

continued

Pour the cake batter on top of the fruit and caramel in the prepared pan and smooth to the edges with an offset spatula. Give the pan a few hard raps on the counter to knock out any air bubbles from the batter.

Bake the cake until it has risen and become a deep golden brown color, and a cake tester inserted into the center comes out clean, about 1 hour. It might require more time. Let cool in the pan on a wire rack for 30 minutes. To unmold, run a small, thin knife around the sides to detach any hardened bits of caramel from the cake pan. Place an inverted serving dish onto the surface of the cake, and, using a towel or oven mitts, flip the cake pan and dish and carefully slide the pan from the cake. Gently peel off the parchment and allow the cake to continue cooling at room temperature for 1 hour before serving.

The cake will keep, covered at room temperature, for up to 3 days.

RUSSIAN NAPOLEON CAKE

YIELD ONE 8 IN [20 CM] CAKE, 8 TO 10 SERVINGS

Flaky Tart Dough (page 286)	2 recipes	
Pastry Cream (about 2 batches, page 300)	4 cups	1 L
Heavy cream, very cold	2 cups	480 ml
Sugar	4 tsp	

FRUIT FOR SERVING (OPTIONAL)

Berries	4 cups	600 g
Sugar	1 to 2 Tbsp	
Fresh lemon juice		

The Napoleon Cake is a Russian creation drawing on the classic French pastry. The Russian version is made in a larger cake format, assembled then refrigerated long enough that its layers soften and meld. It's similar in concept to American icebox cakes made with cookies and whipped cream. If you prefer your filling and layers to remain distinct, as I do (and as the photograph illustrates), serve within three hours of assembly. This showstopper of a dessert is even more delicious and beautiful when served with a simple fruit purée and fresh fruit.

⋯⋯

Preheat the oven to 375°F [190°C]. Line four baking sheets with parchment paper, and have four more sheet pans ready to use as weights.

Working in batches, roll the flaky dough into ten 8 in [20 cm] rounds, each ¹⁄₁₆ in [2 mm] thick.

Place two discs of dough on each prepared baking sheet. Place a second sheet of parchment on top, then a sheet pan for weight.

Bake for 4 minutes. Remove from the oven, press down gently on the weight and dough, and rotate the sheet. Bake until light golden in color, an additional 3 to 4 minutes. If they're not brown enough, uncover and continue to bake. Cool completely on a baking rack.

Once the rounds have cooled, crumble and set aside two rounds to use for finishing. To assemble, place a round on top of a cardboard cake round or plate. Spread a thin layer of pastry cream smooth to the edge with an offset spatula. It should be a little less than ¼ in [6 mm] thick. Repeat for eight layers of flaky rounds. Do not cover the last round with pastry cream; this is the top of your Napoleon.

Whisk the heavy cream and sugar at medium speed in the bowl of a stand mixer fitted with the whisk attachment until medium peaks form. Cover the top of the cake and spread with a spatula. Gently push out the whipped cream over the edges and cover the sides evenly. Press handfuls of the crumbled crust against the surface to fully coat the cake.

Refrigerate until well chilled and set throughout, at least 2 hours and up to overnight. Cooling overnight will yield a traditional, soft-textured cake. If you want the layers to retain some crunch, serve the cake the same day that you bake it.

If serving with berries, mix the berries with sugar to your desired sweetness, and add a squeeze of lemon to taste. Cut the cake into slices to serve, topping with the fruit, if using. This cake is best served within 24 hours of baking.

CAKE AUX OLIVES

YIELDS ONE 9 BY 5 IN [23 BY 12 CM] LOAF; 6 TO 8 SERVINGS

Bread flour	2 cups + 2 Tbsp	275 g
Baking powder	2½ tsp	
White wine	½ cup	120 ml
Dry white vermouth	½ cup	120 ml
Large eggs	4	
Olive oil	¾ cup + 2 Tbsp	210 ml
Ham, chopped	7 oz	200 g
Gruyère cheese, grated	5 oz	140 g
Olives, pitted and coarsely chopped	4 oz	115 g
Fresh thyme leaves	1½ Tbsp	
Salt	1 tsp	
Black pepper, freshly ground	½ tsp	

Cake aux olives is a traditional savory cake recipe, similar to our quick breads. It is rich with olive oil, cheese, and ham, and has a moist crumb and crispy crust. It makes a good appetizer or an entrée with a salad, and, because it is so sturdy, it is perfect picnic food.

KITCHEN NOTES: This is an unusual recipe in that you actually want to develop the gluten structure in the dough. Because of the high amount of olive oil, you don't have to worry about a tough crumb; when mixing, look for elasticity when you raise the paddle out of the dough.

Preheat the oven to 325°F [160°C]. Lightly butter the bottom and sides of a 9 by 5 in [23 by 12 cm] loaf pan and line with parchment paper, leaving a few inches of overhang.

Using a stand mixer fitted with the paddle attachment or by hand with a wooden spoon, combine the flour, baking powder, wine, vermouth, and eggs, and mix on medium speed to combine. With the mixer running on medium speed, slowly add the olive oil in a thin, steady stream until it is thoroughly incorporated and the dough looks elastic.

In a separate bowl, combine the ham, Gruyère, olives, thyme, salt, and black pepper. Fold into the batter with a rubber spatula or wooden spoon until just combined.

Transfer the batter to the prepared loaf pan and smooth the surface with an offset spatula. Bake until a cake tester inserted into the center comes out clean, about 1 hour. Let cool in the pan on a wire rack for about 20 minutes, and then invert onto the rack, turn right-side up, and let cool completely. Serve the cake at room temperature. It will keep, well wrapped, at room temperature for 2 days or in the refrigerator for about 1 week.

CHAPTER FOUR

COOKIES

SHORTBREAD

YIELDS ONE 6 BY 10 IN [15 BY 25 CM] DISH, ABOUT FORTY-EIGHT 2 BY ½ IN [5 CM BY 12 MM] BARS

Unsalted butter, very soft	1 cup + 2 Tbsp	255 g
Salt	½ tsp	
All-purpose flour	2 cups	260 g
Cornstarch	⅔ cup	75 g
Granulated sugar	⅓ cup	70 g
Superfine or granulated sugar for topping	¼ cup	50 g

Finely textured and very tender, the traditional Scottish shortbread is my favorite cookie for its simplicity and as a vehicle for premium butter. Many recipes include some kind of starch—potato, tapioca, cornstarch—although rice flour is what is most commonly used and contributes to the "short" or sandy texture that is the hallmark of the cookie, and gives it that melt-in-your-mouth quality.

KITCHEN NOTES: The butter must be very soft for this recipe. It can be softened in a microwave or by mixing on low speed in a metal bowl and using a kitchen torch to gently warm the sides of the bowl.

. . . . . .

Preheat the oven to 325°F [160°C]. Butter a 6 by 10 in [15 by 25 cm] glass baking dish.

Place the butter in a mixing bowl. The butter must be very soft—the consistency of mayonnaise or whipped cream. Add the salt to the butter and mix well. Sift the flour and cornstarch together into another bowl. Add the granulated sugar to the butter and mix just until combined. Add the flour mixture and mix just until a smooth dough forms.

Pat the dough evenly into the prepared baking dish. The dough should be no more than ⅔ in [1.5 cm] deep. Bake until the top and bottom are lightly browned, about 30 minutes. The middle of the shortbread should remain light. Let cool on a wire rack until warm to the touch.

Sprinkle the shortbread with the superfine sugar. Tilt the dish so that the sugar fully and evenly coats the surface and then tip out the excess sugar. With a very thin, sharp knife, cut the shortbread into rectangular fingers about ½ in [12 mm] wide and 2 in [5 cm] long. If the cookies have become cold they will not slice well, so they must still be warm to the touch at this point. Chill thoroughly before removing from the baking dish.

The first cookie is difficult to remove, but the rest should come out easily with the aid of a small, thin offset spatula. The cookies will keep in an airtight container in a cool place for up to 2 weeks.

WHOLE GRAIN SHORTBREAD WITH EINKORN AND RYE FLOUR

YIELDS ONE 6 BY 10 IN [15 BY 25 CM] BAKING DISH, ABOUT FORTY-EIGHT 2 BY ½ IN [5 CM BY 12 MM] BARS

Unsalted butter, very soft	1 cup + 2 Tbsp	255 g
Salt	½ tsp	
Einkorn flour	1 cup + 1 Tbsp	140 g
Rye flour	¾ cup + 1 Tbsp	115 g
Rice flour	⅓ cup	45 g
Cornstarch	5 Tbsp	35 g
Granulated sugar	⅓ cup	70 g
Superfine or granulated sugar for topping	¼ cup	50g

These are similar to our classic Shortbread (facing page), but with the warm, slightly nutty flavor of einkorn and rye. These little-used flours also make a great choice for baking due to their naturally lower gluten profile, which is exactly what you want in a sandy-style cookie for a tender crumb. Delicious on their own, they would be great dipped in melted dark chocolate.

· · · · · ·

Preheat the oven to 325°F [160°C]. Butter a 6 by 10 in [15 by 25 cm] baking dish.

Place the butter in a mixing bowl. The butter must be very soft—the consistency of mayonnaise or whipped cream. Add the salt to the butter and mix well. Sift the flours and cornstarch together into another bowl. Add the granulated sugar to the butter and mix just until combined. Add the flour mixture and mix just until a smooth dough forms.

Pat the dough evenly into the prepared baking dish. The dough should be no more than ⅔ in [1.5 cm] deep. Bake until the top and bottom are lightly browned, about 30 minutes. The middle of the shortbread should remain light. Let cool on a wire rack until warm to the touch.

Sprinkle the shortbread with the superfine sugar. Tilt the dish so that the sugar fully and evenly coats the surface and then tip out the excess sugar. With a very thin, sharp knife, cut the shortbread into rectangular fingers about ½ in [12 mm] wide and 2 in [5 mm] long. If the cookies have become cold they will not slice well, so they must still be warm to the touch at this point. Chill thoroughly before removing from the baking dish.

The first cookie is difficult to remove, but the rest should come out easily with the aid of a small, thin offset spatula. The cookies will keep in an airtight container in a cool place for up to 2 weeks.

Chocolate Dipped Variation: Skip sprinkling the shortbread with sugar. Temper 8 oz [225 g] milk, dark, or white chocolate, using the method on page 272. Dip half of the cookie in the melted chocolate, letting excess chocolate drip back into the bowl, and let set. Alternatively, you can use melted, untempered chocolate, but refrigerate the cookies after dipping to set the chocolate.

CHOCOLATE-OATMEAL-WALNUT COOKIES

YIELDS TWENTY-FOUR 3 IN [7.5 CM] COOKIES

Bittersweet chocolate	12 oz	340 g
All-purpose flour	2 cups + 3 Tbsp	285 g
Rolled oats	2¼ cups	200 g
Baking powder	1 tsp	
Baking soda	1 tsp	
Unsalted butter, at room temperature	1 cup	225 g
Sugar	1¾ cups	350 g
Blackstrap or other dark molasses	4 tsp	
Large eggs	2	
Whole milk	2 Tbsp	
Vanilla extract	1 Tbsp	
Salt	1 tsp	
Walnuts, coarsely chopped	1 cup	120 g

This version of chocolate chip cookies is like most of the cookies we make at the bakery: familiar flavors, but in a slightly different size or shape than you usually find, or with an additional ingredient that sets them apart from the average. I like delicate, petit four–size cookies best (see Variation; we also make this cookie in a 5 in [12 cm] version, but it is still very thin and delicate). These are to my mind a perfect little cookie, with chunks of chocolate and nuts and some oats for texture.

KITCHEN NOTES: Keep a small bowl of water nearby for dipping your fingers when you are shaping the cookies. The moisture keeps the dough from sticking to your fingers as you flatten the cookies.

Preheat the oven to 350°F [180°C]. Line a baking sheet with parchment paper or a nonstick liner.

Coarsely chop the chocolate into ¼ to ½ in [6 to 12 mm] pieces. A serrated knife works well for this task. Chill in the freezer until needed.

In a mixing bowl, stir together the flour, oats, baking powder, and baking soda. Set aside. Using a stand mixer fitted with the paddle attachment, beat the butter on medium-high speed until light and creamy. Slowly add the sugar and mix on medium speed until light in color and fluffy. Stop the mixer and scrape down the sides of the bowl with a rubber spatula as needed. Add the molasses and beat until well combined. Add the eggs one at a time, beating well after each addition before adding the next egg. Beat in the milk, vanilla, and salt, and then stop the mixer again and scrape down the sides of the bowl. Add the flour mixture and beat on low speed until well incorporated. Stop the mixer, scrape down the sides of the bowl, and fold in the chocolate chunks and the walnuts with the spatula.

Have a small bowl of water ready. Scoop the dough onto the prepared baking sheet. An ice-cream scoop works well (about 3½ oz [100 g] for each scoop). Dip your fingers into the water and press out each scoop into a thin, flat 3 in [7.5 cm] circle.

Bake until the edges of the cookies are lightly browned but the centers remain pale, 10 to 12 minutes. Transfer the cookies to a wire rack and let cool. They will keep in an airtight container at room temperature for up to 2 weeks.

Variation: To make smaller cookies, shape the dough into a log about 1½ in [4 cm] in diameter. Wrap the log in parchment paper, waxed paper, or plastic wrap and place in the freezer for at least 4 hours or up to overnight. Remove from the freezer, unwrap, slice into ¼ in [6 mm] thick rounds, and arrange on the lined baking sheet. Bake as directed, reducing the baking time to 6 to 10 minutes. You can also make the 3 in [7.5 cm] cookies this same way, shaping the log 3 in [7.5 cm] in diameter, slicing it into rounds ¼ in [6 mm] thick, and then baking as directed for 10 to 12 minutes.

OAT DIGESTIVE BISCUITS

YIELDS 24 COOKIES

Milk	3 Tbsp	45 ml
Molasses	1 tsp	
Rolled oats	3⅓ cups	300 g
Oat flour	scant ¾ cup	80 g
Dark brown sugar	⅓ cup + 1 Tbsp	70 g
Salt	1 tsp	
Baking soda	½ tsp	
Unsalted butter, cold	¾ cup	170 g

This little workhorse of a cookie, developed by Jen, is as wonderful on its own as it is sandwiched with jam, covered in chocolate, or crumbled into a pie crust. It is tender and flaky, but still satisfying. It's a little sweet and a little savory, and full of delicious whole oats. The origins of digestive biscuits are British; they are still the most popular cookie in England to have with tea. Victorians believed that the sodium bicarbonate aided digestion, hence the name. They were originally made with the brown castoffs (bran and germ) from sifting white flour, which gave them a distinctive nutty sweetness and crumbly texture.

Preheat the oven to 350°F [180°C] and line a baking sheet with parchment paper or a nonstick liner.

In a small bowl, stir together the milk and molasses.

The dough can be made in a food processor or by hand. If using a food processor, place the rolled oats in the bowl and process until finely ground. Add the oat flour, brown sugar, salt, and baking soda and process until well combined. Cut the butter into ¼ in [6 mm] cubes. Add the butter and process until sandy. Add the milk-molasses mixture and process until the dough starts to come together.

If you are not using a food processor, mix the oats in a spice grinder or blender until finely ground. Place the ground oats into a large bowl and add the oat flour, brown sugar, salt, and baking soda. Whisk together until well combined. Cut the butter into ¼ in [6 mm] cubes. Add the butter and rub it in with your fingers until it reaches a sandy texture. Add the milk-molasses mixture and combine with a spatula until the dough starts to come together.

Turn the dough out onto a work surface and knead a few times to bring it together into a cohesive mass. Take 1 Tbsp of dough at a time and roll it between your hands to form a ball. Flatten the ball into a disc and place it on the prepared baking sheet, flattening it more if needed to form a flat disc about ¼ in [6 mm] thick.

Bake for 7 minutes. Rotate the sheet and bake for 7 minutes more, or until the biscuits are golden brown on the bottom and the edges. Cool on the baking sheet for 5 minutes before transferring the biscuits to a wire rack. These biscuits can be stored in an airtight container at room temperature for up to 1 week.

COCONUT MACAROONS

YIELDS ABOUT 28 SMALL COOKIES

Large egg whites	5	
Sugar	¾ cup + 2 Tbsp	175 g
Salt	½ tsp	
Orange zest	1 Tbsp	
Unsweetened shredded coconut	2½ cups	235 g

The modest little coconut-and-egg white macaroon we think of today is a descendant of the now very fancy sandwiched almond macaron, which can be traced to monks in ninth century Italy. The cookie spread with pastry chefs and nuns throughout France, changing along the way from the all-nut version to one made with nuts and coconut. In the United States it appears as an all-coconut cookie. Almost every culture has a coconut/nut meat/sugar/egg white cookie, reflecting the flavors of the region, such as ginger with cinnamon in the Dominican Republic or cashews in India.

KITCHEN NOTES: Once scooped and placed on the baking sheet, these cookies need to be baked immediately, otherwise the sugar and egg whites rest at the bottom of the cookie and cause over-browning or burnt cookies.

. . . . . .

Place the egg whites in a medium bowl. Whisk in the sugar, salt, and orange zest until well combined. Add the coconut and mix with a rubber spatula until it is fully incorporated. Transfer the coconut batter to an airtight container or cover the bowl with plastic wrap, and refrigerate for 6 hours or overnight.

Preheat the oven to 350°F [180°C]. Line a baking sheet with parchment paper or a nonstick liner.

When ready to bake, transfer the coconut batter to a medium bowl. Mix the batter thoroughly, redistributing the egg whites and sugar. Using a small cookie scoop, firmly press the batter into the scoop. Round the bottom of the scoop with the palm of your hand. This will make the cookies slightly larger and help hold their shape. Drop each cookie onto the prepared baking sheet 1 in [2.5 cm] apart. Bake until the macaroons are a nice golden brown, rotating the baking sheet halfway through baking, 23 to 25 minutes. Remove from the oven and transfer the cookies to a wire rack to cool. They will keep in an airtight container for 1 week.

SALTED CHOCOLATE BUCKWHEAT COOKIES

YIELDS 24 COOKIES

Buckwheat flour	⅓ cup	45 g
Baking powder	½ tsp	
Dark chocolate, cut into chunks	8 oz	225 g
Unsalted butter	2 Tbsp	
Large eggs	2	
Sugar	¾ cup	150 g
Salt	½ tsp	
Vanilla extract	1 tsp	
Cacao nibs	2 Tbsp	
Flaky sea salt, such as Maldon	1 tsp	

This is a rich, dark chocolate cookie that takes advantage of buckwheat's affinity for chocolate.

KITCHEN NOTES: The temperature of the chocolate greatly affects how the batter flows from the pastry bag when you pipe the cookies. If the chocolate is too hot, the batter will be too runny to pipe; if it is too cold, it will be too stiff.

......

Line two baking sheets with parchment paper. Sift the flour and baking powder into a bowl. Set aside.

Pour water to a depth of about 2 in [5 cm] into a saucepan, place over medium heat, and bring to a simmer. Put the chocolate and butter into a stainless-steel bowl that will rest securely on the rim of the pan and place it over, but not touching, the water. Heat, stirring occasionally, just until the chocolate and butter melt and the mixture is smooth. Remove from the heat and let cool.

In the bowl of a stand mixer fitted with the whisk attachment, combine the eggs, sugar, and salt. Beat on high speed until the mixture thickens, becomes pale in color, and falls from the beater in a wide ribbon that folds back on itself and slowly dissolves on the surface, 5 to 6 minutes. Using a rubber spatula, fold the cooled chocolate mixture and vanilla extract into the whipped egg mixture. Add the flour mixture and fold it in quickly but gently with a rubber spatula so as not to deflate the egg mixture. Fold in the cacao nibs.

Preheat the oven to 350°F [180°C].

Immediately fill a pastry bag fitted with a ½ in [12 mm] plain round tip with cookie batter. Pipe cookies 1½ to 2 in [4 to 5 cm] in diameter and 1 in [2.5 cm] apart onto the prepared baking sheet. Let the cookies set at room temperature for 15 minutes. Sprinkle each cookie with a pinch of flaky sea salt. Bake the cookies until the edges are set, but the center remains slightly soft, 10 to 12 minutes. Remove from the oven and allow to cool for 3 to 4 minutes before transferring to a wire rack to cool completely. Store in an airtight container for 2 to 3 days.

MEXICAN WEDDING COOKIES

YIELDS 24 SMALL COOKIES

Walnuts	1¼ cups	150 g
All-purpose flour	2 cups + 3 Tbsp	285 g
Unsalted butter, at cool room temperature	1 cup	225 g
Confectioners' sugar, plus more for coating	⅓ cup	40 g
Salt	½ tsp	
Vanilla extract	1 tsp	
Water	1 tsp	

These cookies have roots in so many cultures, as evidenced by countless customers who tell us their Russian, Hungarian, Italian, or Austrian grandmother used to make them. They are meltingly tender nut cookies, rolled in confectioners' sugar after baking, which gives them a festive, holiday look.

. . . . . .

Preheat the oven to 325°F [160°C]. Line a baking sheet with parchment paper or a nonstick liner.

Using a food processor, process the walnuts until finely ground, about 30 seconds. Sift the flour into a small bowl; set aside. Using a stand mixer fitted with the paddle attachment, beat the butter, confectioners' sugar, and salt on medium speed until creamy, 1 minute. With the mixer on medium speed, add the vanilla extract and water. Scrape down the sides and bottom of the bowl with a rubber spatula. On low speed, add the walnuts, and mix for about 30 seconds before adding the flour. Turn off the mixer once all of the ingredients are completely combined.

Using a small cookie scoop, drop the cookies onto the prepared baking sheet 1 in [2.5 cm] apart. Bake until golden brown, 25 minutes. Transfer the baked cookies to a wire rack to cool.

Sift confectioners' sugar into a medium bowl. Toss the cookies in the sugar to coat. For a cleaner, whiter finish, wait 30 minutes and toss them in sugar again. The cookies will keep in an airtight container for 1 week at cool room temperature or 2 weeks in the refrigerator.

THUMBPRINT COOKIES

YIELDS 24 SMALL COOKIES

Walnuts	½ cup	60 g
Mexican Wedding Cookies dough (page 212)	1 recipe	
Seasonal fruit jam	¼ cup	80 g

KITCHEN NOTES: Make sure the cookie dough is at a cool room temperature. If the dough is too cold, the nuts will not stick to the dough, and the dough will crack when you form the thumbprint.

. . . . . .

Preheat the oven to 325°F [160°C]. Line a baking sheet with parchment paper or a nonstick liner.

Using a food processor fitted with the steel blade, process the walnuts for about 30 seconds until finely ground. Transfer the nuts to a small bowl.

Scoop up the dough with a small cookie scoop and roll into balls. Roll each ball in the ground nuts to coat. Place the cookies on the prepared baking sheet 1 in [2.5 cm] apart. With your thumb, make a cavity in the center of each cookie. If the side of the cookie cracks, press the dough back together. Fill each cookie with ½ tsp of jam. Bake until golden brown and the jam has just started bubbling around the edges, 25 minutes.

Transfer the cookies to a wire rack to cool. The cookies will keep for 4 days in an airtight container at room temperature.

PEANUT BUTTER HONEY COOKIES

YIELDS 36 COOKIES

Raw peanuts	1 cup + 3 Tbsp	170 g
All-purpose flour	2 cups	260 g
Baking powder	1 tsp	
Baking soda	½ tsp	
Light brown sugar	1 cup + 2 Tbsp	200 g
Unsalted butter, at cool room temperature	½ cup	115 g
Peanut butter	scant ½ cup	115 g
Honey	2 Tbsp	
Salt	¾ tsp	
Large egg	1	
Large egg yolk	1	
Milk	2 Tbsp	
Vanilla extract	1 Tbsp	

SUGAR COATING

Granulated sugar	¼ cup	50 g
Salt	¼ tsp	

Lynn, our head of pastry, developed this crispy and chunky peanut butter cookie. It has a bit of honey and salt to balance the richness of the nuts. A wonderful reference for anyone looking into peanut history is George Washington Carver's writing on the peanut in a 1925 bulletin for the Tuskegee Institute (now Tuskegee University) titled "How to Grow the Peanut and 105 Ways of Preparing It for Human Consumption." Carver's passionate support of the peanut came from his research into crop rotation and soil depletion caused by the repeated planting of cotton crops. He helped farmers find better cash crops, the peanut being one of the best. He made research into the peanut part of his life's work, with many early recipes coming from these early publications in Alabama. The peanut butter cookie was one of several in his treatise, picking up momentum as an American favorite after being published in newspapers in the early 1920s. Lynn added the honey to our version, but kept the classic fork-tine crosshatch design, which is how the first published versions were made.

. . . . . .

Preheat the oven to 350°F [180°C]. Line a baking sheet with parchment paper.

Spread the peanuts on the prepared baking sheet and toast for 8 to 10 minutes. Let cool. Once cooled, remove the peanut skins by placing the peanuts in a clean tea towel and rubbing briskly. Chop coarsely.

In a small bowl, sift together the flour, baking powder, and baking soda; set aside. Using a stand mixer fitted with the paddle attachment, cream together the brown sugar, butter, peanut butter, honey, and salt for 1 minute on medium speed. Add the egg, mixing until incorporated, then add the egg yolk and mix to incorporate. Stop the mixer and scrape down the sides and bottom of the bowl with a rubber spatula. With the mixer on medium speed, add the milk and vanilla extract. Decrease the mixer speed to low, add the sifted flour mixture and the chopped peanuts, and mix until completely incorporated. Remove the bowl from the mixer and scrape down the sides and bottom of the bowl. Transfer the cookie dough to an airtight container or cover the mixing bowl with plastic wrap. Refrigerate until firm, at least 2 hours or up to 2 days.

Preheat the oven to 350°F [180°C]. Line two baking sheets with parchment paper or a nonstick liner. Mix the granulated sugar and salt in a shallow bowl.

Scoop up the dough with a small to medium cookie scoop and roll each cookie into 1 in [2.5 cm] balls. Toss in the sugar mixture to coat and place the cookies 1 in [2.5 cm] apart on the prepared baking sheets. Flatten each ball with the tines of a fork, making a crosshatch pattern.

Bake until the edges just start to get some color but the center is still soft, about 11 minutes, rotating the baking sheets halfway through baking. Let cool on the baking sheets for 10 minutes and then transfer to a wire rack. The cookies will keep in an airtight container at room temperature for 5 days.

HAZELNUT BISCOTTI

YIELDS 54 COOKIES, 2½ IN [6 CM] LONG

Hazelnuts	½ cup	70 g
Unsalted butter, very soft	½ cup	115 g
Sugar	¾ cup	150 g
Large eggs	2	
Grand Marnier or other orange-flavored liqueur	4 tsp	
Orange zest	2 tsp	
Aniseeds	1 tsp	
All-purpose flour	2⅓ cups	310 g
Baking powder	1½ tsp	
Salt	¼ tsp	
Large egg for egg wash (optional)	1	

This recipe generously comes from Chez Panisse, where Lindsey Shere originally made them with almonds and grappa (the original version follows). It is one of the few recipes that I have not been compelled to change or recreate except for a slight flavor variation. The basic dough works well with many types of nuts, though my favorite choice is the incredible hazelnuts we get from Oregon. If you dip one of these biscotti into a glass of red wine, the cookie tastes exactly like zabaglione. Of course, the more traditional drink would be grappa or vin santo.

Preheat the oven to 350°F [180°C]. Spread the hazelnuts on a baking sheet. Place in the oven and toast lightly just until fragrant, about 3 minutes. Remove from the oven, place in the center of a kitchen towel, and rub off the skins while the nuts are still warm. Coarsely chop the nuts and set aside. Reduce the oven temperature to 325°F [160°C]. Line a baking sheet with parchment paper or a nonstick liner.

This recipe is easily mixed by a stand mixer fitted with the paddle attachment on medium speed or by hand with a spoon. In a mixing bowl, cream the butter until light and creamy, about 2 minutes. Slowly add the sugar and beat until light in color and fluffy, about 2 minutes. Scrape down the sides of the bowl with a rubber spatula. Add the eggs and beat until the mixture is smooth. Beat in the liqueur, orange zest, and aniseeds. Add the flour, baking powder, and salt and mix until just combined. Stir in the chopped nuts.

On a lightly floured work surface, divide the dough into two equal portions. Shape each portion into a log about the length of your prepared baking sheet and about 2 in [5 cm] in diameter. Set the logs on the baking sheet, spacing them about 2 in [5 cm] apart. If you want to glaze the biscotti, whisk the egg and brush it evenly over the logs.

Bake the logs until they are set to the touch and lightly browned on top, about 25 minutes. Let the logs cool on a wire rack for 5 minutes, then transfer to a cutting board and cut on the diagonal into slices about 2½ in [6 cm] wide and ½ in [12 mm] thick. Return the slices cut-side down to the baking sheet.

Bake the cookies until the edges are lightly toasted, 5 to 7 minutes longer. Let the cookies cool completely on a wire rack. They will keep in a tightly covered container at room temperature for several weeks.

Original Almond Biscotti from Chez Panisse: Omit the orange zest. Substitute almonds for the hazelnuts (there is no need to rub off their skins) and grappa for the liqueur, adding 1 tsp of anise extract with the grappa. Proceed as directed.

TARTINE FRANCISCOS

YIELDS TWENTY-TWO 3½ IN [9 CM] SANDWICH COOKIES OR 44 INDIVIDUAL COOKIES

Unsalted butter, very soft	10 Tbsp	140 g
Sugar	½ cup	100 g
Vanilla bean, split and scraped	1	
Large eggs, at room temperature	2	
Cornstarch	1½ cups	170 g
Rice flour	⅓ cup	50 g
Salt	⅛ tsp	
Nuts, chopped if large (optional)	½ cup	70 g
Chocolate, coarsely chopped (optional)	4 oz	115 g

These are light, crisp, and very buttery, with an affinity for being sandwiched. They are a close cousin to the French cookie *langue de chat*, although those are made with egg whites and these have whole eggs and are a touch thicker. Franciscos happen to be gluten free—they are one of the pastries that has such a short texture they want to be made with a very starchy flour. Try them sandwiched with your favorite chocolate or jam, or with nuts embedded on top. Pine nuts are amazing here. This is a beautiful cookie for the holidays.

KITCHEN NOTES: It is important to make sure all of your ingredients are at room temperature. If your eggs are cold, place them in a bowl of hot water for 10 minutes. When piping cookies to be sandwiched, as a visual aid to ensure all of your cookies are equal in length, pipe starting at the top of the tray and use the first one as your guide. If you are using parchment, you can use a pencil to make length marks with a ruler, turning the paper over before you pipe.

. . . .

Preheat the oven to 350°F [180°C]. Line a baking sheet with parchment paper or a nonstick liner. Have a piping bag ready with a ¾ in [2 cm] cut end or fitted with a ½ in [12 mm] piping tip.

In a medium bowl, beat the butter, sugar, and vanilla seeds until very light and creamy. Add the eggs one at a time, beating until smooth after each addition.

Add the cornstarch, rice flour, and salt and stir by hand until very smooth. Fill the piping bag with a comfortable amount to work with and pipe logs that are 3 in [7.5 cm] long. In order to not have a tail of cookie dough, ease up on the pressure at the end, make a quick downward movement with the bag, and quickly pull up. Any imperfections or tails can be smoothed over with a dampened finger, patting the dough gently into place.

Bake until the edges are light golden and the tops still light, 9 to 12 minutes, rotating the baking sheet halfway through baking. Transfer to a wire rack to cool. The cookies will keep in an airtight container for up to 2 weeks in the refrigerator or 1 week at room temperature.

With Nuts: If topping with nuts, bake the cookies for 1½ minutes (the cookies should have spread but still look wet), remove them from the oven, and sprinkle the nuts over the tops of the cookies. Return them to the oven and bake until the edges are golden, about 9 minutes, depending on the size of cookie.

With Chocolate: If making a chocolate-filled sandwich cookie, temper 4 oz [115 g] chocolate using the method on page 272, or melt the chocolate in a microwave-safe bowl. Match up cookie tops and bottoms, lining them up on a pan. Pipe or spoon a stripe of chocolate down the center of the first few to get a feel for how much chocolate to use. Sandwich so that a little chocolate is visible around the edges. Put the cookie sandwiches in a cool place or the refrigerator to firm up. The sandwich cookies will keep in an airtight container for up to 1 week or in the refrigerator for 2 weeks.

With Matcha: If making a matcha-dipped cookie, prepare the glaze (see page 47) and dip half of the cookie in the glaze, letting the excess drip back into the bowl. Let set.

ORANGE-OATMEAL-CURRANT COOKIES

YIELDS EIGHTY 2 IN [5 CM] COOKIES

Zante currants	1⅓ cups	190 g
All-purpose flour	2 cups + 3 Tbsp	285 g
Baking soda	½ tsp	
Nutmeg, freshly grated	½ tsp	
Unsalted butter, at room temperature	1 cup	225 g
Sugar	1¼ cups	250 g
Large egg	1	
Large egg yolk	1	
Light corn syrup	2 Tbsp	
Blackstrap or other dark molasses	1 Tbsp	
Orange zest	4 tsp	
Vanilla extract	1 tsp	
Salt	½ tsp	
Rolled oats	1⅔ cups	150 g

Some of the simplest recipes are the ones we've wrestled with the longest, like these oatmeal cookies. Soft, with a little spice, orange, and touch of molasses, they have a flavor of childhood. Make them on the larger side and they make an exceptional base for an ice cream cookie.

KITCHEN NOTES: The molasses and corn syrup make a slightly sticky dough that has to chill thoroughly before slicing.

. . . . . .

In a small bowl, combine the currants and enough warm water to cover and set aside for about 10 minutes until the currants are plumped. Drain well and set aside.

Sift together the flour, baking soda, and nutmeg into a mixing bowl and set aside. Using a stand mixer fitted with the paddle attachment, beat the butter on medium-high speed until light and creamy. Slowly add the sugar and mix on medium speed until light in color and fluffy. Stop the mixer and scrape down the sides of the bowl with a rubber spatula as needed. Add the whole egg, egg yolk, corn syrup, molasses, orange zest, vanilla, and salt and beat until well mixed. Stir in the flour mixture, currants, and oats until incorporated.

Divide the dough into two equal portions. Working on a large sheet of parchment paper, shape each portion into a log about 14 in [35 cm] long and 2 in [5 cm] in diameter. Gently press each log to give it an oval shape. Wrap tightly in parchment paper or plastic wrap and place in the refrigerator or freezer overnight.

Preheat the oven to 350°F [180°C]. Line two baking sheets with parchment paper or a nonstick liner.

Unwrap the logs. Using a sharp knife, slice the logs into ovals about ¼ in [6 mm] thick. Arrange the ovals on the prepared baking sheets. Bake until the edges of the cookies are lightly browned but the centers remain pale, 7 to 10 minutes. You may bake both pans at the same time, but rotate them 180 degrees at the midway point if they are not baking evenly. Transfer the cookies to wire racks to cool. The cookies will be soft when they cool. They will keep in an airtight container at room temperature for up to 2 weeks.

WALNUT CINNAMON SLICES

YIELDS 36 COOKIES

All-purpose flour	2 cups	260 g
Ground cinnamon	½ tsp	
Baking soda	¼ tsp	
Unsalted butter, at cool room temperature	⅔ cup + 1 Tbsp	160 g
Sugar	⅔ cup	135 g
Large egg	1	
Salt	½ tsp	
Walnuts, coarsely chopped	¾ cup	90 g

SUGAR COATING

Large egg yolks	2	
Heavy cream	2 Tbsp	
Sugar	1 cup	200 g

These are light, crisp, thin, butter cookies that we form into long, rectangular logs to slice and bake. The walnuts don't need to be toasted ahead of time; they get perfectly browned in the short amount of baking time, with a coating of sugar crystals on the edges providing extra crunch.

KITCHEN NOTES: Any softer nut works well in this recipe—pine nuts, pecans, or pistachios. If using a firmer nut like almond, make sure they are coarsely chopped first.

......

Sift together the flour, cinnamon, and baking soda into a mixing bowl. Set aside. In a stand mixer fitted with the paddle attachment, beat together the butter and sugar on medium speed just until blended and creamy without adding a lot of air. In a small bowl, whisk together the egg and salt until blended.

Slowly pour the egg mixture into the butter mixture, still beating on medium speed until well mixed. Add the flour mixture and beat on low speed just until a dough forms. Mix in the walnuts.

Turn the dough out onto a baking sheet lined with parchment paper, waxed paper, or plastic wrap. Form into a rectangle about 1 in [2.5 cm] thick. Wrap tightly and refrigerate until firm, about 4 hours. If you want to make round cookies, shape the dough into a log of the desired diameter, wrap in parchment paper or plastic wrap, and chill until firm.

Preheat the oven to 325°F [160°C]. Butter a baking sheet or line it with parchment paper or a non-stick liner.

Unwrap the rectangle and, using a sharp knife, slice lengthwise into 2 in [5 cm] wide rectangular logs.

To make the sugar coating, in a small bowl, whisk together the egg yolks and cream to make an egg wash. Spread the sugar on a baking sheet. Brush the rectangular logs well but sparingly with the egg wash. One at a time, dredge the logs in the sugar, coating evenly on all sides. Cut crosswise ⅛ to ¼ in [3 to 6 mm] thick, creating rectangles measuring 2 in [5 cm] by 1 in [2.5 cm], and arrange the rectangles on the prepared baking sheet. If you have made a round log, brush it with the egg wash, coat it evenly with the sugar, cut crosswise ⅛ to ¼ in [3 to 6 mm] thick, and arrange the rounds on the baking sheet.

Bake the cookies until the edges are golden but the centers remain pale, about 7 minutes. Transfer the cookies to a wire rack and let cool. The cookies will keep in an airtight container for up to 2 weeks in the refrigerator or 1 week at room temperature.

RUGELACH

YIELDS 16 RUGELACH

Cream cheese, at room temperature	8 oz	225 g
Unsalted butter, at room temperature	1 cup	225 g
All-purpose flour	2 cups	260 g
Einkorn flour	½ cup	65 g
Salt	1 tsp	
Large egg	1	
Melted butter, cooled	3 Tbsp	
Walnut Currant filling (facing page), or jam	1 recipe	
Sugar for topping		

Flaky cream cheese dough, rolled into little crescents with either preserves or a nut and sugar filling, ruge-lach are a Jewish baking delicacy with numerous recipes passed down in families, some with sour cream, others pareve and made without dairy. Our baker Davita developed these with one important difference, however, making them lighter and flakier than any version I've had: the dough is made with part einkorn flour. Testing this version along with doughs made with five other flours, the einkorn stood out clearly from the rest with flakier, more discernible layers, and a lighter texture and higher rise. You can use any type of jam for filling; our favorite in the test kitchen was fig.

. . . . . .

In the bowl of stand mixer fitted with the paddle attachment, beat the softened cream cheese on medium speed for 5 minutes to soften and aerate slightly. Add the softened butter and mix on medium speed until smooth, 1 to 2 minutes, stopping the mixer to scrape down the sides of the bowl a few times. Add the flours and salt and mix on medium speed until the dough just comes together and begins to ball around the paddle. Do not overmix; you should still see some specks of loose flour in the dough, which will be moist, with some chunks, and not totally cohesive. Turn the dough out onto a sheet of plastic wrap and form a 1 in [2.5 cm] thick disc. Wrap tightly and refrigerate for 1 hour or overnight.

Preheat the oven to 350°F [180°C]. Line a baking sheet with parchment paper or a nonstick liner. Whisk the egg in a small bowl and set aside.

Dust your work surface with flour, and turn the dough out onto it. Using a rolling pin, roll out the dough to form a circle that is 11 in [28 cm] in diameter and a little thicker than ⅛ in [3 mm]. Very lightly brush the dough with butter and spread with a thick layer of the nut or jam filling, equal in thickness to the dough. Leave a ½ in [12 mm] border around the edge. With a pizza cutter or sharp knife, cut the dough round in half, then each half into quarters, and so on until you get sixteen equal triangular pieces. Starting at the base of a triangle, tightly roll up the dough so that the tip of the triangle ends tuck up at the base of the cookie, lightly pushing down to secure the shape. Place the rugelach on the prepared baking sheet and transfer to the freezer for 10 to 15 minutes. Remove from the freezer and brush each cookie with the egg wash, then sprinkle with sugar. Bake until they are golden brown and the base of each cookie is set and slightly darker than the tops, 20 to 25 minutes.

WALNUT-CURRANT FILLING

Walnuts	1 cup	120 g
Brown sugar	⅔ cup	120 g
Ground cinnamon	1 Tbsp	
Currants	½ cup	70 g

Pulse the walnuts in a food processor fitted with the steel blade until the pieces are small, about the size of sunflower seeds. Add the brown sugar and cinnamon and pulse again. Stir in the currants.

ALMOND ROCHERS

YIELDS 30 SMALL COOKIES

Sliced almonds	1⅓ cups	115 g
Large egg whites, at room temperature	2	
Confectioners' sugar	1 cup	125 g
Salt	pinch	
Vanilla extract	½ tsp	

We pipe our rocher batter—a simple meringue with any number of additional nuts, chocolate, or flavorings—into a "kiss," where they puff up and crack, staying soft on the inside, with a crunchy outer shell. With its sweet nature, it pairs well with ingredients that are bitter, such as cacao nibs, or savory, like nuts. They also make a surprisingly delicious two-ingredient tart filling that you can top with any kind of fruit by mixing the crushed cookies with unsweetened, softly whipped cream. The cookie absorbs the excess moisture in the cream, perfectly sweetening and thickening it to a nice, sliceable consistency.

KITCHEN NOTES: Egg whites won't whip in the presence of protein, so make sure no broken yolk or residual oil in a bowl comes into contact with them. If you prefer completely dry, perfectly crisp meringues, bake at 200°F [90°C] for about 45 minutes with the oven door ajar.

. . . . . .

Preheat the oven to 350°F [180°C]. Line a baking sheet with parchment paper or a nonstick liner.

Spread the almonds on an unlined baking sheet. Place in the oven and toast until golden brown, 7 to 10 minutes. Let cool completely. Break up the almonds with your hands into ¼ in [6 mm] pieces (or use a rolling pin). If piping, keep in mind that any large bits of almond will clog the pastry tip.

Pour water to a depth of about 2 in [5 cm] into a saucepan, place over medium heat, and bring to a simmer. Combine the egg whites, confectioners' sugar, and salt in the stainless-steel bowl of a stand mixer that will rest securely on the rim of the saucepan over, but not touching, the water. Whisk together and then place over the saucepan and continue to whisk until the whites are hot to the touch (120°F [50°C]), about 5 minutes or so. Remove the bowl from over the water and place on the stand mixer. Fit the mixer with the whisk attachment and mix on high speed until the mixture is very thick and holds glossy, stiff peaks when you lift the beater. Fold in the almonds and vanilla with a rubber spatula.

Immediately scoop the meringue into a pastry bag fitted with a ½ in [12 mm] (no. 6 or 7) plain tip and pipe onto the prepared baking sheet, forming "kisses" about 1 in [2.5 cm] in diameter and spacing them about 1½ in [4 cm] apart. Or, you can drop the meringue by the tablespoon onto the baking sheet.

Place the baking sheet in the oven and keep the oven door ajar with the handle of a wooden spoon to allow moisture to escape. Bake the cookies until they puff slightly, crack along the sides, and feel dry on the outside but soft to the touch, 15 to 20 minutes. Transfer the cookies to a wire rack and let cool. They will harden as they cool. The cookies will keep in an airtight container at room temperature for up to 2 weeks.

CHEDDAR CHEESE OAT CRACKERS

Oat flour	¾ cup + 2 Tbsp	95 g
Pine nuts	½ cup	70 g
Fresh marjoram, chopped	1 tsp	
Fresh thyme leaves	1 tsp	
Salt	¾ tsp	
Black pepper, freshly ground	¾ tsp	
Grated sharp Cheddar cheese	2 cups	230 g
Unsalted butter, at room temperature	¼ cup	60 g
Cumin seeds	2 Tbsp	
Caraway seeds	2 Tbsp	
White sesame seeds	2 Tbsp	
Poppy seeds	2 Tbsp	

I used to find homemade crackers a little disappointing in that they are often bland or the texture doesn't seem right. Many recipes are based on bread dough, which seems like much too much trouble to go through for a cracker unless you are making a loaf of bread as well. This recipe overcomes all of those problems. It calls for a large amount of cheese, so make sure to use a flavorful one. If you use a sharp Cheddar or even a well-aged Gruyère, the crackers will reflect the pronounced flavor of the cheese, and you'll have a cracker that needs no other accompaniment than a glass of good wine.

KITCHEN NOTES: Be careful with cheese substitutions. A cheese with a high butterfat content such as Brie or even a very soft Fontina will not work. Neither will

very hard cheeses such as pecorino, although you may add a few tablespoons of hard cheese for flavor.

. . . .

In a medium bowl, use a wooden spoon to combine the flour, pine nuts, marjoram, thyme, salt, and black pepper.

In the bowl of a stand mixer fitted with the paddle attachment, combine the Cheddar cheese and butter on low speed. Turn the mixer off, add the flour mixture, and beat on low speed until incorporated.

Dust your work surface lightly with flour, and turn the dough out onto it. Roll the dough into a log about 8 in [20 cm] long and 2½ in [6 cm] in diameter. In a small bowl, combine the cumin seeds, caraway seeds, sesame seeds, and poppy seeds. Spread the seed mixture onto your work surface and roll the log of dough in it, pressing lightly so the seeds adhere, until the dough log is completely covered on all sides. Wrap the dough tightly with plastic wrap and refrigerate for 1 hour.

Preheat the oven to 350°F [180°C]. Line two baking sheets with parchment paper.

Using a serrated knife, cut the log of dough into slices that are ⅛ in [3 mm] thick. Transfer the slices to the prepared baking sheets and bake until the edges of the crackers are golden brown, 8 to 10 minutes, rotating the baking sheets halfway through baking. Transfer the crackers to a wire cooling rack. They will keep in an airtight container at room temperature for up to 1 week.

CHAPTER FIVE

PASTRIES AND CONFECTIONS

ÉCLAIRS

YIELDS 12 ÉCLAIRS

CHOUX PASTE

Nonfat milk	½ cup	120 ml
Water	½ cup	120 ml
Unsalted butter	½ cup	115 g
Sugar	1 tsp	
Salt	¼ tsp	
All-purpose flour	1 cup + 1 Tbsp	140 g
Large eggs	5	

GLAZE

Bittersweet chocolate, coarsely chopped	4 oz	115 g
Light corn syrup	1 Tbsp	
Heavy cream	½ cup	120 ml

FILLING

Pastry Cream (page 300) or Matcha Pastry Cream (page 302), cold	1¼ cups	300 ml

For some people, a true éclair must have a chocolate filling. I think the topping makes it chocolaty enough, and the contrast of a beautiful, cold, vanilla pastry cream filling makes a more compelling pastry. Finishing éclairs with fondant is also traditional, but I find fondant far too sweet and without flavor, even with added chocolate. At our bakery, we simply dip the éclairs into some chocolate ganache that has a small amount of corn syrup for shine. You can also use the Matcha Glaze found on page 47.

KITCHEN NOTES: Remember, when piping choux paste, every little bump and mistake is exaggerated when the dough is baked. The better your piping, the better your shell. This is a forgiving dough to work with, however, and you can scoop up your mistake and try again. Any small bumps can be smoothed with a dampened fingertip.

• • • • • •

Preheat the oven to 425°F [220°C]. Butter a baking sheet or line it with parchment paper.

To make the choux paste, in a heavy saucepan, combine the milk, water, butter, sugar, and salt and place over medium heat until the butter melts and the mixture comes to a full boil. Add the flour all at once, stirring vigorously with a wooden spoon. Keep stirring until the mixture has formed a smooth mass and pulls away from the sides of the pan and some of the moisture has evaporated. This will take about 3 minutes.

Transfer to the bowl of a stand mixer fitted with the paddle attachment or to a heatproof mixing bowl. If using a mixer, add the eggs one at a time and mix on medium-high speed, incorporating each egg before adding the next. When all the eggs have been added, the mixture will be thick, smooth, and shiny. If making by hand, add the eggs one at a time and mix with a wooden spoon, incorporating each egg before adding the next.

continued

Transfer the contents of the bowl to a pastry bag fitted with a ½ in [12 mm] (no. 6 or 7) plain tip, adding only as much to the bag as is comfortable to work with. Pipe out fingers about 5 in [12 cm] long and 1 in [2.5 cm] wide, spacing them about 2 in [5 cm] apart. If you end up with a bulge or a "tail" at the end of the piping, you can smooth it over with a damp fingertip.

Bake until puffed and starting to show some color, about 10 minutes. Reduce the oven temperature to 375°F [190°C] and continue to bake until the shells feel light for their size and are hollow inside, about 12 minutes longer. They should be nicely browned all over. Remove from the oven and, using a metal skewer, poke a small hole in the end of each shell to allow steam to escape. This keeps the shells from collapsing. Let cool on wire racks. They should be used as soon as they are cool enough to fill. You can also wrap them tightly and freeze them for up to 3 weeks. When you are ready to fill them, recrisp them directly from the freezer in a 450°F [230°C] oven for about 10 minutes and then let cool before filling.

To make the glaze, combine the chocolate and corn syrup in a heatproof bowl. Bring the cream to just under a boil in a small saucepan. Pour the cream over the chocolate. Let the mixture sit for about 2 minutes without stirring until the chocolate melts, and then stir gently with a rubber spatula (so as to incorporate as little air as possible) until smooth and shiny. Let cool until just warm.

To fill and glaze the éclairs, stir the pastry cream (it must be very cold) until smooth and then spoon the cream into a pastry bag fitted with a plain tip with a very small opening. It is easiest to start with a hole in each end of the shell and to fill from both ends if necessary. Sometimes pockets inside the shell prevent the pastry cream from filling the entire shell from a single hole. Fill the shells until they feel heavy. To glaze the éclairs, dip the top of each filled éclair into the glaze, shaking gently to allow the excess to drip off, and then place upright on a wire rack and allow the glaze to set.

Alternatively, you can fill the shells by splitting them in half with a serrated knife. Dip the top half in the glaze, allowing the excess to drip off, and then place upright on a wire rack and allow the glaze to set. Spoon the pastry cream into the bottoms of the shells and replace the glazed tops.

Serve the pastries at once, or refrigerate for up to 6 hours before serving. They should be eaten the same day they are filled.

CANELÉS

Confectioners' sugar	1½ cups + 2 Tbsp	200 g
All-purpose flour	¾ cup	100 g
Salt	¼ tsp	
Milk	1⅔ cups	400 ml
Unsalted butter	2 Tbsp + 2 tsp	
Vanilla bean, split and scraped	1	
Large eggs	2	
Large egg yolk	1	
Dark rum	2 Tbsp	

BEESWAX COATING FOR CANELÉ MOLDS

Unsalted butter	¾ cup	170 g
Food-grade beeswax (organic, if possible)	4 oz	115 g

Canelés are unlike any other pastry, in a class of their own. They were originally a specialty of the Bordeaux region of France, where you still see stores devoted to selling only these unique pastries. They are made in a mold that looks like a miniature 2 in [5 cm] Bundt form that is coated in a mixture of beeswax and butter, creating a pastry with a caramelized crust and a soft, almost pudding-like interior.

They can also be terribly challenging even for the most skilled baker, so it is with a slight amount of caution but with a very trusty recipe that Lynn has developed that we offer you the canelé. If you have patience and love a baking challenge, this is your recipe.

. . . . . .

In a large bowl, sift together the confectioners' sugar, flour, and salt. Set aside. Combine the milk and butter in a medium, heavy saucepan and place over medium heat. As soon as the butter is melted, remove the saucepan from the heat and add the vanilla bean seeds. Set aside. In a small bowl, whisk together the eggs and yolk. Pour the egg mixture and the rum into the warmed milk and stir. Gently pour the milk mixture through a fine-mesh sieve set over the sifted dry ingredients. Whisk gently to combine. Pass the batter through the sieve two more times. Add the vanilla pod and refrigerate the batter in a covered container for 48 hours before baking.

To prepare the mold coating, clarify the butter by placing it in a small, heavy saucepan and melting it slowly over medium-low heat. The foamy white milk solids will rise to the surface; using a spoon, skim the milk solids from the top of the melted butter. Slowly pour the hot butter through a cheesecloth-lined strainer. Some of the milk solids may remain in the pot. Take care not to let them mix into the clarified butter. You should have ½ cup [115 g]. Store, well wrapped, in the refrigerator for up to 2 weeks.

To prepare the canelé molds for baking, preheat the oven to 350°F [180°C]. Place a wire rack over a foil-lined baking sheet. Have oven mitts or heat-resistant baking gloves ready to protect your hands. In a small, heavy saucepan, heat the clarified butter and beeswax together until completely melted and hot. Arrange the canelé molds on the wire rack. Very carefully, one at a time, pour the hot beeswax mixture into each mold, filling it completely before tipping the hot mixture back into the pot. Flip and place the

continued

empty mold onto the wire rack to allow any excess beeswax to drip out onto the foil-lined sheet, and set upright before the wax sets. Continue this process until all of the molds are filled, flipped, and drained. If the beeswax mixture begins to cool and set in the pot, place over low heat to melt thoroughly before continuing. There should be a very thin coat of beeswax lining each mold. Line the baking sheet with a fresh sheet of foil. Place the molds directly on the pan, evenly spaced in three rows of four.

Remove the vanilla pod from the canelé batter and gently stir to combine. Some flour may have settled to the bottom of the container. Carefully fill each mold three-fourths of the way. Bake until the batter has risen slightly and is a very dark mahogany color, about 45 minutes, rotating the baking sheet halfway through baking. Test for doneness: if the crown of the canelé is still light in color, replace the mold and continue cooking in 5-minute increments, checking after each round. They should be evenly colored. Some canelés may be ready before others; continue baking the lighter ones. Turn the canelés out of their molds immediately. Cool for 20 minutes before serving. They are best eaten the day they are baked.

Matcha Canelé Variation: When making the batter, omit the vanilla bean and add 1 tsp sifted matcha powder to the milk mixture. Bake as directed.

Citrus Canelé Variation: When making the batter, omit the vanilla bean. Substitute orange liqueur, such as Grand Marnier, for the rum. Add the finely grated zest of half an orange and half a lemon when pouring the batter into the storage container. Bake as directed.

LEMON BARS ON BROWN BUTTER SHORTBREAD

YIELDS ONE 9 BY 13 IN [23 BY 33 CM] BAKING PAN; TWELVE 3 BY 3¼ IN [8 BY 8.25 CM] BARS

CRUST

Confectioners' sugar, plus more for topping	⅓ cup + 2 Tbsp	55 g
All-purpose flour	1½ cups + 2 Tbsp	215 g
Unsalted butter, at room temperature	¾ cup	170 g
Pine nuts (optional)	⅓ cup + 1 Tbsp	55 g

FILLING

All-purpose flour	½ cup	65 g
Granulated sugar	2¼ cups	450 g
Lemon juice	1 cup + 3 Tbsp	285 ml
Lemon zest	from 1 small lemon	
Large eggs	6	
Large egg yolk	1	
Salt	pinch	

Although we love having these bars fill our pastry cases in the fall and winter since they are one of the few bright colors in the sea of chocolate and caramel, a really cold lemon bar in the heat of the summer is very refreshing. I find the bases of most lemon bars to be undercooked and too thick, and the filling usually too scant. Just as we like to bake a lot of our pastries a little darker than many bakeries, we do the same with these bars: we bake the shortbread base until it turns golden brown, producing a deeper butter flavor and crispier crust. We also fill the crust with a little more custard than is typical. You will find that the base of these bars not only has a nice toothsome bite but also will stay crisp beyond the day the bars are made.

If you can find a bergamot orange (a sour, aromatic variety), use the zest in place of the lemon zest. You may also want to try adding pine nuts to the crust. Their earthy flavor is delicious with lemon.

. . . . . .

Preheat the oven to 350°F [180°C]. Butter a 9 by 13 in [23 by 33 cm] baking pan.

To make the crust, sift the confectioners' sugar into the bowl of a stand mixer fitted with the paddle attachment. Add the flour and stir to mix. Add the butter and pine nuts, if using, and beat on low speed just until a smooth dough forms.

Transfer the dough to the prepared pan and press evenly into the bottom and ½ in [12 mm] up the sides of the pan. It should be about ¼ in [6 mm] thick. To help even out the crust, use the flat bottom of any type of cup, pressing down firmly. Line the crust with parchment paper and fill with pie weights. Bake the crust until it colors evenly to a deep golden brown, 25 to 35 minutes. Rotate the pan 180 degrees if the crust appears to be baking unevenly.

While the crust is baking, make the filling. Sift the flour into a mixing bowl. Add the granulated sugar and whisk until blended. Add the lemon juice and zest and stir to dissolve the sugar. In a separate mixing bowl, whisk the whole eggs and egg yolk with the salt. Add the eggs to the lemon juice mixture and whisk until well mixed.

continued

When the crust is ready, pull out the oven rack holding the crust, remove the pie weights and parchment paper, and pour the filling directly into the hot pan. (It is easiest to pour the custard into the pan if the pan is in the oven.) If the crust has come out of the oven and cooled before you have finished making the filling, put it back in for a few minutes so that it is hot when the custard is poured into it. Reduce the oven temperature to 300°F [150°C] and bake just until the center of the custard is no longer wobbly, 30 to 40 minutes.

Let cool completely on a wire rack, then cover and chill well before cutting. Using a sharp knife, cut into twelve squares, or as desired. If you like, dust the tops of the squares with confectioners' sugar. They will keep in an airtight container or well covered in the baking dish in the refrigerator for up to 4 days.

CHOCOLATE FRIANDS

YIELDS 24 MINI CAKES

Bittersweet chocolate, coarsely chopped	6 oz	170 g
Unsalted butter	1 cup	225 g
Large eggs	4	
Sugar	1⅓ cups	265 g
All-purpose flour, sifted	¾ cup	100 g
Cornstarch	2 Tbsp	
Salt	¼ tsp	

GANACHE TOPPING

Bittersweet chocolate, chopped	4 oz	115 g
Heavy cream	½ cup + 2 Tbsp	150 ml

Friand is French for "small mouthful," and these friands, although they look like tiny cupcakes, are rich and toothsome, more moist and more chocolaty than a typical cupcake. They make a perfect little individual party cake, as they are baked in small paper cups and topped with a lovely, shiny, chocolate glaze. I recommend using a bitter chocolate, such as Askinosie, or a chocolate that is at least 70 percent cacao or higher, and I've reduced the amount of sugar a bit from the first version.

KITCHEN NOTES: You can use a pastry bag or a small ice-cream scoop for filling the paper cups. If you can find 1½ by ½ in [4 cm by 12 mm] glassine cups, you can use them for baking and serving the friands, or just cut down paper cupcake cups.

. . . . . .

Preheat the oven to 350°F [180°C]. Line up 24 mini-muffin-cup paper liners on a baking sheet, or butter and flour 24 mini-muffin-tin wells, knocking out the excess flour.

To make the batter, place the chocolate in a large mixing bowl. In a small saucepan, melt the butter over medium heat until very hot. Pour the butter over the chocolate and whisk until smooth. Add the eggs, one at a time, whisking until incorporated before adding the next egg. In a medium mixing bowl, combine the sugar, flour, cornstarch, and salt and whisk together. Add the chocolate mixture to the dry ingredients and whisk well to combine. Transfer the batter to a liquid measuring cup for pouring, and fill the cups almost to the top. Bake until the cakes just start to crack on top, 12 to 15 minutes, depending on the fill level. Let cool for 10 minutes on a wire rack, then unmold them if you have baked them in the muffin tins and let cool completely. If you have baked them in the paper cups, just let them cool in the cups.

continued

To make the ganache, place the chocolate in a small heatproof bowl. Bring the cream to just under a boil in a small saucepan over medium heat. Pour the cream over the chocolate and let sit for a minute or two. Stir gently with a rubber spatula until the chocolate is melted and smooth.

Holding each friand by its sides, dip the top into the ganache and then shake gently to let the excess run off the side. Return the friand to the rack and let the ganache set up in a cool place for about 1 hour. I don't recommend putting them in the refrigerator to set up if your kitchen is hot because condensation will form on the top when you take them out. You can avoid the condensation problem by putting them in an airtight container first, refrigerating, and then leaving them in the container as they come back to room temperature, or serving them right away.

Serve the friands within a day of making, or store them in an airtight container in the refrigerator for up to 5 days.

PECAN DIAMONDS

Chilled Sweet Tart Dough round (page 290)	½ recipe	

FILLING

Sugar	1½ cups	300 g
Unsalted butter	1 cup	225 g
Honey	½ cup	170 g
Salt	1½ tsp	
Pecans, coarsely chopped	4½ cups	450 g
Heavy cream	¼ cup	60 ml
Orange zest	¼ cup	55 g
Ground cardamom (optional)	1 tsp	

With a slightly salty caramel filling on a pastry base, these nutty bites are completely addictive. Cooking the filling in a pot first and then finishing it in the oven creates a foolproof confection, yielding many for little work, making this a perfect holiday or group sweet. The filling will reflect the honey and nuts you choose—you can also try a mixture of nuts or adding a few tablespoons of sesame seeds. Instead of the cardamom here, try adding cinnamon, nutmeg, or allspice. These cookies make a perfect dessert plate alongside tangerines and chocolate.

KITCHEN NOTES: The amount of cardamom called for is very subtle; you can use one and a half times or twice the amount if you prefer a spicier sweet. If adding cinnamon, use the amount suggested for cardamom; for allspice or nutmeg, use half the amount; and for cloves, use one-quarter the amount. If you like your caramel sweets on the salty side, sprinkle with flaky salt when they come out of the oven.

Preheat the oven to 350°F [180°C]. Line an 8 by 12 in [20 by 30 cm] rimmed baking sheet with parchment paper.

Lightly flour your work surface. Roll out the dough into a ⅛ in [3 mm] thick rectangle (see page 289). Carefully transfer the dough to the prepared baking sheet, easing it into the bottom, sides, and corners and then pressing gently into place. Do not stretch the dough or the sides will shrink during baking. If the dough has become too soft to work with, put it in the refrigerator for a few minutes to firm before transferring it to the pan. If the dough develops any tears, patch with a little extra dough, pressing firmly to adhere. With a sharp knife, trim off any dough overhang, using the rim of the sheet as a guide. Refrigerate the dough until it is firm, about 15 minutes. Place in the oven and bake until golden brown, 20 to 25 minutes. Check after 15 minutes; if there are any tears, patch with dough and continue baking.

To make the filling, combine the sugar, butter, honey, and salt in a heavy saucepan. Place over medium-high heat. Once the sugar reaches a rapid boil, cook for 10 minutes. Remove from the heat and add the chopped nuts, cream, orange zest, and cardamom, if using. Stir and return to a boil. Immediately remove from the heat and pour the mixture into the baked pastry. Smooth the surface with a spatula. Bake until the caramel is bubbling, about 10 minutes. Cool completely on a wire rack. Turn the entire batch out of the pan onto your work surface and flip to caramel-side up. Trim the edges with a very sharp knife. Cut 1 in [2.5 cm] rows, then cut vertically into diamonds. The diamonds will keep for 1 week, well wrapped at room temperature.

CHOCOLATE ALMOND TOFFEE

YIELDS ABOUT 1½ LB [680 G]

Sliced almonds	2⅓ cups	200 g
Sugar	1¾ cups	350 g
Unsalted butter	½ cup	115 g
Water	3 Tbsp	45 ml
Blackstrap or other dark molasses	1 tsp	
Salt	¼ tsp	
Vanilla extract	1 tsp	
Baking soda	¼ tsp	
Bittersweet chocolate, coarsely chopped	5 oz	140 g

Toffee is no more than caramelized sugar with a little baking soda and butter, which add the flavor and crunch characteristic of the candy. This is an easy, incredibly delicious, and addictive confection to make. As always with recipes that have just a few ingredients, use the best chocolate you can find. The toffee itself is so sweet, I like to use a chocolate that has less sugar, such as Askinosie or another dark bittersweet chocolate. We use toasted, sliced almonds to top the chocolate, but toasted buckwheat and cacao nibs are also great.

KITCHEN NOTES: When you make candy, it is important to read through the whole recipe first, and have all of your ingredients premeasured and ready to go before you start. Once the sugar begins cooking, you don't have a lot of time to stop and read or measure. When cooking sugar to high temperatures, keep a bowl of ice water close by in case of burns.

You can substitute unsweetened chocolate for 20 percent of your bittersweet chocolate if you prefer a slightly more bitter foil for the toffee.

Preheat the oven to 325°F [160°C]. Spread the almonds evenly on a baking sheet and toast until golden brown, 7 to 10 minutes. Let cool completely.

Line a 13 by 18 in [33 by 46 cm] baking pan or a rimmed baking sheet of about the same size with parchment paper or a nonstick liner. Evenly spread half of the almonds over the bottom of the prepared pan. The parchment or liner should not be visible at all. Reserve the remaining almonds for topping.

In a medium, heavy saucepan, combine the sugar, butter, water, molasses, and salt. Place over medium heat and cook, stirring occasionally, until the mixture registers 295°F [146°C] on a thermometer, 5 to 7 minutes. Immediately remove from the heat and stir in the vanilla and baking soda. Be careful at this point: the mixture will bubble up when you add the baking soda. Make sure that you incorporate the baking soda evenly throughout the mixture.

continued

Pour the hot mixture evenly over the almonds. Work quickly, as it will begin setting up immediately. If you need to spread it out at all, use a lightly oiled rubber or metal spatula.

When the toffee has cooled enough to touch, spread the chocolate over the warm toffee and let the heat of the toffee melt the chocolate. Smooth it out evenly with an offset spatula when it is completely melted. Sprinkle the rest of the almonds over the top, covering evenly. Let cool completely.

Break the cooled sheet into pieces. They will keep in an airtight container in a cool, dry place for up to several weeks. Do not freeze.

MAPLE-GLAZED PECANS

YIELDS 2 CUPS [285 G]

Maple syrup	2 Tbsp	
Light or dark corn syrup	2 Tbsp	
Sugar	2 Tbsp	
Salt	1/8 tsp	
Pecan halves	2¼ cups	285 g

Although we make loads of these at the holidays, they make delicious cocktail bites (try them with sherry) or sweets after a meal. You can also chop them for topping ice cream or a sundae, or use them on top of a chocolate tart. This is a good example of how important salt is to a dessert recipe. The nuts taste sweetly bland without it—good but not very compelling or interesting. The salt heightens the toasted flavor of the pecans and brings out the buttery flavor of the nuts.

KITCHEN NOTES: Corn syrup is used in the glaze because it prevents the sugar and maple syrup from crystallizing, which ensures a clear, shiny coating on the nuts.

· · · · · ·

Preheat the oven to 400°F [200°C]. Line a baking sheet with parchment paper or a nonstick liner.

In a mixing bowl, combine the maple syrup, corn syrup, sugar, and salt and mix well. Add the pecans and toss to coat evenly with the syrup mixture. Turn out the contents of the bowl onto the prepared baking sheet and spread evenly.

Toast the nuts, stirring every few minutes with a heat-proof rubber spatula or a wooden spoon once the mixture begins to bubble, 4 to 6 minutes. The nuts are done when they are golden brown and the syrup is thicker and bubbling slowly. Remove from the oven and let cool completely on the baking sheet. The coating on the nuts should be crisp when the nuts are cool. If it isn't, you can put the nuts back in the oven for another couple of minutes.

Separate the cooled nuts that have stuck together. They will keep in an airtight container in a cool, dry place for up to 2 weeks or for 1 month in the refrigerator.

Sweet and Salty Pecans Variation: Prepare Maple-Glazed Pecans as directed, substituting ¼ cup [60 ml] light corn syrup for the maple syrup, increasing the salt to 3/4 tsp, and decreasing the oven temperature to 325°F [160°C].

PEANUT BRITTLE

YIELDS 1¼ LB [570 G]

Sugar	¾ cup + 2 Tbsp	175 g
Water	¼ cup	60 ml
Light or dark corn syrup	⅓ cup	115 g
Salt	¾ tsp	
Raw peanuts	1⅔ cups	235 g
Unsalted butter	1 Tbsp	
Vanilla extract	½ tsp	
Baking soda	½ tsp	

It is easy to add other flavors and textures to this brittle. If you can find cacao nibs, the fermented, crisp, unsweetened chips of unprocessed chocolate before it becomes a smooth bar, they make a great addition. Because they are unsweetened, they balance well with this very sweet candy. Unhulled pumpkin seeds, known as pepitas, are delicious additions, too. Sesame seeds alone give the candy a Middle Eastern flavor reminiscent of halvah, while unsweetened small-flake dried coconut and macadamias are a delicious tropical variation.

KITCHEN NOTES: If you decide to include one of the preceding suggested additions, add a generous handful of each.

Line a baking sheet with aluminum foil and oil lightly, or line with a nonstick liner.

In a heavy, deep saucepan, combine the sugar, water, corn syrup, and salt over low heat. Stir with a wooden spoon until the sugar dissolves. Increase the heat to high, bring to a boil, and cook without stirring until the mixture registers 264°F [129°C] on a thermometer. This will take 5 to 8 minutes. Immediately add the peanuts to the syrup and stir constantly until the mixture registers 310°F [154°C] onthe thermometer.

Remove from the heat and stir in the butter and vanilla until incorporated. Then add the baking soda and stir quickly, making sure you incorporate the baking soda evenly throughout the mixture. Pour the mixture onto the prepared baking sheet, spreading it with the back of an oiled spoon or offset spatula. Let cool just until you can handle it (it helps if you wear rubber gloves), and then pull from the sides until the brittle has a shiny, "lacy" appearance. This incorporates air bubbles into the candy, making it more crisp. Let the candy cool completely.

Break the brittle into pieces. They will keep in an airtight container in a cool, dry place for up to 2 weeks.

BROWNIES

YIELDS ONE 9 BY 13 IN [23 BY 33 CM] BAKING DISH; 12 BROWNIES

Unsalted butter	¾ cup	170 g
Bittersweet chocolate, coarsely chopped	1 lb	450 g
All-purpose flour	1 cup	130 g
Large eggs	5	
Light brown sugar	2¼ cups	400 g
Vanilla extract	1 tsp	
Salt	½ tsp	

TOPPING (OPTIONAL)

Nuts such as walnut or pecan halves	2 cups	200 g

This recipe has been adjusted and developed at Tartine over the years to reflect our preference for "fudgy" brownies. As is traditional for a brownie recipe, the only leavener is beaten egg, and the batter contains very little flour. The same recipe, with minor variations, can be baked in thin layers for an exceptional base for an ice-cream sandwich (see Variation, page 250).

KITCHEN NOTES: You can't use a cake tester to judge doneness for these brownies. Because the batter has a high percentage of chocolate, the tester comes out wet even if the brownies are done.

· · · · · ·

Preheat the oven to 350°F [180°C]. Butter a 9 by 13 in [23 by 33 cm] glass baking dish.

In a small saucepan, melt the butter over low heat. Remove from the heat and add the chocolate. If the heat from the butter does not fully melt the chocolate, put the pan back over the heat for 10 seconds and stir until melted. Set aside to cool.

Sift the flour into a small mixing bowl. Set aside. In a medium mixing bowl, combine the eggs, brown sugar, vanilla, and salt. Using a stand mixer fitted with the whisk attachment, beat on high speed until the mixture thickens and becomes pale in color and falls from the beater in a wide ribbon that folds back on itself and slowly dissolves on the surface, 4 to 5 minutes. Alternatively, use a mixing bowl and a whisk to beat the ingredients until the mixture falls from the whisk in a wide ribbon. Using a rubber spatula, fold the cooled chocolate into the egg mixture. Add the flour and fold it in quickly but gently with the rubber spatula so that you don't deflate the air that's been incorporated into the eggs.

Pour the batter into the prepared dish and smooth the top with the spatula. If you are using nuts, evenly distribute them across the batter. Bake until the top looks slightly cracked and feels soft to the touch, about 25 minutes. Let cool completely on a wire rack.

continued

Using a sharp knife, cut into twelve squares, or whatever size you desire. The brownies will keep in an airtight container in a cool place for up to 1 week.

Ice-Cream Sandwich Brownies Variation: Preheat the oven to 350°F [180°C]. Butter and lightly flour two 9 by 13 in [23 by 33 cm] glass baking dishes, knocking out the excess flour. (If you have only one baking dish, bake the first batch, let cool, turn out of the dish, wash the dish, and then bake the second batch.) Follow the directions for making the Brownies batter, substituting 6 Tbsp [85 g] unsalted butter; 8 oz [225 g] bittersweet chocolate, coarsely chopped; 1/2 cup [65 g] all-purpose flour; 3 large eggs; 1 cup + 2 Tbsp [200 g] light brown sugar; 1/2 tsp vanilla extract; and 1/4 tsp salt for the amounts given. Divide the batter in half, and spread each half in a prepared baking dish, smoothing the surface with an offset spatula or the back of a large spoon. Bake until the top feels set and the batter has just baked through, 7 to 10 minutes. For ice-cream sandwiches, you want a very moist and fudgy brownie, one that is slightly underbaked (the layers will set up and become quite firm when frozen). Let cool to room temperature in the baking dishes on wire racks, then turn out onto the wire racks to continue cooling completely. (You may need to ease out the edges with a flexible spatula.)

To make the sandwiches, let 1 1/2 to 2 pt [750 ml to 1 L] of ice cream sit at room temperature just long enough to become spreadable. Line a 9 by 13 in [23 by 33 cm] baking dish or pan with plastic wrap, allowing enough overhang to cover the top of the sandwich completely when it is assembled. Place one brownie layer, top-side down, in the lined dish. Scoop the ice cream out onto the brownie and spread evenly and quickly with a rubber spatula or an offset metal spatula. Top with the second brownie layer, top side up, and gently and evenly press down on the second layer. Fold the plastic wrap over the top, covering completely. Using a square plate or a book, press down with firm, even pressure to distribute the ice cream evenly. Freeze for at least 3 hours or overnight. Uncover the top, turn the sandwich out onto a cutting board, peel away the plastic wrap, and cut into desired sizes with a large, very sharp knife. Wrap together or individually until ready to serve. The sandwiches will keep, well wrapped, in the freezer for up to 2 weeks.

ROCKY ROAD BROWNIES

YIELDS ONE 9 BY 13 IN [23 BY 33 CM] BAKING DISH; 12 BROWNIES

Marshmallow Meringue (recipe follows)	1 recipe	

TOPPING

Bittersweet chocolate chips	2 oz	60 g
Sweet and Salty Pecans Variation (page 247)	2/3 cup	65 g
Cacao nibs	2 Tbsp	

BROWNIES

Bittersweet chocolate, coarsely chopped	10 1/2 oz	300 g
Unsalted butter	1/2 cup	115 g
Spelt flour	1/2 cup	70 g
Large eggs	4	
Sugar	2/3 cup	270 g
Vanilla extract	1 tsp	
Salt	1/4 tsp	
Dried cherries	2/3 cup	100 g
Sweet and Salty Pecans Variation, coarsely chopped (page 247)	1 cup	100 g
Bittersweet chocolate chips	3 1/2 oz	100 g
Cacao nibs	2 Tbsp	

Brownie lovers divide into two camps: cakey and fudgy. This creation by Carolyn is for the fudgy campers, as well as fans of chunky brownies. They are sweet, nutty, very chocolaty, and ribboned with dramatic swirls of meringue.

• • • • • •

Preheat the oven to 325°F [160°C]. Butter a 9 by 13 in [23 by 33 cm] glass baking dish.

Spoon the meringue into a piping bag and set aside.

To make the topping, combine the chocolate chips, pecans, and cacao nibs in a small bowl. Set aside.

Pour water to a depth of about 2 in [5 cm] into a saucepan, place over medium heat, and bring to a simmer. Put the chocolate and butter into a small stainless-steel bowl that will rest securely on the rim of the pan and place it over, but not touching, the water. Stir the chocolate and butter with a rubber spatula to melt the mixture evenly. Take off the heat and set aside.

Sift the flour into a small mixing bowl. Set aside. In the bowl of a stand mixer fitted with the whisk attachment, combine the eggs, sugar, vanilla, and salt. Whisk on high speed until the mixture thickens, becomes pale in color, and falls from the whisk in a wide ribbon. Using a rubber spatula, fold the cooled chocolate into the egg mixture. Fold in the flour. Fold in the dried cherries, chopped pecans, chocolate chips, and cacao nibs, taking care to work quickly and gently so that you don't deflate the air that has been incorporated into the eggs.

Pour the batter into the prepared dish and smooth the top with the spatula. Snip 1/2 in [12 mm] off the tip of the piping bag filled with the marshmallow meringue, leaving a hole about the size of a dime. Pipe four lines of the meringue lengthwise from end to end in the pan, leaving about 2 in [5 cm] of space between each line. Rotate the pan and pipe four horizontal lines to create a crosshatch pattern. Using

continued

a spoon, swirl the marshmallow into the brownie batter to create a marbled effect. Set aside the piping bag; you will have used about half of the meringue mixture. Garnish the top of the brownie with half of the topping mixture.

Bake the brownie until the top looks slightly puffed and feels soft to the touch, about 25 minutes. Remove from the oven (leave the oven on) and quickly pipe dollops of the remaining marshmallow meringue onto the surface of the brownie and smooth them out with a spoon into an irregular pattern. Garnish with the remaining topping mixture and return to the oven for 5 minutes to toast the marshmallow. Let cool completely on a wire rack.

Using a sharp, oiled knife, cut into twelve squares. Wipe the knife clean between each cut with a damp kitchen towel. The brownies will keep in an airtight container in a cool place for up to 1 week.

MARSHMALLOW MERINGUE

YIELDS 2 CUPS [450 ML]

Large egg whites (3 to 4)	1/2 cup	120 ml
Sugar	3/4 cup + 2 Tbsp	175 g
Salt	1/8 tsp	
Cream of tartar	pinch	
Vanilla extract	2 tsp	

Pour water to a depth of about 2 in [5 cm] into a saucepan, place over medium heat, and bring to a simmer. Combine the egg whites, sugar, salt, and cream of tartar in the bowl of a stand mixer that will rest securely on the rim of the pan and place it over, but not touching, the water. Begin to mix the egg whites with a whisk to combine, then switch to a rubber spatula, mixing and scraping the sides and bottom of the bowl to prevent scrambling. When the mixture reaches 170°F [76°C], carefully remove the bowl from the pan, return to the stand mixer, and immediately begin whipping the meringue on high speed with the whisk attachment.

As the meringue cools, it will become bright white, thick, and glossy. Once the bowl is only slightly warm to the touch, reduce the speed of the mixer to low and add the vanilla extract; increase the mixer speed to high to incorporate. When the meringue is cool and holds stiff peaks when you lift the whisk from the bowl, it is ready to be used immediately.

BLACK TEA BLONDIES WITH CARAMEL SWIRL

YIELDS 16 TO 20 BLONDIES, DEPENDING ON SIZE

All-purpose flour	1½ cups + 2 Tbsp	210 g
Earl Grey tea leaves, finely ground	1 tsp	
Dark brown sugar	2¼ cups	400 g
Unsalted butter, melted	1 cup	225 g
Vanilla extract	2 tsp	
Salt	1 tsp	
Large eggs	3	
Caramel Sauce (page 309)		

Blondies tend to be overly sweet. Including finely ground black tea and lightly salted caramel here elevates what could be a one-note treat, adding a complex flavor.

• • • • • •

Preheat the oven to 350°F [180°C]. Butter a 9 by 13 in [23 by 33 cm] glass baking dish. Sift the flour and ground tea into a small bowl. Set aside.

Using a stand mixer fitted with the paddle attachment, combine the brown sugar, melted butter, vanilla, and salt. Beat on medium speed for 30 seconds. With the mixer running, add the eggs one at a time, incorporating each egg before adding the next. Using a rubber spatula, scrape the bottom and sides of the mixing bowl. Reduce the speed to low, and add the flour mixture. Mix on low speed just until combined.

Pour the batter into the prepared dish and smooth the top with a spatula. Drizzle the caramel sauce over the top and drag a knife horizontally left to right, creating a marbled design. Bake until the center and the sides have risen evenly, about 25 minutes. Let cool completely on a wire rack.

Using a sharp knife, cut the blondies to the desired size. These will keep in an airtight container in a cool place for up to 5 days.

CHAPTER SIX

HOLIDAY

PUMPKIN PIE

YIELDS ONE 10 IN [25 CM] PIE OR SIX TO EIGHT 4 IN [10 CM] TARTLETS; 8 TO 12 SERVINGS

Partially baked and cooled 10 in [25 cm] Flaky Tart Dough shell or six to eight 4 in [10 cm] tartlet shells (page 286)	1	
Pumpkin purée	2 cups	510 g
Large eggs	3	
Large egg yolk	1	
Heavy cream	1 cup	240 ml
Brandy	2 Tbsp	
Light or dark brown sugar	½ cup	90 g
Salt	½ tsp	
Ground cinnamon	1 tsp	
Ground ginger	1 tsp	
Ground cloves	⅛ tsp	
Nutmeg, freshly grated	⅛ tsp	
Black pepper, freshly ground	⅛ tsp	
Lightly sweetened, softly whipped cream for serving		

Customers often ask if we process our own pumpkin for our holiday pies. We tried one year, and it was a fiasco of round-the-clock roasting, blending, and sieving, and the results were never completely satisfying. It was hard to get a totally smooth purée, and the final product didn't have the flavor I wanted.

I recently discovered that pumpkin in the can is actually a blend of one or more types of winter squash with pumpkin. Pumpkin and squash belong to the same genus, hence the wide latitude with labeling, and it explains why my early experiments yielded less than great results. If you want to do some home-roasting, try red kuri or kabocha squash. Both result in a beautiful rich color, make a very smooth purée, and have very good flavor.

Scale the sugar up or down as you like, or use maple syrup as a sweetener.

KITCHEN NOTES: If you do opt to use fresh pumpkin or other squash, follow these steps for a smooth purée: Preheat the oven to 400°F [200°C]. Cut the pumpkin or squash in half, scrape out the seeds and fibers, and discard. Place the halves on a baking sheet lined with parchment paper or aluminum foil, cut-side down, and bake until a paring knife easily pierces the skin and flesh, about 1 hour. Cool, scrape the flesh into the bowl of a food processor fitted with the steel blade, and process until smooth. This will keep in an airtight container in the refrigerator for up to 1 week.

......

Have the pie shell ready for filling. Preheat the oven to 325°F [160°C].

In a mixing bowl, combine the pumpkin purée, whole eggs, egg yolk, cream, and brandy and whisk to mix well. In a second mixing bowl, combine the brown sugar with the salt and all the spices. Stir to mix. Whisk the sugar mixture into the pumpkin mixture.

Pour the filling into the pie shell and smooth the top with a rubber spatula if necessary. Bake the pie until just set but still slightly wobbly in the center, about 1 hour. The filling will continue to set as it cools. Let the pie cool on a wire rack. Serve slightly warm, at room temperature, or cold, with whipped cream. The pie will keep in the refrigerator for up to 4 days.

PECAN MAPLE PIE WITH KUMQUATS AND BOURBON

YIELDS ONE 9 IN [23 CM] PIE; 8 TO 12 SERVINGS

Fully baked and cooled Flaky Tart Dough shell (page 286)	1	
Sugar	¾ cup	150 g
Maple syrup	½ cup	155 g
Light corn syrup	½ cup	170 g
Bourbon	2 Tbsp	
Salt	½ tsp	
Unsalted butter, cubed	¼ cup	60 g
Vanilla extract	1 tsp	
Large eggs, lightly beaten	3	
Pecan halves	2¾ cups	275 g
Kumquats, thinly sliced and seeded	½ cup	85 g
Unsweetened, softly whipped cream for serving		

Have the pie shell ready for filling.

In a saucepan, combine the sugar, maple syrup, corn syrup, bourbon, and salt. Place over medium heat, bring to a rolling boil, and boil for 1 minute. Remove the pan from the heat, add the butter, and whisk as it melts. Let the mixture cool to room temperature. While the mixture is cooling, preheat the oven to 350°F [180°C].

Add the vanilla and eggs to the cooled mixture and stir to mix well. Stir in the pecans and kumquats. Pour into the pie shell.

Bake the pie until the filling is just set, 40 to 60 minutes. If the top is browning too quickly, cover with a piece of aluminum foil. Let cool on a wire rack. Serve warm or at room temperature with the whipped cream. The pie will keep in the refrigerator for up to 1 week.

It's hard to stray from the standards at the holidays, but the addition of kumquats and bourbon to pecan pie really lifts it up from its sticky sweetness to another level. The skin of kumquats is sweet and very thin, so they in effect "candy" in the custard as it bakes, while the tart flesh makes a nice contrast to the sweet, butterscotchy flavor of the pie filling. Bourbon adds a lovely note of vanilla and more depth of flavor.

KITCHEN NOTES: If kumquats are unavailable, use the grated zest of one orange or tangerine, adding it at the same point as the kumquats.

SOFT GLAZED GINGERBREAD

YIELDS 12 TO 20 COOKIES, DEPENDING ON SIZE OF CUTTERS

DOUGH

All-purpose flour	4 cups	520 g
Cocoa powder	1 Tbsp	
Ground ginger	4 tsp	
Ground cinnamon	2 tsp	
Ground cloves	1½ tsp	
Black pepper, freshly ground	1¼ tsp	
Salt	1 tsp	
Baking soda	½ tsp	
Unsalted butter, at room temperature	1 cup	225 g
Granulated sugar	¾ cup + 2 Tbsp	175 g
Large egg	1	
Blackstrap or other dark molasses	⅓ cup + 2 Tbsp	155 g
Light corn syrup	2 Tbsp	

GLAZE

Confectioners' sugar	1 cup	125 g
Water	2 Tbsp	

Several years ago during the holidays, I experimented with different thicknesses of gingerbread dough and patterned rolling pins and cookie molds. I found that the dough I was using made a perfect soft cookie with some adjustments to the butter and sugar, and the addition of a little extra molasses and corn syrup. The dough also kept the impression from an antique pin I had, and when it was glazed and cut into rectangles, the resulting cookies looked like tiles, with the glaze settling into the grooves and turning white from the crystallization of the sugar.

This dough makes a fine crisp gingerbread cookie as well, rolled out thinly, and iced after baking.

The spice mix is very warm with a hint of black pepper, and the small amount of cocoa gives the dough an appealingly dark color.

Originally, I used what is called a thread glaze, meaning that sugar and water are cooked together to the thread stage, cooled slightly, and then brushed on. The brushing action made the sugar crystallize and set. A simple water icing (confectioners' sugar and water mixed together to a thin brushing consistency) is easier and works just as well. The glaze seals in the moisture in the cookie and gives it a perfect amount of extra sweetness.

KITCHEN NOTES: If you are using a pin or cookie forms with a carved design, make sure to flour the top of the dough so that it doesn't stick in the crevices of the design. As long as the flour is lightly and evenly distributed, it will disappear from the surface during baking; you can also use a pastry brush to brush away any excess. The patterned pin and cookie plaques are often sold as springerle molds or pins, after the Scandinavian cookie traditionally made with them.

. . . . . .

To make the dough, stir together the flour, cocoa powder, ginger, cinnamon, cloves, pepper, salt, and baking soda in a mixing bowl. Set aside. Using a stand mixer fitted with the paddle attachment, beat the butter on medium-high speed until creamy. Slowly add the granulated sugar and mix on medium speed until the mixture is completely smooth and soft. Stop the mixer and scrape down the sides of the bowl with a rubber spatula as needed. Add the egg and mix well.

continued

Add the molasses and corn syrup and beat until incorporated. Stop the mixer again and scrape down the sides of the bowl. Add the flour mixture and beat on low speed until a dough forms that pulls away from the sides of the bowl and all the ingredients are well incorporated. Remove the dough from the bowl, flatten it on a large piece of plastic wrap into a rectangle about 1 in [2.5 cm] thick, cover the dough with the plastic wrap, and refrigerate overnight.

Preheat the oven to 350°F [180°C]. Line a baking sheet with parchment paper or a nonstick liner.

Dust your work surface with flour, unwrap the dough, and place it on the work surface. If using a plaque with a design, roll out the dough ⅓ in [8 mm] thick, lightly dust the top with flour, press your cookie molds over the dough, and then cut out the shapes with a small knife and place on the prepared baking sheet, spacing them about 1 in [2.5 cm] apart. Alternatively, using the mold as a guide, cut around it with a small knife, flip the mold over so the design is facing you, and place the dough over it, pressing it into the design. Unmold the shapes onto the prepared baking sheet, leaving about 1 in [2.5 cm] between them.

If using a patterned rolling pin, lightly dust the lined baking sheet with flour and transfer the dough to the pan. Lightly dust the top of the dough with flour and roll it into a rectangle about ⅓ in [8 mm] thick with a plain pin. Then, using the patterned pin, roll over the dough with enough pressure to ensure a clear impression of the design. Trim the sides with a small knife. It is not necessary to cut into smaller sizes before baking.

Bake the cookies until lightly golden along the sides but still soft to the touch in the center, 7 to 15 minutes. The timing will depend on the size of the individual cookies, or if you have made a single large patterned piece that will be cut after baking.

While the cookies are baking, prepare the glaze. In a small bowl, whisk together the confectioners' sugar and water until smooth.

When the cookies are ready, remove from the oven and let cool on the pan on a wire rack for about 10 minutes. Then, while the cookies are still warm, using even strokes, brush a light coat of glaze on the top of each cookie, evenly covering it. Let the cookies cool completely. When the glaze dries, it should leave a shiny, opaque finish. If you have used a patterned pin to make a single large plaque, cut into the desired sizes with a small, very sharp knife. At the bakery, we cut them into 3 by 4 in [7.5 by 10 cm] rectangles, but 1½ by 4 in [4 by 10 cm] makes a nice smaller size. The cookies will keep in an airtight container in a cool place for about 2 weeks. They do not freeze well, however, as the glaze becomes watery when they are thawed.

Icing Variation: If you want to make the traditional thread glaze for finishing the cookies, heat 1½ cups [300 g] of granulated sugar and 1 cup [240 ml] of water over low heat, stirring until the sugar dissolves. Then increase the heat to medium and cook without stirring until the mixture registers 225°F [107°C] on a thermometer. Remove from the heat and let the syrup cool to 180°F [82°C]. Brush the syrup over the cooled cookies with a clean, dry, natural-bristle pastry brush, brushing quickly back and forth to encourage sugar crystals to form. Once the crystallization begins, the glaze will continue to turn opaque over the next hour or so. Store as directed above.

STEAMED GINGERBREAD PUDDING

YIELDS TWO 9 BY 5 IN [23 BY 12 CM] LARGE LOAVES,
OR SIX TO EIGHT 4½ BY 2¾ BY 2½ IN [11 BY 7 BY 6 CM] SMALL LOAVES

GINGERBREAD

All-purpose flour	1½ cups + 2 Tbsp	210 g
Baking soda	1 tsp	
Ground cinnamon	1 tsp	
Black pepper, freshly ground	½ tsp	
Ground cloves	¼ tsp	
Fresh ginger, peeled and coarsely chopped	⅔ cup	100 g
Hot water	¾ cup + 2 Tbsp	210 ml
Granulated sugar	¾ cup	150 g
Blackstrap molasses	⅔ cup	225 g
Vegetable oil such as safflower or sunflower	½ cup + 2 Tbsp	150 ml
Salt	½ tsp	
Large eggs	2	

BOURBON HARD SAUCE

Unsalted butter, at room temperature	½ cup	115 g
Confectioners' sugar	1 cup	125 g
Bourbon, Cognac, or Armagnac	½ cup + 1 Tbsp	135 ml
Salt	pinch	

This is not a true steamed pudding. I don't always have the patience for making those, but I don't mind admitting it because the result of this recipe is miraculously like the real thing. I started out trying David Lebovitz's Fresh Ginger Cake, but mismeasured something and ended up with a super-moist "steamed" cake. It is not what I would call a "light" cake, but its unique, firm, moist texture vindicates all cakes that don't fall into the category of "light and airy." The batter is so wet that it "steams" itself, baking into the firmer style of British pudding that would be logistically impossible for a bakery to make in any large quantity. It's one recipe that we have never changed and is only offered in the fall. Serve with the hard sauce, or more simply with unsweetened, softly whipped cream.

KITCHEN NOTES: You can quickly peel ginger by scraping the edge of a spoon along the length of it. You can also use a vegetable peeler, but you take off more of the ginger. When slicing ginger, always slice against the grain into ⅛ in [3 mm] thick "coins" before chopping. If you cut with the grain, you will end up with tough, hairlike fibers.

· · · · · ·

To make the gingerbread, preheat the oven to 325°F [160°C]. Butter the bottom and sides of two 9 by 5 in [23 by 12 cm] loaf pans or six to eight 4½ by 2¾ by 2½ in [11 by 7 by 6 cm] loaf pans.

This recipe is easily mixed in a stand mixer fitted with the whisk attachment or by hand with a whisk. Sift together the flour, baking soda, cinnamon, pepper, and cloves into a mixing bowl.

continued

Place the ginger in a blender, add enough of the hot water to cover, and process until smooth. Pour into a large mixing bowl. Pour the rest of the hot water into the blender to dislodge any remaining ginger and add to the mixing bowl. Add the granulated sugar, molasses, oil, and salt to the ginger and beat on medium speed until well mixed. Add the flour mixture and beat on low speed until moistened. Then switch to high speed until the batter is perfectly smooth, about 1 minute. Add the eggs and beat on medium speed until incorporated. The batter will be very thin.

Pour the batter into the prepared pans, dividing it evenly. Bake the cakes until a cake tester inserted into the center comes out clean, about 1 hour and 10 minutes for the large pans and 45 minutes for the small pans.

To make the hard sauce, combine the butter, confectioners' sugar, bourbon, and salt in a small mixing bowl and mix with a whisk or wooden spoon until smooth. Serve at room temperature. The sauce will keep in a tightly covered container in the refrigerator for up to 1 week.

When the cakes are ready, let cool in the pans on wire racks for about 20 minutes, and then invert onto the racks, turn right-side up, and let cool. Serve the cakes warm or at room temperature with the hard sauce. The cakes will keep, well wrapped, in the refrigerator for up to 1 week.

BÛCHE DE NOËL

YIELDS ONE 12 IN [30.5 CM] CAKE; 8 TO 10 SERVINGS

CAKE BATTER

All-purpose flour	scant ½ cup	65 g
Cornstarch	2 tsp	
Vegetable oil	scant 2 Tbsp	25 g
Large eggs	2	
Sugar	6 Tbsp	75 g
Salt	pinch	

COFFEE SOAKER

Coffee, brewed double-strength, or espresso	¼ cup	60 ml
Sugar	2 Tbsp	

ESPRESSO BUTTERCREAM

Large egg whites	4	
Sugar	1 cup + 2 Tbsp	225 g
Salt	½ tsp	
Unsalted butter, at cool room temperature, cut into ½ in [12 mm] cubes	1¼ cups	285 g
Espresso, cooled	2 Tbsp	

CHOCOLATE MOUSSE

Dark chocolate, chopped	5 oz	140 g
Heavy cream	1 cup	240 ml
Large eggs	2	
Large egg yolks	2	
Sugar	6 Tbsp	75 g

GANACHE GLAZE

Powdered unflavored gelatin	½ tsp	
Cold water	2 Tbsp	
Dark chocolate, chopped	9 oz	255 g
Heavy cream	1 cup	240 ml
Sugar	¾ cup	150 g

After many years of making our Bûche de Noël the same way, we wanted to modernize the look, working with new flavors and textures, and using new techniques to apply the decorations. The cake is first rolled with buttercream, enrobed in chocolate mousse, and glazed with chocolate. It was a group effort between Lynn working on the cake form—filling it with a light chocolate mousse and espresso soaker—and Carolyn taking on the decorations. My only note to Carolyn was to come up with a new mushroom decoration to put on the clean, poured-chocolate finish that Lynn made for the cake. Carolyn developed an ingenious method of sifting cocoa on tempered white chocolate circles. When pressed, they take on the trompe l'oeil look of mushrooms stacked on tree trunks. The finished cake is unlike any bûche I've seen, arresting in its beautiful simplicity and originality.

KITCHEN NOTES: For a truly professional look, use a bûche mold at least 3 in [10 cm] wide and 14 in [35 cm] long. Bûche molds aren't standard; the important part is that it has the capacity to hold the mousse and the cake. Using an offset spatula, spread the mousse evenly on the cake roll. Freeze the cake for at least 6 hours or overnight before glazing.

· · · · · ·

continued

To make the cake layer, preheat the oven to 375°F [190°C]. Position the rack in the lowest third of the oven and line a 9 by 13 in [23 by 33 cm] rimmed baking sheet with parchment paper.

Follow the instructions on pages 312–13 for making the Génoise recipe, whisking in the oil instead of the butter (the oil does not need to be heated).

With an offset spatula, spread the batter evenly on the prepared baking sheet. Bake until the surface is golden brown and springs back in the center when pressed lightly with your fingers, 12 to 14 minutes. Transfer to a wire rack and let cool in the pan completely.

To make the coffee soaker, warm the coffee and sugar in a small saucepan until the sugar is dissolved; set aside to cool.

To make the buttercream, pour water to a depth of about 2 in [5 cm] into a saucepan, place over medium-low heat, and bring to a simmer. Put the egg whites into the bowl of a stand mixer that will rest securely on the rim of the pan and place it over, but not touching, the water. Whisk in the sugar and salt. Whisk the egg white mixture until hot to the touch, 3 to 5 minutes. Remove the bowl from the heat. Using a stand mixer fitted with the whisk attachment, whip the egg white on high speed for 4 to 5 minutes to maximum volume. Reduce the mixer speed to medium, and whip for another 3 minutes to stabilize the meringue. With the mixer on medium-high speed, add the softened butter one cube at a time, until it is all added. Stop the mixer and scrape the sides and bottom of the bowl. Make sure all the butter is incorporated. Restart the mixer, add the espresso, and mix on medium speed until the buttercream is light and fluffy. The buttercream can be used immediately or stored in an airtight container in the refrigerator for 1 week or in the freezer for 1 month. When ready to use, warm/thaw the buttercream to soft room temperature and, using a stand

mixer fitted with the whisk attachment, whip on high speed until light in texture.

To assemble the cake roll, unmold the cake. Turn the cake over with the parchment paper face up. Carefully peel off the parchment paper. Place the cake on a clean piece of parchment paper. Using a pastry brush, evenly soak the cake with the coffee soaker. Be careful not to oversoak; this could cause the cake to crack when rolled. Measure out about 1 cup [150 g] of the buttercream. Using a small offset spatula, spread the buttercream evenly over the surface of the cake.

Place the cake horizontally in front of you and begin rolling it toward you, rolling tightly until you reach the bottom. Wrap the cake tightly in plastic and refrigerate until firm, about 2 hours or overnight.

If using a mold, line it with plastic wrap to help the case release. Make sure your lining is smooth so your glaze will be, too.

To make the chocolate mousse, pour water to a depth of about 2 in [5 cm] into a saucepan, place over medium-low heat, and bring to a simmer. Put the chocolate into a stainless-steel bowl that will rest securely on the rim of the pan and place it over, but not touching, the water. Stir the chocolate until melted. Set aside to reach room temperature. Whisk the heavy cream to soft peaks by hand in a bowl or in a stand mixer fitted with the whisk attachment. Rest the mixing bowl on the rim of the pan with simmering water so it's over, but not touching, the water. Add the eggs, egg yolks, and sugar and whisk the eggs until hot to the touch (140°F [60°C]), taking care that the eggs don't scramble. In the bowl of a stand mixer fitted with the whisk attachment, whisk the eggs on high speed until the they are pale yellow, tripled in volume, and fall off the whisk in a wide ribbon that folds back on itself and slowly dissolves. Using a rubber spatula, quickly fold the melted chocolate into the egg mixture.

Once the chocolate is almost incorporated, you will still see some streaks of chocolate. Fold in the whipped cream.

Pour two-thirds of the mousse into the prepared mold. Unwrap the cake roll, trim it to fit the mold if needed, and gently place it, seam-side up, into the center of the mold. Gently press the cake down into the mousse so it is centered and the mousse pushes up around the sides. Working quickly, pour the remaining mousse over the top of the cake. With a spatula, smooth out the mousse so it's level with the rim of the mold. Freeze the Bûche de Noël for at least 6 hours or overnight.

Remove the cake from the freezer, unmold and unwrap it, and place it on a wire rack set over a rimmed baking sheet.

To make the glaze, soften the gelatin in a small bowl with the cold water; set aside. Put the chopped chocolate in a deep stainless-steel bowl; set aside. Heat the cream and sugar in a small saucepan until hot but not too hot (about 130°F [55°C]. Add the gelatin and water to the hot cream mixture and stir with a spatula to dissolve. Pour the hot cream mixture over the chopped chocolate and let the chocolate melt for 1 to 2 minutes. Stir the chocolate gently so as not to incorporate any air bubbles. Continue to mix, scraping the sides of the bowl, until the mixture is shiny and smooth.

Immediately pour the glaze over the top of the cake. Starting from one end, pour the glaze in a heavy enough stream to cover the sides as you move slowly across the cake to the other end. Ideally, try pouring the glaze in one pass for the smoothest result. Let the cake rest for 5 to 10 minutes before transferring to a serving plate or board. Letting the glaze rest too long may cause it to tear when moved. Refrigerate until decorating (directions follow) or serving. The cake will keep, covered and refrigerated, for 3 to 4 days.

BÛCHE DE NOËL DECORATIONS

WHITE CHOCOLATE MUSHROOMS, PISTACHIO MOSS, GILDED CRANBERRIES, AND DARK CHOCOLATE TWIGS

WHITE CHOCOLATE MUSHROOMS

Cocoa powder	2 Tbsp	
White chocolate	5 oz	140 g

KITCHEN NOTES: Use care when melting the white chocolate. Its high sugar and milk content will cause it to seize rapidly. Use a digital thermometer for precision.

· · · · · ·

Place a small pot filled with 1 in [2.5 cm] of water over medium-low heat. Prepare a piping bag or a quart-size resealable plastic bag for filling. Have ready two sheets of parchment paper, exactly the same size, and an object to press the chocolate into discs; the bottom of a measuring cup is perfect.

Fill a small sieve with the cocoa powder and set aside. Place three-quarters of the chocolate in a heatproof mixing bowl (reserve the remaining chocolate at room temperature). Place the bowl over the simmering water and gently stir the chocolate with a rubber spatula to ensure that it melts slowly and evenly. Using a thermometer, bring the chocolate to 113°F [45°C]. Immediately remove the bowl from the heat and place it onto a folded kitchen towel or trivet on the counter. Add the remaining room temperature chocolate and gently mix with the rubber spatula to melt and cool the chocolate. This is called "seeding," which will help temper the chocolate. Stir the chocolate occasionally until it cools to 79°F [26°C], then place it quickly back over the pot of steaming water to raise the temperature to 83°F [28°C], the working temperature of white chocolate. Use care—this will only take a few seconds. If the

continued

chocolate is heated beyond its working temperature, the process must be restarted from the beginning with new chocolate. At 83°F [28°C], the chocolate is now tempered and ready to work with.

Pour the chocolate into the prepared piping bag and use scissors to snip off the tip to create a small hole, about ¹⁄₁₆ in [2 mm] in diameter. Pipe mounds of white chocolate in rows onto a sheet of parchment paper. The size of the piped chocolate should range from the size of a quarter to the size of a dime; more variation is better for lifelike mushroom garnishes. Quickly use the small sieve to tap cocoa powder onto the chocolate mounds, completely covering each round. Lay the second sheet of parchment over the piped chocolate. Working quickly, press each mound with a measuring cup until it is very flat, and smooth it out using a circular motion to create uneven, frilly edges. Slide the parchment paper onto a cutting board and refrigerate or let sit in a cool place for 1 to 4 hours. Finished mushrooms can be stored in an airtight container at a cool room temperature for up to 3 days.

PISTACHIO MOSS

Raw pistachios	2 Tbsp
Matcha powder	¼ tsp

Using a spice grinder, process the pistachios with the matcha powder until a clumpy but fine mixture forms. Store in an airtight container at room temperature for up to 3 days.

GILDED CRANBERRIES

Fresh cranberries	5 to 10
Edible gold luster dust	

Wash and thoroughly dry the cranberries. Using a small paint or pastry brush, dust them with the gold powder until they are glimmering. Store in an airtight container at room temperature for up to 3 days. If they get humid and lose their shine, re-dust right before use.

DARK CHOCOLATE TWIGS

Bittersweet chocolate, chopped	4½ oz	130 g
Cocoa powder for sifting		

Pour water to a depth of about 1 in [2.5 cm] into a saucepan, place over medium-low heat, and bring to a simmer. Prepare a piping bag fitted with a 1 mm tip or snip the corner from a quart-size resealable plastic bag. Line a baking sheet or a cutting board with a sheet of parchment paper, ensuring that it stays flat and the edges do not curl.

Put 3¾ oz [109 g] of the chocolate in a small heatproof bowl and place over, but not touching, the simmering water. Gently stir it with a rubber spatula until melted. Using a thermometer, allow the chocolate to reach approximately 131°F [55°C]. Immediately move the bowl to rest on a folded kitchen towel. Add the remaining chocolate and gently mix with the rubber spatula. Cool to 82°F [28°C], stirring occasionally. Place it back over the simmering water to raise the temperature to 88°F [31°C]. Take care, as this will only take a few seconds. At 88°F [31°C], the chocolate is tempered. If the chocolate is heated beyond 88°F [31°C], the process must be restarted from the beginning.

Pour the chocolate into the prepared piping bag or plastic bag. Steadily pipe long, thin lines of dark chocolate from end to end on the prepared baking sheet, in close proximity to one another. This can be done in a long zigzag fashion, as the untidy ends will be trimmed away. Once the parchment paper is full of delicate dark chocolate lines, lightly sift cocoa powder over the chocolate to create texture. You may leave some plain, as well, to create a nice contrast between textures.

Once the chocolate begins to harden, but is not set, the twigs can be scored. Use a knife or a bench scraper to trim the piped edges away, and section the chocolate lines into varying lengths, 2 to 4 in [5 to 10 cm]. To remove the twigs from the paper, slide an offset spatula under the twigs, row by row. They will naturally snap where they were scored.

Use the twigs right away, or store them in an airtight container in a cool, low-humidity place for up to 2 weeks.

To decorate the Bûche de Noël, position several of the discs of white chocolate mushrooms—of various sizes—in a line along the top of the cake. We cut ends off of the discs for variation and to make it easier to press them onto the cake. At the base of the cake, arrange as many twigs as you like. Sprinkle the top of the cake with pistachio moss, and cluster several gilded cranberries at the base to resemble holly berries.

LINZER TORTE

YIELDS ONE 9 IN [23 CM] TART, 12 TO 15 SERVINGS;
OR 14 SANDWICH COOKIES

All-purpose flour	1¾ cups	230 g
Ground cinnamon	1 tsp	
Ground cloves	¼ tsp	
Baking soda	¼ tsp	
Hazelnuts, almonds, pecans, walnuts, or a combination, toasted, or nut flour	about 2 cups	225 g
Unsalted butter, at cool room temperature	10 Tbsp	140 g
Granulated sugar	½ cup	100 g
Salt	½ tsp	
Large egg	1	
Vanilla extract	1 tsp	
Seasonal fruit jam, chilled	1 cup	280 g
Large egg for egg wash	1	
Confectioners' sugar for dusting	¼ cup	30 g

If we are adding desserts to the Tartine collection that use a simple pastry base and jam—Thumbprint Cookies, Victoria Sponge, or jam buns—we would be remiss in not including Linzer Torte. It is considered the oldest pastry in the world, with recipes from Austria and Verona going back to the mid-1600s, but it didn't make its way to America until the 1850s, when an Austrian émigré first brought it to Wisconsin. Linzer dough is known for its lightly spiced crust and crumbly, fork-tenderness, owing its texture to the egg and high percentage of ground nuts in the dough, usually in the form of hazelnuts, or a combination of hazelnuts and almonds. Try it with pecans or walnuts or a combination of nuts. This recipe is adapted from Michelle Lee.

KITCHEN NOTES: The dough can be frozen for up to 1 month. Defrost in the refrigerator for 1 day before baking. Rolled dough can be re-rolled two times more (total of three times). If using nut flour, lightly toast in a 350°F [180°C] oven before using.

• • • • • •

Sift the flour, cinnamon, cloves, and baking soda into a bowl and set aside.

In a food processor fitted with the steel blade, process the toasted nuts until very fine, but not clumping, about 30 seconds.

In a mixing bowl fitted with a paddle attachment, cream the butter, granulated sugar, and salt on medium speed until combined, about 1 minute. Add the ground nuts and mix on medium speed until combined. Add the egg and vanilla and mix until incorporated, 1 to 2 minutes. Stop the mixer and use a rubber spatula to scrape down the sides and bottom of the bowl. With the mixer on low speed, add the flour mixture and mix for about 1 minute to incorporate the dry ingredients until a dough forms. Shape the dough into two small disks that are ½ in [12 mm] thick and wrap in plastic wrap. Refrigerate for at least 1 hour or overnight.

Lightly dust your work surface with flour and place one dough disk on it. Roll out the dough to ⅛ in [3 mm] thick, rolling from the center toward the edge in all directions. Lift and rotate the dough a quarter turn after every few strokes, dusting with flour underneath as necessary to prevent sticking, and working quickly to keep the dough from getting warm. Cut out a circle with an 11 in [28 cm] diameter. Transfer the circle to a 9 in [23 cm] tart pan, easing it into the bottom and sides and then pressing gently into place. (If the dough has become too soft to move, make sure it is well floured and fold the dough in quarters and transfer to the refrigerator to chill for 15 minutes.) If the dough develops any tears, patch with a little extra dough, pressing firmly to adhere. With a sharp knife, trim the dough level with the top of the tart pan. Place the tart shell in the refrigerator or freezer until it is firm, about 15 minutes.

Preheat the oven to 350°F [180°C]. Dock the bottom of the tart shell by pricking with a fork or the tip of a knife, spacing the holes 2 in [5 cm] apart. Spread the chilled jam evenly into the bottom of the tart shell using an offset spatula. Set aside.

Lightly dust your work surface and roll out the second disk of dough as directed. Using a rolling pizza cutter or a sharp knife, cut long strips that are ½ in [12 mm] wide. To form the lattice, starting at one edge of the tart, lay parallel strips of dough across the tart about 1 in [2.5 cm] apart. The dough strips should slightly overhang the edges of the tart. Rotate the tart 180 degrees, and lay strips across the tart, on top of and perpendicular to the first set. Using your fingers, gently press the edges of the tart shell where the strips overlap to adhere them. Trim off the excess dough that hangs over from the strips, then press the dough strips against the tart shell edges to seal.

Beat the egg in a small bowl. Using a pastry brush, gently brush the beaten egg onto the lattice top. Bake the tart until the dough is golden brown and the jam starts to bubble, about 45 minutes. Transfer the tart to a wire rack to cool. If you've used a pan with a removable bottom, unmold, then slice. If not, slice in the pan. The tart can be served cold or at room temperature. Wrap or store in an airtight container in the refrigerator or at room temperature for up to 1 week.

To make linzer sandwich cookies, preheat the oven to 350°F [180°C] and line a baking sheet with parchment paper. Roll out the dough ⅛ in [3 mm] thick. Cut out cookies to the desired size and shape; I like to use a 2 in [5 cm] fluted round cutter. Remember you will need two dough cutouts per cookie. To create a "window" for the jam to show through, cut out a small shape from half of the cookies. Arrange the dough cutouts 1 in [2.5 cm] apart on the prepared baking sheet. Bake until golden brown, 10 to 12 minutes. Let the cookies cool on the baking sheet for 2 to 3 minutes before transferring to a wire rack to cool completely.

To finish the cookies with jam, spread ½ tsp of jam onto the cookies without the center cutout, stopping about ⅛ in [3 mm] from the edges. Line up the top cookies (with the center cutouts) on a piece of parchment paper, flat-side down, and lightly dust them with confectioners' sugar. Sandwich a sugared cookie atop each jam-covered cookie (you should see the jam through the cutout). The cookies will keep in an airtight container for 3 to 4 days at room temperature or 1 week in the refrigerator.

FRUIT AND NUT CAKE

YIELDS ONE 9 BY 5 IN [23 BY 12 CM] LOAF; 6 TO 8 SERVINGS

Tapioca flour	½ cup	55 g
Oat flour	¼ cup	25 g
Sea salt	1 tsp	
Baking soda	¼ tsp	
Baking powder	¼ tsp	
Dried dates or figs	2¼ cups	335 g
Dried apricots, nectarines, plums, peaches, or cherries (halve large fruits such as figs or peaches)	1¼ cups	200 g
Assorted nuts, such as walnuts and pecans	1¼ cups	300 g
Brown sugar, firmly packed	¾ cup + 2 Tbsp	160 g
Large eggs	3	
Vanilla extract	1 tsp	

I tried a version of this cake when visiting a friend's shop, Talbott and Arding, in Hudson, New York. It's a charming little shop, full of warmth and delicious smells, selling cheeses as well as beautiful prepared foods and baked goods. This cake, originally from Alice Medrich, is displayed in giant, 7 lb [3 kg] loaves. I bought a huge chunk of it, and ate the entire thing on my train ride home along the Hudson River to New York City through the snow. It's full of dried summer fruits—cherries, apricots, and golden raisins—warm, tart fruits that lend their acidity to lift this cake from the usual overly sweet holiday fruitcake. I pressed bits of cheese into this as I snacked on it on the train, and I still eat it this way; it's a wonderful addition to a cheeseboard.

KITCHEN NOTES: This recipe is my variation, which is gluten free and has a small amount of spice and my preferred fruit and nut combination. Alice's was first published with an equal amount of wheat flour.

. . . . . .

Position a rack in the lowest position of the oven and preheat to 300°F [150°C]. Grease and line a 9 by 5 in [23 by 12 cm] loaf pan with parchment paper.

In a large bowl, whisk together the flours, salt, baking soda, and baking powder to combine. Add the fruit, nuts, and brown sugar and mix thoroughly with your fingers.

In a small bowl, whisk together the eggs and vanilla. Pour the egg mixture into the fruit and nut mixture and thouroughly combine with your hands until the fruits and nuts are covered. Scrape the mixture into the prepared pan and place in the oven.

Bake until deep brown in color and a knife inserted into the center of the loaf comes out crumb free, 1½ to 2 hours. If the cake gets too dark, loosely cover it with foil.

Cool completely on a wire rack. To serve, slice with a sharp, heavy knife. Store, tightly wrapped, at room temperature for 1 week. The loaf also freezes beautifully for up to 1 month.

SWEET POTATO TEA CAKE WITH MERINGUE

YIELDS ONE 9 BY 5 IN [23 BY 12 CM] LOAF; 6 TO 8 SERVINGS

All-purpose flour	1⅓ cups + 1 Tbsp	185 g
Baking powder	1½ tsp	
Baking soda	½ tsp	
Ground cinnamon	2 tsp	
Ground nutmeg	1 tsp	
Ground cloves	¼ tsp	
Sweet potato, boiled and puréed	1 cup	255 g
Sugar	1⅓ cups	265 g
Vegetable oil	¾ cup	180 ml
Salt	1 tsp	
Large eggs	3	

MERINGUE TOPPING

Large egg whites	3	
Sugar	⅔ cup	135 g
Vanilla extract	1 tsp	

This is a version of our popular Pumpkin Tea Cake (the original recipe is on page 283). It has a soft, even, moist crumb and a slight spiciness. The roasted, puréed sweet potato is a nice change from pumpkin, the subtle difference in flavor not overpowered by spice. It is finished with a thick swirl of meringue that is swooped into the top of the cake. Baker Michelle Lee added this delicious dramatic effect.

KITCHEN NOTES: If you are making the sweet potato purée, try to make it the same consistency as canned pumpkin purée. The water content of any vegetable can vary, making your cake wetter or drier.

. . . . . .

Preheat the oven to 325°F [160°C]. Lightly butter the sides and bottom of a 9 by 5 in [23 by 12 cm] loaf pan.

This recipe is easily mixed with a stand mixer fitted with a whisk attachment, or by hand with a whisk. Sift together the flour, baking powder, baking soda, cinnamon, nutmeg, and cloves into a mixing bowl and set aside.

In another mixing bowl, beat together the sweet potato purée, sugar, oil, and salt on medium speed or by hand until well mixed. Add the eggs one at a time, beating well after each addition until incorporated before adding the next egg. Scrape down the sides of the bowl with a rubber spatula. On low speed, add the flour mixture and beat until combined. Scrape down the sides of the bowl, then beat on medium speed for 5 to 10 seconds to make a smooth batter. The batter should be the consistency of a thick purée.

Transfer the batter to the prepared loaf pan and smooth the surface with an offset spatula. Set aside.

To make the meringue topping, pour water to a depth of about 2 in [5 cm] into a saucepan, place over medium heat, and bring to a simmer. Whisk together the egg whites and sugar in the bowl of a stand mixer fitted with the whisk attachment that will rest securely on the rim of the saucepan, but not touch the water.

continued

Continue to whisk until the whites are hot to the touch (120°F [50°C]), about 5 minutes. Carefully remove the bowl from the pan, return to the stand mixer, and immediately begin to mix on high speed until the mixture is very thick and stiff, and holds stiff peaks when you lift out the whisk. This will take 5 to 7 minutes. Add the vanilla and mix to combine.

Spoon the meringue over the batter in the loaf pan and drag a knife through the meringue and batter to create a marbled pattern. Don't thin out the meringue too much, though. The meringue bakes best when left in thicker patches. Bake until a paring knife inserted into the center comes out clean, about 1½ hours. Let the cake cool in the pan on a wire rack for about 20 minutes, then run a sharp knife around the sides and invert onto the rack, turn right-side up, and let cool completely. Serve the cake at room temperature. It will keep, well wrapped, at room temperature for 4 days or in the refrigerator for 1 week.

PUMPKIN TEA CAKE

All-purpose flour	1¾ cups	230 g
Baking powder	1½ tsp	
Baking soda	½ tsp	
Ground cinnamon	1 Tbsp + 2 tsp	
Nutmeg, freshly grated	2 tsp	
Ground cloves	¼ tsp	
Pumpkin purée	1 cup	255 g
Vegetable oil such as safflower or sunflower	1 cup	240 ml
Sugar, plus more for topping	1⅓ cups	265 g
Salt	¾ tsp	
Large eggs	3	

The recipe has ended up on many "best of" lists for pumpkin tea cakes. It is reliable, easy, and super-moist, and has a nice balance of pumpkin to spice. The flavor will differ depending on the brand of pumpkin purée you use—some resulting in a lighter-colored cake, and others a more pronounced pumpkin flavor. If you want to process your own, red kuri or kabocha squash work well; both have good flavor and a nice, smooth texture when puréed. This cake isn't too sweet, so a dollop of Bourbon Hard Sauce (page 265) is a delicious addition on a slice of this cake. If you can find raw pepitas (hulled pumpkin seeds), they make a beautiful crunchy topping, along with the sugar.

KITCHEN NOTES: As with all quick breads, make sure not to overmix the batter, or you will develop a coarse, tough crumb.

Preheat the oven to 325°F [160°C]. Lightly butter the bottom and sides of a 9 by 5 in [23 by 12 cm] loaf pan.

This recipe is easily mixed with a stand mixer fitted with the whisk attachment, or by hand with a whisk. Sift together the flour, baking powder, baking soda, cinnamon, nutmeg, and cloves into a mixing bowl and set aside.

In another mixing bowl, beat together the pumpkin purée, oil, sugar, and salt on medium speed or by hand until well mixed. Add the eggs one at a time, mixing well after each addition until incorporated before adding the next egg. Scrape down the sides of the bowl with a rubber spatula. On low speed, add the flour mixture and beat just until combined. Scrape down the sides of the bowl, then beat on medium speed for 5 to 10 seconds to make a smooth batter. The batter should have the consistency of a thick purée.

Transfer the batter to the prepared loaf pan and smooth the surface with an offset spatula. Sprinkle evenly with 2 Tbsp of sugar. Bake until a cake tester inserted into the center comes out clean, about 1 hour. Let cool in the pan on a wire rack for about 20 minutes, and then invert onto the rack, turn right-side up, and let cool completely. Serve the cake at room temperature. It will keep, well wrapped, at room temperature for 4 days or in the refrigerator for about 1 week.

CHAPTER SEVEN

BASIC BAKERY RECIPES

FLAKY TART DOUGH

—

YIELDS TWO 9 OR 10 IN [23 OR 25 CM] TART OR PIE SHELLS OR TWELVE 4 IN [10 CM] TARTLET SHELLS

Salt	1 tsp	
Water, very cold	½ cup + 2 Tbsp	150 ml
All-purpose flour	3½ cups	455 g
Unsalted butter, very cold	1⅓ cups	300 g

This is an example of a baker's recipe that you will never have to look up if you just remember the basic ratio of three:two:one—flour to butter to water. It can be scaled up and down as needed, and it always makes a perfect flaky dough if you handle it gently and keep the butter and water ice cold. At Tartine, we make this dough two different ways: one is quickly mixed together, and the other is a bit more lengthy but yields an even flakier dough that is like a rough puff pastry. We use the second method for our galettes, which is detailed with the Fruit Galettes recipe (page 127).

KITCHEN NOTES: There are two things that you can do to ensure a flaky crust: work the dough very briefly, making sure that some of the butter remains in pea-size pieces (when the dough is rolled out, you should see faint streaks of butter), and chill the dough well before baking. Chilling creates little pockets (made by the flour and water) where the butter is, which will remain after baking and is what creates the light and fork-tender texture in a well-made dough.

· · · · · ·

In a small bowl, add the salt to the water and stir to dissolve. Keep very cold until ready to use.

To make the dough in a food processor, put the flour in the bowl. Cut the butter into 1 in [2.5 cm] pieces and scatter the pieces over the flour. Pulse briefly until the mixture forms large crumbs and some of the butter is still in pieces the size of peas. Add the water-salt mixture and pulse for several seconds until the dough begins to come together in a ball but is not completely smooth. You should still be able to see some butter chunks.

To make the dough by hand, put the flour in a mixing bowl. Cut the butter into 1 in [2.5 cm] pieces and scatter the pieces over the flour. Using a pastry blender or two knives, cut the butter into the flour until the mixture forms large crumbs and some of the butter is still in pieces the size of peas. Drizzle in the water-salt mixture and stir with a fork until the dough begins to come together in a shaggy mass. Gently mix until the dough comes together into a ball but is not completely smooth. You should still be able to see some butter chunks.

On a lightly floured work surface, divide the dough into two equal balls and shape each ball into a disk 1 in [2.5 cm] thick. Wrap well in plastic wrap and chill for at least 2 hours or overnight.

To line a tart pan or pie dish, place a disk of dough on a lightly floured surface and roll it out ⅛ in [3 mm] thick, rolling from the center toward the edge in all directions. Lift and rotate the dough a quarter turn every few strokes to discourage sticking, and work quickly to prevent the dough from becoming warm. Lightly dust the work surface with extra flour as needed to prevent sticking. If lining a pie dish, cut out a circle 2 in [5 cm] larger than the dish. If lining a tart pan with a removable bottom, cut out a circle 1½ in [4 cm] larger than the pan. Carefully transfer the round to the pie dish or tart pan (fold it in half or into quarters to simplify the transfer if necessary), easing it into the bottom and sides and then pressing gently into place. Trim the dough even with the rim of the pan with a sharp knife. If you are lining a pie dish, you can trim the dough so that there is a ½ in [12 mm] overhang, fold the overhang under, and flute or crimp the edge, though at the bakery we leave the edge plain.

For recipes that call for unbaked shells, refrigerate until ready to use. If refrigerating overnight, cover the shell with plastic wrap. For recipes that call for a partially baked or fully baked shell, chill the shell until firm to the touch, 30 minutes to 1 hour, before baking. This ensures the flakiest crust. The shells may also be well wrapped and frozen for up to 2 weeks at this point. It is not necessary to thaw them before continuing with the following steps for baking.

Preheat the oven to 375°F [190°C].

Line the pastry shells with parchment paper and fill with pie weights. For a partially baked crust, bake until the surface looks dry and pale, with no dense or opaque areas left, about 20 minutes; to check, lift a corner of the paper. Remove from the oven and remove the weights and paper. Return the shells to the oven and bake for a few minutes longer. Check the dough while it is baking. If it is rising up in the middle, gently pierce it with the tip of a knife (be careful not to make a large hole in case you use a very liquid filling).

For a fully baked shell, bake the shells until the surface looks light brown, about 25 minutes; to check, lift a corner of the paper. Remove from the oven and remove the weights and paper. Return the shells to the oven and bake until golden brown, about 5 minutes longer.

Let the shells cool completely on wire racks before filling. They will keep, well wrapped, in the refrigerator for up to 1 week or in the freezer for up to 2 weeks.

Einkorn Variation: Follow the directions for Flaky Tart Dough, substituting equal parts pastry flour and einkorn flour for the all-purpose flour.

FLAKY DOUGH FOR SLAB PIES

YIELDS ONE 9½ BY 13 BY 1 IN [23 BY 33 BY 2.5 CM] DOUBLE CRUST SLAB PIE

Salt	1½ tsp	
Water, very cold	1 cup	240 ml
All-purpose flour	5¼ cups	680 g
Unsalted butter, very cold	2 cups	450 g

KITCHEN NOTES: When wrapping and storing your dough, be sure to divide the dough into two equal halves. For slab pies, shape the halves into rectangles. When the time comes to roll out the dough and form your shells, this step makes it easier to form the desired shape for your pie pan.

. . . . . .

In a small bowl, add the salt to the water and stir to dissolve. Keep very cold until ready to use.

To make the dough in a food processor, put the flour in the bowl. Cut the butter into 1 in [2.5 cm] pieces and scatter the pieces over the flour. Pulse briefly until the mixture forms large crumbs and some of the butter is still in pieces the size of peas. Add the water-salt mixture and pulse for several seconds until the dough begins to come together in a ball but is not completely smooth. You should still be able to see some butter chunks.

To make the dough by hand, put the flour in a mixing bowl. Cut the butter into 1 in [2.5 cm] pieces and scatter the pieces over the flour. Using a pastry blender or two knives, cut the butter into the flour until the mixture forms large crumbs and some of the butter is still in pieces the size of peas. Drizzle in the water-salt mixture and stir with a fork until the dough begins to come together in a shaggy mass.

Gently mix until the dough comes together into a ball but is not completely smooth. You should still be able to see some butter chunks.

On a lightly floured work surface, divide the dough into two equal balls and shape each ball into a rough square 1 in [2.5 cm] thick. Wrap well in plastic and chill for at least 2 hours or overnight.

To line a baking sheet, place a disk of dough on a lightly floured surface and roll out ⅛ in [3 mm] thick, rolling from the center toward the edge in all directions. Lift and rotate the dough a quarter turn every few strokes to discourage sticking, and work quickly to prevent the dough from becoming warm. Lightly dust the work surface with extra flour as needed to prevent sticking. Gently press the dough into a rectangular shape as you roll.

To line a rimmed baking sheet, roll to a rectangle 2 to 3 in [5 to 8 cm] larger than your 9 by 13 in [23 by 33 cm] pan. Transfer to the prepared sheet pan, following the instructions in the recipes on pages 115 to 123. Refrigerate until ready to use. If refrigerating overnight, cover with plastic wrap.

Einkorn Variation: Follow the directions for Flaky Dough for Slab Pies, substituting equal parts pastry flour and einkorn flour for the all-purpose flour.

SWEET TART DOUGH

YIELDS FOUR 9 IN [23 CM] TART SHELLS OR TWELVE 4 IN [10 CM] TARTLET SHELLS

Unsalted butter, at room temperature	1 cup + 2 Tbsp	255 g
Sugar	1 cup	200 g
Salt	¼ tsp	
Large eggs, at room temperature	2	
All-purpose flour	3¾ cups + 2 Tbsp	500 g

EGG WASH (OPTIONAL)

Large egg	1
Salt	pinch

Also called *pâte sucrée*, this dough is used for most of the tart shells we make at Tartine. The recipe is from a bakery in the south of France where Chad and I worked, Boulangerie Artisanale des Maures. When I asked Patrice, the pastry chef, if I could write down the recipe, he said, "Of course, but isn't it the same as a sucrée dough in America?" This is the same recipe that just about every baking-school student learns in France, and what most pastry shops and restaurants use, with minor variations. Like so many recipes in baking, there are few secrets here. Rather, it is the individual baker's touch that makes each product unique, and what you do with it.

This is also a dough that a baker would say "behaves well," meaning that it can be rolled very thin, it is easy to handle, and it bakes beautifully, holding its shape without slumping down into the tart pan like some doughs do, yet is "fork tender" to eat. It also may be rolled out multiple times without losing its quality, a valuable aspect for a bakery that makes so many tarts. One trick that we employ at the bakery is to brush egg wash lightly on the bottom and sides of partially baked shells. This thin coating seals the shell, creating a barrier that will keep the crust crisp longer.

KITCHEN NOTES: Eggs can be brought to room temperature quickly by placing them in a bowl and running lukewarm water over them for about 5 minutes. Any leftover dough can be used as a simple cookie dough. This dough keeps exceptionally well, so make some for use now and freeze ready-to-roll discs of it for future use (it will keep for up to 1 month).

. . . . . .

Using a stand mixer fitted with the paddle attachment, combine the butter, sugar, and salt and mix on medium speed until smooth. Mix in 1 egg. Add the remaining egg and mix until smooth. Stop the mixer and scrape down the sides of the bowl with a rubber spatula. Add the flour all at once and mix on low speed just until incorporated.

On a lightly floured work surface, divide the dough into four equal balls and shape each ball into a disk ½ in [12 mm] thick. Wrap well in plastic wrap and chill for at least 2 hours or overnight.

To line a tart pan, place a dough disk on a lightly floured surface and roll out ⅛ in [3 mm] thick, rolling from the center toward the edge in all directions. Lift and rotate the dough a quarter turn after every few strokes, dusting underneath as necessary to discourage sticking, and work quickly to prevent the dough from becoming warm. Cut out a circle 2 in [5 cm] larger than the pan. If the dough is still cool, carefully transfer the circle to the pan, easing it into the bottom and sides and then pressing gently into place. Do not stretch the dough, or the sides will shrink during baking. (If the dough has become too soft to work with, put it in the refrigerator for a few minutes to firm up before transferring it to the pan.) If the dough develops any tears, just patch with a little extra dough, pressing firmly to adhere. Trim the dough level with the top of the pan with a sharp knife. Place the pastry shell in the refrigerator or freezer until it is firm, about 15 minutes.

If you are making tartlet shells, roll out the dough in the same way, cut out circles according to the size of your pans, and line the pans. The rest of the dough, including the scraps, can be frozen for future use.

Preheat the oven to 325°F [160°C].

Dock (make small holes in) the bottom of the tart shell or tartlet shells with the tines of a fork or the tip of a knife, making tiny holes 2 in [5 cm] apart. Place in the oven and bake for 7 to 10 minutes for a partially baked large shell or 5 to 7 minutes for tartlet shells. The pastry should be lightly colored and look dry and opaque. Check the shell(s) during baking and rotate the pans if necessary for even color. If you want to brush the shell(s) with an egg wash (see headnote), beat the egg with the salt in a small bowl.

A minute or two before the desired color is reached, remove the shell(s) from the oven and lightly brush the bottom and sides with the egg wash. Return the shell(s) to the oven and bake until the desired color is reached and the coating is set.

For a fully baked shell, proceed as directed for a partially baked shell, but bake until golden brown, about 5 minutes longer.

Let cool completely on wire racks. The pastry shells will keep, well wrapped, in the refrigerator for up to 1 week or in the freezer for up to 2 weeks.

CHOCOLATE BUCKWHEAT TART DOUGH

YIELDS ONE 9 IN [23 CM] TART SHELL OR FOUR 4 IN [10 CM] TARTLET SHELLS

Einkorn flour	scant 1½ cups	175 g
Buckwheat flour	⅓ cup	45 g
Almond flour	⅓ cup	30 g
Cocoa powder	2 Tbsp	
Unsalted butter, at room temperature	10 Tbsp	140 g
Confectioners' sugar, sifted	⅔ cup	85 g
Large egg	1	
Large egg white, beaten	1	

Sift the flours and cocoa powder into a small bowl. Set aside.

Using a stand mixer fitted with the paddle attachment, beat the butter and confectioners' sugar on low speed until smooth. Stop the mixer and scrape down the sides of the bowl with a rubber spatula. Increase the speed to medium-low and mix in the whole egg. Stop the mixer and scrape down the bowl once again. Turn the mixer back to low speed and mix in the dry ingredients just until incorporated.

Turn the dough out onto a lightly floured work surface and gently knead in any dry ingredients that have not been fully incorporated. Shape the dough into a ½ in [12 mm] thick disk. Wrap well in plastic wrap and chill for at least 1 hour or overnight.

To line a tart pan, place a dough disk on a lightly floured surface and roll out ⅛ in [3 mm] thick. Roll from the center toward the edge in all directions. Lift and rotate the dough a quarter turn after every few strokes, dusting flour underneath as necessary to discourage sticking, and working quickly to prevent the dough from becoming warm. Cut out a circle 2 in [5 cm] larger than the pan. If the dough is still cool, carefully transfer the circle to the pan, easing it into the bottom and sides and then pressing gently into place. Do not stretch the dough, or the sides will shrink during baking. (If the dough has become too soft to work with, put it in the refrigerator for a few minutes to firm up before transferring it to the pan.) If the dough develops any tears, patch with a little extra dough, pressing firmly to adhere. Trim the dough level with the top of the pan with a sharp knife. Place the pastry shell in the refrigerator or freezer until it is firm, about 15 minutes.

If you are making tartlet shells, roll out the dough in the same way, cut out circles according to the size of your pans, and line the pans. The rest of the dough, including the scraps, can be frozen for future use.

Preheat the oven to 325°F [160°C].

Dock (make small holes in) the bottom of the tart shell or tartlet shells with the tines of a fork or the tip of a knife, making tiny holes 2 in [5 cm] apart. Place in the oven and bake for 13 to 15 minutes for a partially baked large shell or 8 to 10 minutes for tartlet shells. The pastry should be lightly colored and look dry and opaque. Check the shell(s) during baking and rotate the pans if necessary for even color.

A minute or two before the desired color is reached, remove the shell(s) from the oven and lightly brush the bottom and sides with the egg white. Return the shell(s) to the oven and bake until the desired color is reached and the egg white is set.

For a fully baked shell, proceed as directed for a partially baked shell, but bake until golden brown, 12 to 15 minutes longer.

Let cool completely on wire racks. The pastry shells will keep, well wrapped, in the refrigerator for up to 1 week or in the freezer for up to 2 weeks.

RYE TART DOUGH

YIELDS TWO 9 IN [23 CM] TART SHELLS OR SIXTEEN 3 IN [8 CM] TARTLET SHELLS

Unsalted butter, at cool room temperature	1⅓ cups	300 g
Confectioners' sugar	1 cup	125 g
Salt	½ tsp	
Large egg	1	
Large egg yolk	1	
Rye flour	1⅓ cups	185 g
Einkorn or all-purpose flour	1¼ cups	165 g
Large egg white, beaten	1	

Using a stand mixer fitted with the paddle attachment, beat the butter, confectioners' sugar, and salt on medium speed until smooth. Mix in the egg. Add the egg yolk and mix until smooth. Stop the mixer and scrape down the sides of the bowl with a rubber spatula. Add the flours all at once and mix on low speed just until incorporated.

Turn the dough out onto a lightly floured work surface, divide into two equal portions, and shape each ball into a disk that is ½ in [12 mm] thick. Wrap well in plastic wrap and chill for at least 1 hour or overnight.

To line a tart pan, place a dough disk on a lightly floured surface and roll out ⅛ in [3 mm] thick, rolling from the center toward the edge in all directions. Lift and rotate the dough a quarter turn after every few strokes, dusting flour underneath as necessary to discourage sticking, and working quickly to prevent the dough from becoming warm. Cut out a circle 2 in [5 cm] larger than the pan. If the dough is still cool, carefully transfer the circle to the pan, easing it into the bottom and sides and then pressing gently into place. Do not stretch the dough, or the sides

will shrink during baking. (If the dough has become too soft to work with, put it in the refrigerator for a few minutes to firm up before transferring it to the pan.) If the dough develops any tears, patch with a little extra dough, pressing firmly to adhere. Trim the dough level with the top of the pan with a sharp knife. Place the pastry shell in the refrigerator or freezer until it is firm, about 15 minutes.

If you are making tartlet shells, roll out the dough in the same way, cut out circles according to the size of your pans, and line the pans. The rest of the dough, including the scraps, can be frozen for future use.

Preheat the oven to 325°F [160°C].

Dock (make small holes in) the bottom of the tart shell or tartlet shells with the tines of a fork or the tip of a knife, making tiny holes 2 in [5 cm] apart. Place in the oven and bake for 13 to 15 minutes for a partially baked large shell or 8 to 10 minutes for tartlet shells. The pastry should be lightly colored and look dry and opaque. Check the shell(s) during baking and rotate the pans if necessary for even color.

A minute or two before the desired color is reached, remove the shell(s) from the oven and lightly brush the bottom and sides with the egg white. Return the shell(s) to the oven and bake until the desired color is reached and the egg white is set.

For a fully baked shell, proceed as directed for a partially baked shell, but bake until golden brown, 12 to 15 minutes longer.

Let cool completely on a wire rack. The pastry shells will keep, well wrapped, in the refrigerator for up to 1 week or in the freezer for up to 2 weeks.

MATCHA TART DOUGH

YIELDS TWO 9 IN [23 CM] TART SHELLS OR EIGHT 4 IN [10 CM] TARTLET SHELLS

Einkorn or all-purpose flour, sifted	1¾ cups + 2 Tbsp	245 g
Almond flour	¼ cup	30 g
Matcha powder, sifted	1 Tbsp + 1 tsp	
Unsalted butter, at room temperature	⅔ cup + 1 Tbsp	160 g
Confectioners' sugar, sifted	¾ cup	95 g
Large egg, at room temperature	1	
Large egg white, beaten	1	

Sift the flours and matcha powder into a small bowl. Set aside.

Using a stand mixer fitted with the paddle attachment, beat the butter and confectioners' sugar on low speed until smooth. Stop the mixer and scrape down the sides of the bowl with a rubber spatula. Add the egg and mix on medium-low speed. Stop the mixer and scrape down the bowl once again. Turn the mixer back to low speed and add the flour mixture. Mix until just incorporated.

Turn the dough out onto a lightly floured work surface and gently knead in any dry ingredients that have not been fully incorporated. Divide the dough into two equal portions and shape each piece into a ½ in [12 mm] thick disk. Wrap well in plastic wrap and chill for at least 1 hour or up to overnight.

To line a tart pan, place a dough disk on a lightly floured surface and roll out ⅛ in [3 mm] thick, rolling from the center toward the edge in all directions. Lift and rotate the dough a quarter turn after every few strokes, dusting flour underneath as necessary to discourage sticking, and working quickly to prevent the dough from becoming warm. Cut out a circle 2 in [5 cm] larger than the pan. If the dough is still cool, carefully transfer the circle to the pan, easing it into the bottom and sides and then pressing gently into place. Do not stretch the dough, or the sides will shrink during baking. (If the dough has become too soft to work with, put it in the refrigerator for a few minutes to firm up before transferring it to the pan.) If the dough develops any tears, patch with a little extra dough, pressing firmly to adhere. Trim the dough level with the top of the pan with a sharp knife. Place the pastry shell in the refrigerator or freezer until it is firm, about 15 minutes.

If you are making tartlet shells, roll out the dough in the same way, cut out circles according to the size of your pans, and line the pans. The rest of the dough, including the scraps, can be frozen for future use.

Preheat the oven to 325°F [160°C].

Dock (make small holes in) the bottom of the tart shell or tartlet shells with the tines of a fork or the tip of a knife, making tiny holes 2 in [5 cm] apart. Place in the oven and bake for 13 to 15 minutes for a partially baked large shell or 8 to 10 minutes for partially baked tartlet shells. The pastry should be lightly colored and look dry and opaque. Check the shell(s) during baking and rotate the pans if necessary for even color.

A minute or two before the desired color is reached, remove the shell(s) from the oven and lightly brush the bottom and sides with the egg white. Return the shell(s) to the oven and bake until the desired color is reached and the egg white is set.

For a fully baked shell, proceed as directed, but bake until golden and the green color of the matcha is still coming through, 12 to 15 minutes longer.

Let cool completely on a wire rack. The pastry shells will keep, well wrapped, in the refrigerator for up to 1 week or in the freezer for up to 2 weeks.

GLUTEN-FREE CRUMB CRUST

Oat Digestive Biscuits, baked and cooled (page 208)	about 10	150 g
Unsalted butter, melted	4 Tbsp	
Brown sugar	1 Tbsp + 2 tsp	
Salt	½ tsp	
Cinnamon (optional)	1 tsp	

Preheat the oven to 350°F [180°C]. In a food processor, grind the cookies to a fine crumb, about 30 seconds. Pour the melted butter evenly on top of the crumbs and add the brown sugar, salt, and cinnamon (if using). Process until the crumb mixture will hold together when squeezed in the palm of your hand, about 10 seconds.

Transfer the crumb mixture to a pie or springform pan and press evenly onto the bottom and up the sides of the pan. Using the flat bottom of a cup, firmly press the crumbs into the pie shell or cheesecake base.

Bake until golden brown, 5 to 10 minutes. Let cool completely before adding filling, or store, covered, in the refrigerator for up to 2 days.

PASTRY CREAM

YIELDS 2½ CUPS [600 ML]

Whole milk	2 cups	480 ml
Vanilla bean	½ bean	
Salt	¼ tsp	
Sugar	½ cup + 1 Tbsp	115 g
Cornstarch	4 to 5 Tbsp	30 to 35 g
Large eggs	2	
Unsalted butter	¼ cup	60 g

Pastry cream is used often in this book, for simple tart fillings, for trifle and cake layers, and for filling éclairs. If you have some on hand, it makes a delicious spur-of-the-moment sauce, thinned with a bit of cream or milk and served alongside cake or fresh fruit. You can also make a quick frangipane-flavored tart filling by crushing four Almond Rochers (page 224) and mixing them with a batch of pastry cream, or serve plain as a simple vanilla pudding.

This recipe calls for whole eggs, which makes a lighter cream than some traditional French versions that call for only yolks. If you like a richer cream, use four yolks instead of the two whole eggs in the recipe.

KITCHEN NOTES: While the milk is heating, the milk solids want to adhere to the bottom of the pan, so make sure to whisk or stir the milk well every now and again. If any burn spots appear on the bottom of the pan, they can flavor the entire batch of milk. Taste the milk if you see any spots and discard it if it has an acrid flavor. There is no rescuing burned milk. The biggest concern when making pastry cream is to keep the eggs from curdling. There is a fine line between pastry cream that has cooked long enough to be properly thick and a moment later when it has cooked too long and the eggs have developed a grainy, curdled look. If the cream is only slightly grainy, use an immersion blender or a countertop blender, although this solution doesn't always save the batch. Never use an aluminum pan for pastry cream. The yolks react with the metal and turn the cream gray. Have a lightly dampened kitchen towel on hand to help stabilize the bowl of eggs as you whisk the milk into it, freeing both of your hands for pouring and whisking.

Have a bowl ready for cooling the pastry cream with a fine-mesh sieve resting on the rim.

Pour the milk into a heavy saucepan. Split the half vanilla bean in half lengthwise and use the tip of a sharp knife to scrape the seeds from the pod into the milk. Add the salt, place over medium-high heat, and bring to just under a boil, stirring occasionally and making sure that the milk solids are not sticking to the bottom of the pan. The larger the batch, the more careful you need to be.

Meanwhile, in a mixing bowl, whisk together the sugar and cornstarch. Use the larger amount of cornstarch for a firmer pastry cream for making Banana Cream Pie with Caramel and Chocolate (page 94) or the coconut variation that accompanies it and the smaller amount for other uses. Add the eggs and whisk until smooth.

When the milk is ready, slowly ladle about one-third of the hot milk into the egg mixture, whisking constantly. Pour the egg-milk mixture back into the hot milk and continue whisking over medium heat until the custard is as thick as lightly whipped cream, about 2 minutes. In order for the cornstarch to cook and thicken fully, the mixture must come just to the boiling point. You want to see a few slow bubbles. However, if the cream is allowed to boil vigorously, you will curdle the pastry cream. Remove from the heat and immediately pour through the sieve into the bowl. (If the custard stays in the hot pot, it will continue to cook.) Let cool for 10 minutes, stirring occasionally to release the heat and prevent a skin from forming on top.

Cut the butter into four pieces. When the pastry cream is ready (it should be about 140°F [60°C]), whisk the butter into the pastry cream one piece at a time, always whisking until smooth before adding the next piece.

To cool the cream, cover the bowl with plastic wrap, pressing the wrap directly onto the top of the cream (the plastic wrap prevents a skin from forming on the surface). To cool it very quickly, place it in a shallow dish and press plastic wrap directly on top. Be careful whisking the cream once it is cold. Overmixing will break down the starch and thin the cream. Pastry cream will keep, well covered, in the refrigerator for up to 5 days.

continued

MATCHA PASTRY CREAM VARIATION

YIELDS 2½ CUPS [600 ML]

Whole milk	2 cups	480 ml
Salt	¼ tsp	
Matcha powder	1 tsp	
Cornstarch	3 Tbsp + 1 tsp	25 g
Sugar	½ cup + 1 Tbsp	115 g
Large eggs	2	
Unsalted butter	¼ cup	60 g

Follow the directions for Pastry Cream (page 300), sifting the matcha powder into the cornstarch and sugar mixture. Cook and cool as directed.

FRANGIPANE CREAM

YIELDS 3 CUPS [750 ML]

Confectioners' sugar	1 cup	125 g
Unsalted butter, at room temperature	½ cup	115 g
Sliced almonds	¾ cup + 2 Tbsp	75 g
Large egg, at room temperature	1	
Large egg yolk, at room temperature	1	
Pastry Cream (page 300), at room temperature	¾ cup	180 ml
Cornstarch	4 tsp	
Brandy (optional)	4 tsp	
Salt	pinch	

Sift the confectioners' sugar into the bowl of a stand mixer fitted with the paddle attachment. Add the butter and beat together on low speed to combine. Increase the speed to medium and beat until smooth and creamy. Stop the mixer and scrape down the sides of the bowl with a rubber spatula. Add the almonds, egg, egg yolk, pastry cream, cornstarch, brandy (if using), and salt and beat on low speed until all the ingredients are evenly incorporated, stopping to scrape down the bowl as needed. The mixture may have a slightly "broken" appearance, which is normal.

The cream will keep in an airtight container in the refrigerator for up to 1 week.

I have included two versions of frangipane cream, also called *crème d'amandes* (almond cream). This one is a traditional recipe that includes pastry cream as one of its ingredients. The pastry cream produces a lighter and more moist filling than the usual mixture of eggs, butter, sugar, and almond flour, but it does take longer to prepare if you do not already have pastry cream on hand.

KITCHEN NOTES: We use natural sliced almonds (with their skins on). They add a little flavor, but mostly they contribute an attractive speckled look to the cream. If you prefer a filling with a lighter color, use sliced blanched almonds.

FRANGIPANE CREAM VARIATION

YIELDS 3 CUPS [720 ML]

Sliced almonds	2⅓ cups	200 g
Sugar	1 cup	200 g
Unsalted butter, at room temperature	¾ cup + 2 Tbsp	200 g
Brandy (optional)	4 tsp	
Salt	pinch	
Large eggs	2	
Whole milk	2 Tbsp	

This variation is a classic French recipe and makes a slightly more "cakey" filling. Usually you see this version made with equal parts butter, sugar, and almonds. We add the small amount of milk for a slightly moister filling.

· · · · · ·

In a food processor, combine the almonds with ¼ cup [50 g] of the sugar and process until finely ground. Set aside.

In the bowl of a stand mixer fitted with the paddle attachment, beat the butter on medium speed until creamy. Add the remaining ¾ cup [150 g] of sugar and mix to incorporate. Add the almond-sugar mixture and beat until thoroughly combined. Add the brandy (if using), salt, and 1 egg and mix until incorporated. Add the remaining egg and the milk and mix until light and fluffy.

The cream will keep in an airtight container in the refrigerator for up to 1 week.

LEMON CREAM

Lemon juice	½ cup + 2 Tbsp	150 ml
Large eggs	3	
Large egg yolk	1	
Sugar	¾ cup + 2 Tbsp	175 g
Salt	pinch	
Unsalted butter, cool	1 cup	225 g

This recipe creates a soft, luscious, delicate, and creamy filling with many uses. It is the base for one of our most popular tarts, Lemon Cream Tart (page 93).

A particular French technique creates an even softer filling than typical curd, and it should come as no surprise therefore that pastry chef Pierre Hermé developed it. His technique is genius and yet common sense: after making the curd, you "mount" butter into the very warm (but not hot) mixture as you would for a buerre blanc sauce, whisking continuously as it melts. This technique keeps the butter in emulsion and creates the softer, lighter look of this lemon cream. Use the cream in trifles, with unsweetened yogurt, or spread between cake layers (Lemon Meringue Cake, page 155). I've also frozen it in ice pop molds, creating a sort of lemon pudding pop. If you fold it with an equal volume of whipped cream, it makes a lovely cake filling.

KITCHEN NOTES: Never use an unlined aluminum pan when heating lemon juice or any mixture containing acidic ingredients. The acid in the juice reacts with the metal, giving the dessert a metallic flavor. The finished cream keeps well in a sealed container in the refrigerator, and may be quickly re-softened in a bowl set over simmering water, whisking to keep the emulsion from breaking.

......

Pour water to a depth of about 2 in [5 cm] into a saucepan, place over medium heat, and bring to a simmer. Combine the lemon juice, eggs, egg yolk, sugar, and salt in a stainless-steel bowl that will rest securely on the rim of the saucepan over, but not touching, the water. Whisk the ingredients together. (Never let the egg yolks and sugar sit together for more than a moment without stirring; the sugar will "cook" the yolks and turn them granular.) Place the bowl over the saucepan and continue to whisk until the mixture becomes very thick and registers 180°F [82°C] on a thermometer. This will take 10 to 12 minutes. Remove the bowl from over the water and let cool to 140°F [60°C], stirring from time to time to release the heat.

Meanwhile, cut the butter into 1 Tbsp pieces. When the cream is ready, leave it in the bowl if using an immersion blender, or pour it into a countertop blender. With the blender running, add the butter 1 Tbsp at a time, blending after each addition until incorporated before adding the next piece. The cream will be pale yellow and opaque and quite thick.

You can use the cream immediately, or pour it into a storage container with a tight-fitting lid and refrigerate for up to 5 days. To use after refrigeration, gently heat in a stainless-steel bowl set over simmering water until it has softened.

MATCHA ALMOND CREAM

YIELDS 1¾ CUPS [420 ML]

Almond flour	1 cup	100 g
Einkorn flour	2 Tbsp	
Matcha powder	heaping 1 tsp	
Confectioners' sugar, sifted	¾ cup	95 g
Unsalted butter, at room temperature	7 Tbsp	100 g
Large eggs, at room temperature	2	
Vanilla extract	1 tsp	

Sift together the flours and matcha powder into a small bowl. Set aside. Sift the confectioners' sugar into the bowl of a stand mixer fitted with the paddle attachment. Add the butter and beat together on low speed to combine. Increase the speed to medium and beat until smooth and creamy. Stop the mixer and scrape down the sides of the bowl with a rubber spatula. Add 1 egg and mix on medium speed until it is fully incorporated. Scrape down the bowl once more. Add the remaining egg and the vanilla extract, and mix on medium speed until combined and creamy. Add the dry ingredients and mix until almost fully incorporated. Scrape down the bowl once more, and finish mixing until smooth and creamy.

The cream will keep in an airtight container in the refrigerator for up to 1 week.

CARAMEL SAUCE

YIELDS ABOUT 1½ CUPS [360 ML]

Heavy cream	²/₃ cup	160 ml
Vanilla bean	¼ bean	
Sugar	1¼ cups	250 g
Water	¼ cup	60 ml
Light corn syrup	2 Tbsp	
Salt	¼ tsp	
Lemon juice	³/₄ tsp	
Unsalted butter	4 Tbsp	60 g

This is an incredibly versatile sauce and cake filling, with enough body to stay put when spread over cake layers, and just thin enough to sauce ice cream. It is layered in the Lemon Meringue Cake (page 155) and Devil's Food Layer Cake (page 157), and it is delicious if a little is spooned onto the tart shell of Chocolate Hazelnut Tart (page 105) before its chocolate filling. We add some to the bottom of Banana Cream Pie with Caramel and Chocolate (page 94) and its coconut variation, too, where it tempers the overall sweetness of the tart and adds another layer of flavor. When I spoon it over simple baked fruits, like apples or figs, it becomes a whole new sauce as it mixes with the concentrated fruit juices from the roasting pan. This recipe also perfectly demonstrates how the addition of a couple of simple ingredients to a base heightens its flavor. A squeeze of lemon juice and a little salt bring out deeper flavors of the butter and caramelized sugar.

KITCHEN NOTES: Be sure to use a good-size pan for cooking the caramel. When you add the hot cream, the caramel will boil furiously at first, increasing dramatically in volume. As always when caramelizing sugar, have ice water close by in case of burns.

......

Pour the cream into a small, heavy saucepan. Split the vanilla bean in half lengthwise and use the tip of a sharp knife to scrape the seeds from the pod halves into the milk. Place over medium-high heat and bring to just under a boil, stirring occasionally. Reduce the heat to low to keep the cream warm.

In a medium, heavy saucepan, combine the sugar, water, corn syrup, and salt. Bring to a boil over medium heat, stirring to dissolve the sugar. Then cook, without stirring, until the mixture is amber colored, 5 to 8 minutes. Remove from the heat.

The mixture will continue to cook off the heat and become darker, so make sure to have your cream close by. Carefully and slowly add the cream to the sugar syrup. The mixture will boil vigorously at first. Let the mixture simmer down, and then whisk until smooth. Add the lemon juice. Let cool for about 10 minutes.

Cut the butter into 1 in [2.5 cm] chunks and add them to the caramel one at a time, whisking constantly after each addition. Then whisk the caramel periodically as it continues to cool.

The caramel will keep in an airtight container in the refrigerator for up to 1 month.

CHOCOLATE PUDDING

YIELDS 3¾ CUPS [1.02 KG]; 4 TO 6 SERVINGS

Whole milk	1¾ cups	420 ml
Heavy cream	½ cup + 2 Tbsp	150 ml
Cornstarch	¼ cup	30 g
Sugar	¾ cup	150 g
Cocoa powder	3 Tbsp	15 g
Large eggs	3	
Salt	¼ tsp	
Bittersweet chocolate, coarsely chopped	2½ oz	70 g

The thick texture of this pudding is the result of the high amount of chocolate melted into the pudding at the end, firming up the custard as it cools. There is cocoa powder in the mix as well, giving it an even more intense chocolate flavor. Use in the Chocolate Pudding Pie (page 97) or eat with unsweetened, softly whipped cream—without question.

KITCHEN NOTES: What you are making here is essentially pastry cream. Any time that you add a hot liquid to eggs, it is called tempering or a *lié*, meaning that you must add the hot liquid very slowly so the eggs don't cook.

Have ready a fine-mesh sieve placed over a large heatproof container. Combine the milk and cream in a heavy, medium saucepan and heat to just under a boil. Meanwhile, in a mixing bowl, combine the cornstarch and sugar, and sift in the cocoa powder. Whisk until blended. In another mixing bowl, whisk the eggs with the salt until blended, then add to the sugar mixture and whisk until well combined.

Slowly add half of the hot milk mixture to the egg mixture while whisking constantly. Pour the egg mixture back into the pan with the rest of the milk mixture and cook over medium heat, whisking constantly, until the mixture has visibly thickened and registers 208°F [98°C] on a thermometer. This should take 5 to 7 minutes, depending on how cold your eggs are.

Immediately pour the contents of the pan through the sieve. Add the chocolate and let the heat of the milk-egg mixture melt it. When the chocolate has melted, blend with an immersion blender for a full 5 minutes until no lumps are visible. Stop the blender and scrape down the sides of the container with a rubber spatula as needed. Alternatively, you may use a blender and work in small batches, or use a whisk to blend by hand, being extremely careful with the hot mixture. The pudding will keep, well covered, in the refrigerator for up to 4 days.

GÉNOISE

YIELDS ONE 10 IN [25 CM] CAKE

Unsalted butter	5 Tbsp	75 g
All-purpose flour	1⅓ cups + 1 Tbsp	185 g
Cornstarch	1 Tbsp	
Large eggs	6	
Sugar	1 cup + 1 Tbsp	210 g
Salt	pinch	

When made well, this classic French cake base (sometimes erroneously termed sponge cake) has a perfectly uniform and delicate crumb structure. It has less sugar and butter than sponge cake, so it relies on the use of simple syrup, flavored or neutral, for its moisture. The benefit of génoise is its strong structure, which is why you see it for cakes that are layered. Traditionally, this cake is paired with mousses, curds, Bavarians, buttercreams, or simply with whipped cream for a more refined version of strawberry shortcake.

KITCHEN NOTES: This is the one piece of invaluable advice that I give all bakers about mixing a génoise batter: when you add the flour, some of it invariably ends up along the sides of the bowl. The inclination is to scrape it down with your spatula, but this is what causes lumps, which are impossible to smooth out. Instead, using your rubber spatula, push some of the batter up the side of the bowl where the flour is stuck and let the batter pull the flour away. If some stays, leave it. The second most common problem happens when you transfer the batter to the cake pan. If you scrape the sides of the bowl where there is a little batter clinging, you will be dislodging a little flour, too, creating lumps.

Preheat the oven to 350°F [180°C]. Line the bottom of a 10 in [25 cm] springform pan with 3 in [7.5 cm] sides with parchment paper cut to fit exactly. Do not butter the sides of the pan.

In a small saucepan, melt the butter over low heat, remove from the heat, and keep warm. Sift together the flour and cornstarch into a bowl and set aside.

Pour water to a depth of about 2 in [5 cm] into a saucepan, place over medium heat, and bring to a simmer. Combine the eggs, sugar, and salt in the bowl of a stand mixer that will rest securely on the rim of the saucepan over, but not touching, the water. Whisk together and then place over the saucepan and continue to whisk until the mixture is hot to the touch (120°F [50°C]), 5 to 7 minutes.

Remove the bowl from over the water and place on the stand mixer. Fit the mixer with the whisk attachment and mix on medium-high speed until the batter is pale yellow, has tripled in volume, and falls from the beater in a wide ribbon that folds back on itself and slowly dissolves on the surface, 3 to 5 minutes. Using a rubber spatula, fold in the flour mixture in three batches, making sure you reach all the way down to the bottom of the bowl where the flour likes to sink, and pulling it all the way to the top. Scoop out a small portion of the batter into a small bowl and whisk in the warm melted butter. Gently and quickly fold the butter mixture into the batter, being careful not to deflate the batter.

Pour the batter immediately into the prepared cake pan. Bake until the top springs back when lightly touched, 40 to 45 minutes. Let cool in the pan (the sides of the pan will help hold the structure of the cake as it cools) on a wire rack. To unmold, run a small, thin knife around the sides of the pan to loosen the cake and then release and lift off the pan sides. Invert the cake, peel off the parchment, and then use as directed in individual recipes. The cake will keep, well wrapped, in the refrigerator for up to 3 days or in the freezer for up to 1 month.

To split the cake into layers: The easiest way to divide the cake into layers is to use a long, thin, serrated knife. Place the cake on a flat surface and mark the desired thickness all the way around the cake. Work from the top to the bottom of the cake if making more than two layers. Holding the knife parallel to the work surface and using a sawing motion, cut through the cake, checking that the tip end and handle end of the knife are level and slicing where you marked. If you are making more than two layers, take off the first layer and set it aside before you begin to cut the next layer. If you aren't using the layers right away, cover with plastic wrap so they don't dry out.

CANDIED FENNEL

―――――――――

YIELDS ABOUT 3 TBSP

Superfine sugar	½ cup	100 g
Fennel seed stalk	1 (or as many as you have)	
Egg white, beaten	1	

There is wild fennel growing all over California, on roadsides and in backyards. It's one of the most easily foraged wildflowers in California. These candied edible seeds remind me of the breath-sweetening treat—called *mukhwas*—offered at Indian restaurants. When left on the stalk, the seeds make a beautiful presentation as a garnish on a tart.

Have a tall glass at hand and place the superfine sugar on a rimmed plate. Using a pastry brush, paint the seeds with just enough egg white to cover, gently wiping away excess with a paper towel. Working in sections of 10 to 20 seeds at a time, dip them into the sugar to coat, gently tapping off the excess. Stand the stalk in the glass until dry, about 1 hour. Use within 24 hours.

ON GRAINS

When Liz and I began to study baking and pastry professionally at the Culinary Institute of America in the early 1990s, there were only a few types of flours in use. We used bread flour for bread—it was mostly a strong, "white" (refined) variety. For pastry, we used a few softer flours: pastry and cake, and sometimes "all purpose"—all also white and refined. All of these were made from very few varieties of commodity wheat selected and cultivated to optimize yield and production.

For most of the history of agriculture, hundreds of thousands of grain types were grown, chosen for their flavor and suitability to the communities where they were cultivated. But this is not the case in the modern commercial agricultural system, which favors varieties that yield the largest harvest from the smallest plot of land. The flours milled from this wheat are almost universally bleached and refined. The germ and bran are removed, which essentially turns a fresh-milled, dynamic product with a shelf life of a few weeks into an inert white powder that can sit on the shelf for over a year without going rancid.

So much of pastry and baking is about technique—learning and practicing different ways to achieve tender, flaky scones; airy, layered croissants; and crisp tart shells. In the beginning, we didn't think of pastry flour as a flavoring ingredient. The flavor in our pastries came from butter, sugar, fruit, creams, nuts, chocolate, spices, and the rest of the arsenal in the pastry chef's pantry. The flour was just the blank canvas.

Our reflection on flour as flavor first started several years ago, though its roots came from our first mentors. Richard Bourdon and Dave Miller introduced us to a small group of diverse and ancient grains in the mid-1990s. Our education continued when we went to work in the south of

France and Savoie for Daniel Collin and Patrick LePort—French bakers who embraced both organic and ancient grains (highly unusual in France at that time).

When Liz and I returned to open our first bakery in Point Reyes Station, just north of San Francisco, we used high-quality organic flour milled nearby in Petaluma. It was good stuff, but still mostly of the "white" variety. We milled some of our own flour for a short time, but the demands of building and growing a financially sustainable bakery forced us to simplify and focus on what customers wanted. Over the years, Tartine became well known for our signature crusty, burnished, country bread, along with flaky croissants, morning buns, lemon tarts, galettes, cakes, gougères, and a tight range of cookies. We've always pushed hard to maintain the highest level of quality and freshness, baking our pastries and breads throughout the day and continually restocking the case from the oven.

After publishing our recipes in our books and celebrating the spread of wonderful artisanal bakeries across the country, it was time to take another look at why and how we do what we do. I had originally trained as a chef, and I wanted to bring a chef's sense of play and attention to the grains we were using. Considering the source in a more profound way opened a whole new universe to us.

In 2014, I visited the Bread Lab in Skagit Valley, Washington, north of Seattle. At the time, the Bread Lab was working closely with Washington State University (WSU) and their grain-breeding program. The Bread Lab had several different types of mills for testing small-scale batches of grain, and the team of breeders and graduate students there began to cultivate small test plots of grains, enlisting a handful of chefs and bakers to help select for flavor, nutrition, and baking qualities. There were tens of thousands of varieties of grains in the vault and dozens in the ground growing. It took some time to build up enough grain for us to test in bread, pastry, pizza, and pasta—and several years until there was enough for us to actually put into bakery production. The results were groundbreaking. From a flavor perspective, it was as if we had been baking in black and white and now were able to work in color.

The other major breakthrough was taking a hard look at how the grains were being milled. Historically, the two most popular types of mills were the ancient stone mill, which grinds the whole grain, crushing germ and bran together with the starch, and the more modern roller mill. Grain can be used "whole" (100 percent) or sifted to remove some of the bran and germ, leaving a whiter, more refined flour (with less flavor and arguably less nutrition). Roller mills are on the other end of the spectrum. They enable the grain to be stripped apart into individual components. They are best known for heavily refined industrial flour, but that's certainly not the only way they can be used.

The holy grail for lots of bakers (us included) is to achieve a flour that has the flavor, fiber, and nutrition gained from whole grain, but with the baking qualities more associated with refined flour: light texture, open and tender crumb, and thin, defined layers. Working closely with our friends and partners at Cairnspring Mills, we've found just that. Two years ago, we switched to using a collection of flours freshly milled from several varieties of wheat selected by us and grown by a small group of farmers who work closely with Cairnspring in Skagit Valley. Cairnspring mills the flour and ships it immediately, which allows us to use it within a few weeks of being milled. This preserves the flavor and nutrition in noticeable and impactful ways.

We no longer refer to the flours as bread, pastry, or cake. We call them by their variety names, determining through initial lab testing and then in-house bake testing what we think the best use would be at Tartine. We have a core group in constant use, and several new varieties to test each year. The ones we like get developed further, and over time they become part of our daily production of pastry, bread, and pasta. Some are ancient, some are modern, and some are combinations bred together through traditional means to achieve the most sustainable growing, harvesting, and disease-resistant characteristics, as well as the most flavor and individual character.

While the recipes in this book are all built from Tartine DNA, they now are made with fresh-milled varieties of wheat and other grains (several gluten free) that we've selected for flavor. The way the grains are milled ensures more fiber from the bran, along with fat, nutrients, and flavor from the germ. Transforming Tartine by starting from the source—the grain—and building end-to-end relationships with breeders, farmers, and millers, we arrive at what I consider to be the most authentic version of Tartine since we started this journey over twenty-five years ago, one that pushes us forward while honoring and staying connected to the past.

Chad Robertson

ACKNOWLEDGMENTS

I'm grateful to Chronicle Books and the many people who bought the first edition for their desire to see more Tartine recipes!

This version has more recipe and idea collaborations from our bakers than any other book; my being gluten-free necessitated a new approach, an approach I found to be the most fulfilling work experience I've had to date. I'd like to thank our whole bakery and commissary team for their assistance. In particular, I'd like to thank assistants Kristen Adele, Andrea Echeverria, and Michael Orson. New recipes and recipe development were done by bakers Kelsey Brito, Scarlett Cisneros, Kristina Costa, Fausto Echeverria, Lynn Echeverria, Nicole Green, Jen Latham, Carolyn Nugent, Alexa Prendergast, and Davita Spencer.

Many thanks to Andrea Gentl and Martin Hyers, who photographed this book, as well as their assistant Francesca Crichton; you were a pleasure to work with, wonderful human beings, and supremely talented and patient. Quietly talking for hours on end while concentrating on the creativity we each bring to something we all enjoy is one of the rare pleasures of life, which don't come along often enough.

To my agent, Katherine Cowles, who knows how to get a project done, how to inspire, and who to bring together to do it all.

Many thanks to the team at Chronicle Books for the very rare opportunity to update a cookbook.

To Vanessa Dina, Chronicle Books designer, the person who made this book come alive with a perfect balance of design and simplicity.

To Sarah Billingsley, my editor and best test-baker, who corralled all of the ideas, slips of paper with handwritten recipes, and bakers into one cohesive form. You are always a pleasure to work with.

To Alice Waters, for her enduring support of us and thoughtful foreword; you always inspire.

My gratitude to Chad Robertson, who never lets an initial idea be merely "good" without finding a way to push it (or me) to be the best version possible.

INDEX

Chronicle Books publishes distinctive books and gifts. From award-winning children's titles, bestselling cookbooks, and eclectic pop culture to acclaimed works of art and design, stationery, and journals, we craft publishing that's instantly recognizable for its spirit and creativity. Enjoy our publishing and become part of our community at www.chroniclebooks.com.